Between Two Worlds

Whispers Across the Ocean

Janise Bailey Mitchell

Dedication

To my muse—
*the spark that shows up when the house is quiet, the coffee is
cold, and the page is still blank.*

*Though miles and seas stretch far and wide,
Our hearts find ways to never hide.
In whispers soft, I dream of you,
A love so pure, so sweet, so true.*

*I've never heard your gentle voice,
Yet in my heart, you are my choice.
I've never felt your touch so near,
But still you are everything I hold dear.*

*Two souls apart, yet still so near,
You've made the distance disappear.
For every time we talk, I find
You are the love that fills my mind.*

Unattributed (original author not confirmed)
If you are the original author, please contact the publisher
for proper credit.

Table of Contents

Chapter 1

The Night the Vow Broke

Marcus came home around 4:00 a.m. He headed straight for the den and collapsed on the sofa. He woke the next day around noon. His head was pounding, and his throat was parched from too much alcohol the night before. He stumbled to the fridge, yanked open the door, and grabbed a sports drink. He gulped it down in greedy swallows, liquid spilling from the corners of his mouth.

Something didn't feel right. He went back to the den, sat down on the couch, and turned on the television. He couldn't shake the feeling that something was wrong. He felt it like a splinter under the skin. The silence was too sharp, too heavy. He climbed the stairs, each step a drumbeat in his skull. He shoved open the bedroom door, empty.

He stumbled down the hall to Micah's room. The bed was made. The room was too neat. Toys gone, books missing, shelves hollowed out. He ripped open drawers, finding only scraps, a sock, an undershirt, and a forgotten crayon. He rushed back to the primary bedroom, threw open the closet door, and found Celeste's clothes were missing, the hangers rattling like bones.

"Celeste?" His voice cracked, raw, swallowed by the silence.

The truth struck him in a jagged instant, tearing through his chest. They were gone, really gone.

And then the quiet horror followed, slow and crushing, wrapping around him like a vice. He stood in the empty doorway, panting, the walls tilting, his body refusing to move. The rage came in waves, but beneath it was something worse, emptiness, vast and final.

He stopped, tried to tell himself he was overreacting. She was visiting her parents. She needed space. She'd be back. The days passed. He called her cell, but there was no answer. Then weeks. He left messages, but she didn't respond. Then months.

Reality finally set in. And with it came more rage. She left him. Just like that. After everything. Marcus drowned his anger in whiskey. He got into fights, burned bridges, and lost the few friends he had left. He wasted money, blew through his savings, and ignored his financial advisors' calls. He stopped attending charity events, and soon the sponsors stopped calling.

One night, Marcus was arrested outside a nightclub after punching a man who bumped into him. It made the news. Former NFL Star Marcus Hollaway Arrested for Assault. That was the beginning of the end. The endorsements vanished. His reputation was in shambles. He spiraled deeper, convinced the world had turned against him. But the truth was, he had done this to himself.

Driving down the interstate, Celeste thought about the night's events. She had no regrets, no sense of loss, no pain. This time, she was determined that her husband wouldn't find them, and there would definitely be no going back.

With music playing on the radio, her son asleep in the backseat, she felt a twinge of excitement at the thought of starting her life over. The car jolted and bumped as it moved across a series of rumble strips. She checked the rear-view mirror as Micah shifted slightly and clutched his stuffed teddy bear. Nothing in her life had ever led her to believe she would end up in this situation.

The smell of rain mixed with dirt and the arid heat penetrated her senses. Her thoughts drifted as she considered the twists and turns that led her here.

She thought about her parents, her dad, Ronald, a doctor, and her mom, Diane, a literature professor. She made a mental note to call them so they wouldn't worry. She owed them so much for their strong work ethic and the values they instilled in her and her siblings. Although their family was one of privilege, it was also one of discipline.

Education and excellence were non-negotiable; they were deeply ingrained. As a result, she and her siblings thrived. Celeste graduated summa cum laude and was the valedictorian of her high school class. She lettered in track and spoke fluent Mandarin, thanks to her parents' insistence. This language set her apart from her peers in job interviews and opened many doors for her.

A song on the radio reminded her of Eleanor, one of the most important people in her life. Eleanor Monroe was her dad's mother and the heart of their family. She was a woman of strength and faith whose love seemed endless. Celeste could see her sitting on the front pew in church. Her church crown on her head, singing and clapping her hands. She always promised to leave all of her church hats to Celeste. The thought made her smile. She could still hear the lessons Eleanor would whisper to her as a child. Eleanor was the one who taught Celeste how to pray, sit quietly in the face of grief, and find beauty in the little things.

Her grandmother was her biggest fan. Celeste frowned as she remembered the day she came home from school and found her family gathered in the living room. That's the day she learned her grandmother had pancreatic cancer. During Eleanor's final days, Celeste recalled sitting by her bedside for hours. She read to her, prayed with her, and silently held her hand when words were no longer possible.

As she drove down the highway, she realized that when Eleanor was passing, she didn't really grasp the finality of death, but the burden certainly weighed heavily on her. The memory of her grandmother's final whisper resonates deep inside her even now.

"Death isn't the end, baby. It's just the next step home." Eleanor had said.

Those words always returned to Celeste in quiet moments, like now. As the miles stretched out before her, her eyes burned from the strain, and her back was stiff from hours behind the wheel. She blinked hard, forcing herself awake as the road hummed beneath her tires.

For a brief moment, the thought that she could use the trust fund her grandmother left her to start over flickered in her mind. However, her stubborn resolve to carve out her own path made her dismiss the idea as quickly as it appeared.

To her surprise, her old high school sweetheart came to mind. Charles Baker was her next-door neighbor. She wondered where life had taken him. Their relationship was more of a comfortable convenience than one of love and passion.

They parted for college as friends. Celeste smiled faintly at the memory. She realized how rare it was for two people their age to end a relationship as friends. But Charles was the comfort of routine, not the spark that could change her life. That spark came with Marcus.

As the car passed a highway exit for a university, Celeste's thoughts drifted to her old alma mater, Brookfield University, where she majored in Business Administration and Marketing and minored in Psychology. An image of Marcus appeared in her mind. He was the recipient of a stacked scholarship. One for academics and the other for his athletic abilities. He majored in Kinesiology with plans to become a coach one day.

She remembered how disciplined he had been. His natural charisma and leadership earned him respect both on and off the field. Despite his popularity, he remained humble. He studied hard and kept his grades up. He once told her that his parents expected him to maintain a minimum GPA of 3.5 and that he never wanted to disappoint them.

They met in a study group during their freshman year. Marcus was drawn to Celeste's quiet confidence and intrigued by the fact that she wasn't impressed by who he was. Instead, she challenged him intellectually, just like she did with everyone else.

Their friendship kept growing. Then came late-night walks around campus, sharing coffee before exams, and slipping notes into textbooks. Running was something they both enjoyed. Marcus ran as part of his athletic training, and Celeste ran to clear her mind. She remembered the kindness of his gestures: flowers on her pillow, tickets to poetry readings, and handwritten notes left before away games.

By junior year, Marcus's name had been on several watch lists. His trophy case was filled with awards, including the Heisman. Scouts filled the stands, and his dream of the NFL was at his fingertips. Coaches were recruiting him on and off campus during breaks.

His parents were at every home game and traveled to some of his away games. Like his parents, she had been at his side through it all, proud of his accomplishments as a rising star, all while chasing her own ambitions.

She remembered his parents always asking about his grades. And his dad told him, "Never forget there is more to life than football, son."

Celeste squinted. Obviously, Marcus had forgotten those words. She now realized how a single tragedy, like the unexpected death of Marcus's parents, could set off a chain reaction, a domino effect that could send a person's entire life spiraling out of control.

By their senior year, they were inseparable, and Marcus had received multiple offers from professional teams. She smiled when she recalled the look on his face when he proposed. After she said yes, they discussed the pros and cons of each team's offer.

They set the date for their wedding just before the draft announcements were made. At that time, she had believed entirely in the love they shared and the future they had imagined together.

Celeste blinked, letting the memories settle like dust on a windowsill. The warmth of nostalgia lingered, but the hum of the road beneath her reminded her that she was here, in the present, moving forward one mile at a time.

The fuel gauge dipped low, and Celeste eased the car off the interstate into the bright sprawl of a Buc-ee's. The parking lot stretched wide, packed with travelers, big rigs, and SUVs, all pulling in for gas and food.

Inside, the air was thick with the smell of roasted nuts, smoked brisket, and coffee. She held Micah's hand as they navigated the aisles. She let him choose his snacks. He grabbed a bag of gummy bears and a neon-colored slushie. Celeste picked up two breakfast tacos and a black coffee, then stepped outside to fill the tank.

Micah sipped on his slushie as she filled the tank. She watched him with a faint smile, realizing they would need to stop sooner than she planned so he could use the restroom and burn off some energy. For a brief moment, it felt like they weren't running at all—just traveling, just passing through.

Back in the car, Celeste smiled as Micah ate his breakfast sandwich. He had not asked about his dad or where they were going. Micah seemed content eating and playing with his toy.

The highway unfolded quietly before her, the steady hum of the engine settling into a familiar rhythm. With nothing but open road ahead, the stillness wrapped around her, loosening memories she had tucked away for so long.

As they continued their journey, her thoughts once again returned to happier times with the man she had spent so much time with. The man with whom she built her hopes and dreams. The father of that sweet little boy in the back seat.

For a brief moment, tears began to fill her eyes, but she bit her lip and forced herself to think about happier times.

Her mind quickly jumped to her and Marcus's wedding. It had felt like a fairytale, the stone church, her grandmother's church. Its stained-glass windows spilled beautiful color where her grandmother always sat. Her father's arm steadied her as she walked down the aisle toward Marcus. Church bells rang out triumphantly, announcing the joy echoing in Marcus and Celeste's hearts.

The reception was lavish, with music, laughter, and promise. Marcus's first contract funded the celebration. She thought of it now as if she were standing at a distance, watching a younger version of herself stepping into a dream. Her hands ached from gripping the wheel too tightly, the tendons sore as if the tension had settled into her bones.

They honeymooned on the Amalfi Coast. It lived in Celeste's memory like a painting of a villa by the sea, with mornings spent on balconies savoring espresso, evenings filled with pasta and wine, and sunsets over the water. She remembered Marcus whispering he was lucky to have her, and she had believed him. She had carried that light home with her, ready for the life they were to build together.

They began their life together in Texas, young and ambitious, holding fast to dreams that seemed just within reach. Marcus pursued football with a single-minded devotion, his body bruised but his spirit ablaze every time he stepped onto the field. Celeste, equally determined, enrolled at St. Alistair University to complete her MBA.

She recalled her pregnancy through her final year of study. A period when she carried the weight of textbooks and her and Marcus' child at the same time. Her professors admired her grit. But it was her quiet determination, studying late into the night, typing papers with one hand pressed to her growing belly, that became her own private triumph.

Not long after graduation, she gave birth to their son, Micah. Marcus cried when he held him for the first time, his broad shoulders trembling as the tiny infant curled into his chest. From that moment, he was a father overcome by love for his son.

Even in the chaos of training schedules and games, Marcus rushed home at every chance, kicking off his sneakers as he came through the door, eager to cradle his son before sleep. He changed diapers without complaint, whispered to Micah as though the baby already understood the world, and made it clear to everyone that no victory on the field could match the quiet joy of fatherhood.

The warmth of those early family memories lingered at the edges of her mind, soft and insistent, before giving way to the steady rhythm of the road. The endless stretch of highway slowly drew her back to the present, grounding her in the here and now.

A few hours later, the horizon shimmered in the heat. When the gauge dropped again, Celeste pulled into a quiet roadside gas station, its single row of pumps glowing under fluorescent lights. She stepped out, shoulders stiff, and filled the tank while Micah stretched his legs.

The cool air inside smelled faintly of disinfectant and popcorn. Celeste grabbed another coffee, and Micah picked out a toy car from a rotating rack, holding it as if it were a treasure. Back outside, Celeste spotted the golden arches of a McDonald's. Micah ran a few loops around the car before climbing back into his booster seat, cheeks flushed, his laughter echoing briefly in the empty lot. Then they drove to McDonald's.

Inside, Micah spotted the play area. "Can I, Momma, can I?" Celeste nodded, and off he went. She placed their order and let him play until the food arrived. Once he finished, he hurried back, while Celeste ate in peace.

Sipping on her coffee and staring over at the play area, she thought her life in the beginning with Marcus had been precisely what she expected. She found her place in corporate marketing.

She thought she had it all: a successful husband, a beautiful home, and the promise of a perfect life.

For a time, their home in Texas was filled with that tenderness. A young mother with her degree, a father with his arms full of his child, and a sense that the future was bright enough to blind them.

But as she looked back now, she realized how quickly perfection had begun to fracture. She remembered the pressure Marcus carried, the weight of money, fame, and expectation. At first, he managed it with grace, still writing her letters, still planning quiet nights when he was home.

But as the seasons passed, the demands of football changed him. The injuries began. She remembered the sound of ice packs, the smell of pain cream, the frustration in his eyes each time his body betrayed him.

"Momma," called Micah, interrupting Celeste's thoughts, "I am going to the bathroom."

"Just a second, baby," she said as she cleared the table and followed him to the restroom area. "Don't forget to wash your hands, sweetheart." When he finished, she led him back through the restaurant and out to the car. Micah climbed into his booster seat. Celeste buckled her seatbelt, started the car, and pulled out of the lot onto the highway, thinking he still hadn't asked about his dad or where they were going.

Micah started playing with the toy car he picked up at the gas station and chatted with Celeste about his favorite TV show. They sang songs and played a license plate game until he started to fall asleep. Celeste put on some soft music and focused on getting to the next state safely.

By the twelfth hour of driving, exhaustion pressed down on her like a weight. Her eyes burned, her back ached, and her hands cramped from gripping the wheel. The headlights of passing trucks were too bright for her tired eyes.

From the backseat came a drowsy voice: "Momma, how much longer?" She forced a smile into her words, soft but steady. "Not too much longer, baby. Go back to sleep." Twenty minutes later, she spotted a hotel just off the interstate and pulled in, grateful for the chance to stop.

The car rolled to a stop, and Celeste let out a long breath, her shoulders finally loosening. She paused a moment to stretch, letting the quiet of the hotel parking lot wash over her before stepping toward the lobby, ready to focus on the small comforts that awaited them inside.

The lobby smelled faintly of coffee and polished wood. She moved quickly through check-in, her voice low; rest was the only thing on her mind. In the room, she set Micah's backpack on the bed, ordered room service, ran his bath water, and helped him out of his clothes. His body smelled of sweat and road dust, his hair sticking damply to his forehead.

"Bath time, buddy," she whispered. He didn't argue. The warm water soothed him, and he giggled when she poured cups of water over his head, rinsing the day away. She wrapped him in a fluffy white towel and slipped him into clean pajamas. The food arrived just as she finished.

Micah stayed awake just long enough to eat. The two of them ate in silence, half-finished plates left on the table. When he was done, Celeste tucked him into the cool sheets, and within minutes, he was fast asleep.

She took this opportunity to call her parents. She decided to call the landline and, as she expected, there was no answer. She left a message on their voicemail, her voice thin with fatigue: "Mama, Daddy—it's me. We're on the road. Don't worry, we're safe. I'll call when I can." She hesitated, then ended the call quickly, unwilling to say more.

She stepped into the shower after Micah was asleep, letting the hot water pound against her sore shoulders. It washed away the dust, the gasoline fumes, and the tension she'd been carrying. When she finally slid beneath the covers, she felt the bed swallow her whole, exhaustion pulling her under.

Sunlight slipped in through the heavy curtains, pale and thin. Celeste woke to the sound of Micah humming softly to himself as he played with his toy car on the bedspread. For a moment, she lay still, disoriented, the silence of the room so different from the roar of the highway. Then she sat up, her muscles stiff but her mind steadier than it had been the night before.

"Ready to keep going, Momma?" Micah asked, his voice bright with morning energy.

She smiled faintly, brushing a hand through his hair. "Yes, baby. We've got miles ahead."

They dressed, packed their small bag, and made a quick stop at the hotel restaurant for breakfast—pancakes for Micah, coffee, and toast for her. The ordinary normalcy of it felt almost surreal. Then they were back on the road, the car humming beneath them, the long stretch of interstate opening once more.

Chapter 2

The Calling

The faint sweetness of wildflowers drifting in from the roadside permeated the air, drawing her back to a night she would never forget, the call about Maya.

She had been her best friend since grade school. The drive to the hospital. The sterile room. The cold fear in Maya's eyes. And then the loss. Celeste thought about how it wasn't only death that haunted her, but the fear that went unanswered in her friend's last moments.

She prayed that night with desperation, pleading with God for purpose. And she remembered the answer that came, quiet and undeniable: Be the presence you wish had been there.

Marcus had been there too, standing beside her through the long hours and bringing her stale coffee from the hospital vending machine. He had known Maya well, and the grief on his face mirrored hers. He filled Maya's hospital room with her favorite flowers. Maya was Micah's godmother, a bond that made the loss cut deeper. In those moments, Celeste leaned on Marcus's strength, grateful for his steady presence, even as she realized no one could shield her from the ache of losing Maya.

She remembered how she threw herself into her work afterwards, building a career but never a calling. She thought about how colleagues leaned on her in their moments of crisis, how they admired her calm wisdom, how she prayed with individuals and listened as they confided their innermost feelings. And yet, even then, she had felt the ache of disconnection, sneaking away at lunch breaks to fill her leather-bound journals with poems about time and loss and the fragile residue of love.

That answer, "be the presence you wish had been there," changed everything. Within a year, she left her corporate job and enrolled at Mount Zion Theological Seminary. She remembered those early hospice visits, when she read to strangers, sang gentle hymns, and offered her presence rather than platitudes. She realized something undeniable: what people feared most was not death, but dying alone. And she had vowed to be there for as many people as she could.

Now, just five classes away from finishing her Master's, she could see her hospice ministry taking shape. A ministry rooted in peace, poetry, scripture, and music. She often imagined the book she would someday write, Whispers at the Edge of Heaven. For her, dying was never about letting go. It was about going home.

Her thoughts moved to Reverend Naomi Carter, the retired chaplain who had become her mentor. Celeste remembered the first seminar, "The Ministry of Presence," and how Reverend Carter's raw honesty had pierced her. When a person is dying, they do not need a preacher. They need a witness.

She could still hear Naomi's voice and feel the warmth of that first extended conversation. It was as if the older woman had been waiting for her. Naomi taught her to listen for the subtle language of the dying, to honor the silence, and to grieve without drowning in every loss. Even now, when she speaks with Reverend Carter, she always reminds her, "You were born for this child. One day, you will guide me home, too."

The afternoon dragged on, the monotony of cracked asphalt broken only by glimpses of rest areas and passing semis. When her eyelids grew heavy, Celeste pulled into a travel plaza. Micah ran ahead to a small grassy patch near the picnic tables, chasing his toy car across the concrete and into the grass. She stood by the pump, refueling as the sun lowered in the sky. Inside, the air was filled with the scent of fresh coffee and frying oil. She bought a cup, strong and black, and let the warmth warm her hands before heading back to the car. Micah climbed in again, cheeks flushed, hair damp with sweat, his laughter echoing as the road pulled them onward.

Her mind wandered despite the rhythm of the journey, thoughts drifting like the sunlight flickering across the dashboard. Faces and voices from the past surfaced unbidden, each one a quiet reminder of lessons learned and moments cherished, pulling her gently from the hum of the present.

Once again, Celeste's thoughts were interrupted by the low rumble of passing trucks, the steady sound of tires on asphalt and the sudden roar of a motorcycle speeding past. As the noises subsided, she thought of Sam Brooks, the old jazz musician who had initially pushed her away with his sharp words. "I don't need no prayers, and I don't need no pity." She remembered the way she had noticed his records, how that single question about jazz had opened a door for her. She could still feel the evenings spent with him, notebook in hand, as she scrawled poems while the music played.

She could hear his voice admitting regrets and speaking of unspoken love. She remembered the night she had played his favorite live recording and his whisper: "That's the sound of heaven, isn't it?" He had passed hours later, leaving her with a lesson that shaped her work. Ministry was not always scripture. Sometimes it was music, poetry, or simply being present.

After his passing, Celeste wrote "The Song at the End," a deeply personal poem. It hangs in her office to remind her of why she had chosen this path. With Naomi's wisdom and Sam's memory etched into her, Celeste knew her calling. She was not just called to witness death; she was there to honor life. She reminded herself daily that in the end, it is not about how a person dies. It is about how they are remembered.

She shifted in her seat, reached for the side, and turned on the massage feature. Just as she finished, a soft, familiar song played on the radio. Marcus's parents had loved this artist. Celeste's fingers tightened on the wheel. She thought of how much they loved and supported Marcus. How proud they were of his accomplishments, yet they never lost their humility.

The song carried her back to that silence, to the weight of loss that had reshaped him, and by extension, their marriage.

She remembered the phone call, the night before the accident, his mother's soft request for sweet tea, his father's teasing about a golf game. The next day, they were gone, taken by a drunk driver. Celeste could still hear the guttural sound Marcus made when he dropped the phone. A sound of grief so raw it had cut through her.

After that, everything shifted. She remembered trying to hold him together as he fell apart. He withdrew, drank too much, missed his appointments, and raged against the world. She remembered the sting of his words: "You don't understand. You still have your parents." The resentment in his eyes had frightened her. She had watched him throw himself recklessly into the game, burning himself down with every hit.

Then came the knee injury. She remembered the night he sat with the swelling, the pills untouched beside him, the television blaring with the game he could no longer play. She had seen in his face the hollow recognition that it was over. Football was gone, and with it his sense of self.

The man she had loved became someone else. The abuse didn't begin overnight. It started with emotional withdrawal, then harsh words, and control. The man who once lifted her now tore her down, blaming her for things she couldn't control. She endured it longer than she should have, believing that the man she had fallen in love with was still in there somewhere. She glanced in the mirror at Micah's small face pressed against the window, his breath fogging the glass. He looked peaceful, unaware of the storm she carried inside.

Celeste thought about how long she had tried to hold on. She told herself Marcus was grieving, that this wasn't who he really was. She reminded herself of the man who used to bring her flowers for no reason at all. The man who left notes in her textbooks in college. The man who held their son for the first time with tears in his eyes. But love alone couldn't save them.

The memories of how his drinking escalated. How his anger became unpredictable. She recalled the nights when Marcus didn't come home, and when he did, he reeked of alcohol and bitterness. She chuckled when she thought of how she learned to measure his moods by the way he shut the door; if it slammed, she braced herself for an argument.

The abuse began slowly. First with silence, then with words, cutting, cruel words meant to make her feel as small as he did. "You think you're better than me now? You wouldn't have anything if it weren't for me. If you loved me, you'd understand." The physical abuse came later.

She told herself she could manage it. She kept making excuses for him. It was just the grief talking, and that the man who once left flowers on her pillow was still there. But over time, she could no longer deny that the man she married was gone. Then, one night, he grabbed her arm.

It wasn't hard, not enough to leave a bruise, but enough to make her breath catch. Enough for her to see the look in his eyes. The same wild, untethered anger she'd been ignoring for too long. The first time he hit her, he swore it was a mistake. He begged her forgiveness. He cried.

Celeste believed him until it happened again. And again. Over the years, Marcus grew more controlling, isolating Celeste. He didn't want her to go out with friends. He monitored what she wore and whom she spoke to. Every argument ended in rage, shattered objects, and bruises hidden beneath long sleeves.

Celeste tried to leave twice, but every single time Marcus managed to find her, manipulate her, and pull her back in. "No one will love you like I do. Do you think you can make it without me? You're my wife. That means you stay."

And Celeste, broken and exhausted, stayed until the night that changed everything. That was the moment she knew. The night Celeste finally left was one she would never forget.

Marcus had been drinking heavily, his bitterness boiling over after another rejection from a coaching job. The argument started over nothing. But when Marcus threw a glass against the wall, their son, Micah, flinched from the noise, something in Celeste snapped.

Micah was watching, observing, and learning. She could not, and she would not, let her son grow up in a house where he thought that this was what love looked like. She wouldn't let herself become a shell of the woman she once was. And if she stayed, he would think this was normal.

She remembered the nights of slammed doors, the sharp, angry words designed to cut, the manipulation that kept her tethered. "No one will love you like I do. You are my wife. You stay." For years, she endured. This time would be the last. She waited until Marcus went out drinking, then grabbed her and Micah's things. She packed their bags, took Micah, left the house, and vanished into the night, all while Marcus was out. These thoughts made Celeste angrier with herself than with Marcus. She vowed never to allow herself to excuse abuse of any kind in the future.

Chapter 3

Exit 258

The knock of sunlight against the heavy curtains roused Celeste from sleep. For a moment, she didn't remember where she was. The quiet hum of the air conditioner, the faint scent of clean linen clinging to the sheets, the weight of a hotel mattress instead of her own bed, all of it felt strange and distant. Then she turned her head and saw Micah curled on his side, his stuffed bear tucked close, his small breaths even and soft.

"Morning, buddy," she whispered when his eyes blinked open.

They dressed quickly, Celeste smoothing the wrinkles from her blouse while Micah tugged on his sneakers with sleepy determination. Downstairs, the hotel restaurant smelled of syrup and butter. Micah devoured a plate of pancakes, his cheeks sticky with syrup, while Celeste stirred her coffee slowly, letting the warmth anchor her. She forced down a piece of toast, her appetite muted by the long stretch of road still waiting for them.

Back in the parking lot, the early sun was already hot against her skin. She loaded their overnight bag into the trunk and buckled Micah into his booster seat. He pressed his bear to the glass, watching the world slide by as Celeste pulled up to another gas station pump.

As she fitted the nozzle into the tank, the meter ticked steadily upward. Celeste leaned against the SUV for a moment, rolling her sore shoulders, feeling the weight of miles behind them and miles ahead. Inside, Micah's head tilted as he hummed to himself, making his toy car race across the seat.

The tank clicked full. She capped it, slid back behind the wheel, and started the engine. The road stretched out once again, and with a steadying breath, Celeste merged back onto the interstate. This was the last leg. The end was somewhere up ahead, waiting.

By late afternoon, the miles gave way to coastline, the sky opening into a brighter horizon. The interstate narrowed, then turned into a two-lane road bordered by pines and glimpses of ocean blue. Celeste gripped the wheel tighter as a sign came into view, weathered but welcoming: **Exit 258 — Solmere.**

She eased off the highway, the sound of tires shifting from asphalt to the softer hum of coastal pavement. Micah stirred in the backseat, his stuffed bear slipping from his lap.

They had finally arrived.

She lingered a moment in the quiet of the main street, taking in the gentle sway of the café sign and the distant glint of sunlight on the water. The town felt small, familiar, and yet entirely new, offering a calm she hadn't known in years. Celeste drew in a deep breath, letting the salty air fill her lungs, steadying herself before stepping toward the next chapter of her life. Celeste arrived in Solmere with luggage neatly stacked in the back of her SUV, her son, Micah, and the quiet determination to rebuild her life. Solmere was the last exit on the highway. She chose the town because it was peaceful, tucked away along the coast, far enough from the life she left behind. And she thought Marcus wouldn't think to look for her there.

Celeste parked on the quiet main street of Solmere, the salty ocean air mingled with the scent of coffee drifting from a café down the block, making Celeste crave a strong cup of coffee. But she had to settle down first.

The sign for Solmere Realty swung gently in the breeze, its hand-painted lettering weathered but proud. She pushed the door open and stepped inside.

Behind the desk stood a woman with sharp, kind eyes and the unshakable confidence of someone who had never left this place.

"Hello, I am Elizabeth Warren," she said, extending her hand.

Celeste shook it firmly. "Hello, I am Celeste Monroe. This is my son Micah. We just arrived in town, and I'm looking for a place."

Elizabeth's handshake was warm, her voice welcoming.

"You have come to the right place. I have lived here all my life. Are you looking to rent or buy?"

"I'd like to purchase eventually," Celeste replied, "But for now, I need a place to stay until I find a house."

Elizabeth nodded thoughtfully. "I think I've got the right place for you. A charming little cottage, it's quiet, safe, and near the edge of town, but close enough that you won't feel isolated.

Celeste nodded, hope flickering in her chest.

"And for Micah," Elizabeth continued, her voice practical but caring, "there's a woman I trust who can come to the house and watch him when you need. Solid, dependable. There is also a daycare center I can recommend. I think it's one of the best in town. Small, personal, the kind of place where kids are seen, not just supervised."

Celeste felt her throat tighten, the mix of relief and exhaustion almost overwhelming.

The drive to the cottage wound through narrow streets lined with cedar trees. When they arrived, Celeste paused at the porch steps. From the front porch, she could see the shimmer of the ocean.

The house itself was simple but beautiful, with white siding trimmed in soft blue, weathered shutters, and a crushed seashell path leading to the door.

Inside, the cottage opened into a sunlit living room with warm wood floors and soft neutral tones. There were two bedrooms, a large eat-in kitchen with wide windows, and two bathrooms, one downstairs and one upstairs. A small staircase led to a bonus room with a bunk bed and an open loft area that spilled out onto a rooftop deck overlooking the sea.

Celeste turned slowly, taking it in. "It's beautiful," she whispered. "We'll take it."

On the way back to the office, they stopped at the daycare center. The building was small but cheerful. Micah wandered to the play area, watching the other children with quiet curiosity while Celeste talked with the staff.

When they returned to the realty office, Celeste completed her rental application. Elizabeth reviewed the application. Her gaze lingered on Celeste's work history.

"You wouldn't happen to be looking for a job, would you?"

Celeste raised her eyes.

"Yes, actually. I planned to start looking once we settled in." Elizabeth's smile widened as she read the degrees listed: Marketing, Psychology, and Theology. You have extensive leadership experience.

She smiled, "Good. There's a women's center here in town, good people, but they've been searching for a new director for months. You might be exactly what they're searching for."

Celeste blinked. "A woman's center?"

"Yes. Small, underfunded, but full of heart. They need structure, someone who knows how to rebuild from the ground up."

Celeste swallowed, the possibilities opening before her like a road she hadn't dared imagine. A cottage, safety for Micah, and, even here at the edge of the sea, a chance to rebuild herself.

Elizabeth slid the papers into a folder and stood. "Welcome to Solmere," she said, shaking Celeste's hand while handing her the keys and rental agreement to her new home. "Sometimes the right place finds you before you know you're looking."

Chapter 4

Decompression

The next morning, sunlight poured through the curtains, gentle and gold. The ocean breeze carried the faint cry of gulls as Celeste woke to the sound of Micah's small footsteps paddling across the floor. He was already dressed, his curls tousled and his bear tucked under one arm.

"Mama," he said, grinning. "Can we go get my new room stuff today?"

Celeste smiled, brushing a hand through his hair. "Yes, baby. We've got a lot to do today."

They spent the morning driving through town, stopping first at a small clothing shop where Celeste selected a few outfits for both of them, comfortable and simple pieces. Then they found a home goods store, where Micah helped choose bright throw pillows, a small lighthouse-shaped lamp, and seashell-patterned curtains for his new room. Celeste added soft blankets, candles, and a few framed prints of ocean landscapes, all small touches to make the cottage feel like home.

At lunch, they sat at a café overlooking the water. Micah stirred his chocolate milk with a straw, thoughtful.

"Do we really need a housekeeper, Mama?" he asked.

"Maybe just sometimes," Celeste replied. "She could help while I'm at work."

He nodded, accepting the answer easily. "And the daycare?"

Celeste smiled. "We'll stop by this afternoon. I think you'll like it."

Later that day, they returned to the daycare center Elizabeth had shown them. The building seemed even more cheerful in the daylight, its playground bright with color and laughter. Inside, Celeste completed the necessary paperwork while Micah met the teacher and explored the play area. When it was time to leave, he was already reluctant to go.

"I like it here," he said as they walked back to the car.

"I thought you might," Celeste replied, squeezing his hand. "It's close to home, and everyone seems kind."

Back at the cottage, they unpacked the last of their bags. Micah ran up the stairs to the bonus room, his laughter echoing down the hall.

"I want this one, Mama!" he called. "The bunk beds!"

Celeste climbed halfway up the stairs, smiling.

"All right. But you have to promise me that you won't go out on the deck without me."

"I promise," he said solemnly, holding up his pinky.

They spent the rest of the weekend settling in, washing linens, arranging books, and walking down to the beach in the evenings. Celeste watched Micah run along the shoreline, his footprints washing away with each wave. For the first time in a long while, she felt peace settle into her bones.

Monday morning, Celeste dropped Micah off at the daycare center. She stood for a moment watching until he disappeared inside. He waved from the window, excitement shining on his face. The quiet moment grounded her, reminding her why she had chosen this fresh start. Then she turned and headed toward her next stop.

From there, Celeste drove to Seafoam Spa & Wellness. The soft chime of the door announced her arrival as she stepped inside. The faint scent of eucalyptus and lavender seeped into the air as she stepped inside, leaving the weight of the week on the mat outside. Soft instrumental music drifted through the lobby, blending with the distant hum of a waterfall fountain.

"Welcome, Ms. Monroe," a receptionist greeted, handing her a petite plush robe and slippers. "Your appointment is ready, everything from hair to nails and a pedicure. We'll have you renewed in no time."

Celeste let out a small laugh. "Thank you. I could use it."

The stylist's chair cradled her like a familiar hug. Warm towels wrapped around her shoulders, the scent of shampoo rising in delicate waves. She closed her eyes as her hair was washed, the massage of her scalp loosening knots of tension she hadn't realized were there. The stylist hummed softly as she snipped and trimmed, shaping her hair into a sleek style that framed her face.

Next came the nail station. Celeste sank into a leather chair, the bubbles of a pedicure foot bath warming her toes. She watched the nail technician paint her fingers a soft coral, the color catching the sunlight streaming through the spa's tall windows. Her feet followed, buffed, polished, and smoothed until they gleamed. She flexed them gently, marveling at the sensation of lightness and care.

Between treatments, she sipped a steaming cup of herbal tea, letting the quiet lull of the spa wrap around her. No deadlines, no Micah's small demands, no town errands, just the steady rhythm of breathing, the gentle hum of music, and the warm presence of being fully attended to.

By the time the spa day drew to a close, Celeste felt a tangible shift within her, her shoulders lower, her back straighter, her mind quieter. She stepped out into the bright afternoon sun, carrying a small bag of spa products the receptionist had recommended.

Her next stop was Quill & Ink Bookstore, a cozy shop tucked between the café and the bakery she had noticed earlier. The bell chimed as she entered, and the smell of paper, leather, and ink greeted her like an old friend. Shelves towered high, lined with journals, novels, poetry collections, and hand-lettered notebooks.

Celeste's fingers brushed over the spines, lingering on the smooth texture of a leather-bound journal embossed with gold leaf. She pulled it from the shelf, flipping through blank pages that smelled faintly of cedar and possibility.

"This one," she whispered to herself, placing it gently into her bag. "New beginnings deserve new words."

She wandered further, picking up a few more journals, a collection of poetry she had been meaning to read, and a small sketchbook for Micah to doodle in on rainy afternoons. Each item felt deliberate, a small declaration of intention.

At the counter, she paid and walked outside, the late afternoon sun bathing the street in gold. Bag in hand, hair freshly styled, nails polished, and feet pampered, she felt a rare sense of contentment. It had been a long time since she allowed herself a day that asked nothing of her.

Micah would be waiting to go home, no doubt bursting with tales of his daycare adventures, and she would return to the cottage with a sense of quiet victory, a day entirely for herself, a pause between the responsibilities and the rebuilding.

Chapter 5

New Beginnings

Celeste inhaled deeply, letting the scent of the sea mingle with the crisp autumn air. She had arrived here, truly arrived, and for the first time in a long while, she allowed herself to believe that she deserved every bit of care, joy, and peace that Solmere had to offer.

When Celeste returned to the daycare center to pick up Micah, the sound of children's laughter drifted through the open windows. She stepped inside, spotting him on the floor beside another boy, both bent over a tower of wooden blocks.

"Micah," his teacher called gently. "Your mom's here, sweetheart."

Micah's face lit up. "Mama!" He sprang to his feet, his new friend rising beside him.

"This is Kai," Micah said proudly. "We built the tallest tower, and it didn't even fall when people walked by!"

The other boy grinned shyly. "Hi, Mrs. Monroe."

Celeste smiled warmly. "Hello, Kai. That sounds impressive."

Kai's teacher joined them. "Micah did very well today. Bright, curious, and very polite. The two of them hit it off right away. Inseparable since snack time."

Celeste's chest eased. "That's wonderful to hear."

She thanked the teacher and took Micah's hand as they walked to the car. He was bubbling with stories before they even reached the door.

"Kai's dad builds boats," he said quickly. "And he said I can see one sometime. And we drew superheroes! Mine can fly and has lightning powers."

Celeste laughed softly. "It sounds like you had a big day."

"Yeah," he said, grinning. "I like it there, Mama. And I like Kai."

Celeste squeezed his hand gently. "I'm glad, baby. Sounds like you found a good friend."

As they drove back toward the cottage, the sky blushed pink over the water. Micah's voice filled the car, recounting every small detail of his day, and Celeste let the sound of it wash over her—the laughter, the sunlight, the easy joy of a child finally free to be happy. For the first time in a long time, she felt that they might truly belong.

That evening, after Micah was tucked into bed and the soft rhythm of the ocean drifted through the open window, Celeste sat at the small kitchen table with her laptop open. The glow from the screen lit her face, and she hesitated for a moment before dialing the number Elizabeth had given her earlier that day.

A calm voice answered. "Solmere Women's Resource Center, this is Angela speaking."

"Hello," Celeste said, her voice steady but warm. "My name is Celeste Monroe. Elizabeth Warren referred me. She mentioned there might be a position available."

There was a brief pause, followed by a welcoming tone. "Yes, Elizabeth told us someone might be calling. Are you available to come in for an interview this week?"

Celeste exhaled softly. "Yes, absolutely. Any day that works for you."

"Tomorrow morning at ten would be perfect. Just ask for me when you arrive."

"I'll be there," Celeste said, and when she ended the call, she let out a breath she hadn't realized she'd been holding. It felt like the first step toward something solid.

The next morning, she dressed in a crisp blouse and tailored slacks, smoothing her hair as she glanced in the mirror. Micah, still buzzing from his first day of daycare, tugged at his backpack straps while humming one of the songs they had played in class.

After dropping him off, Celeste parked in front of the Women's Center, a modest brick building with white shutters and a mural of a tree blooming with handprints. The scent of coffee drifted from inside as she stepped through the door.

Angela, the woman she had spoken to, greeted her with a smile. "Ms. Monroe. It's good to meet you finally."

Celeste returned the smile, shaking her hand. "Thank you for seeing me."

They led her into a small conference room lined with bookshelves and community flyers. Two other women were there, a board member and a program coordinator. The questions came gently but with purpose: her experience in nonprofit work, her education, her vision for supporting women rebuilding their lives.

Celeste answered honestly, her voice calm but enthusiastic. She spoke about management, grant writing, community outreach, and her belief that real change began with compassion and structure. When she talked about her time in corporate marketing, she framed it not as wasted years but as training for this: organizing, budgeting, and building relationships.

When the interview ended, Angela smiled again. "You've given us a lot to think about. Thank you, Celeste."

As Celeste stepped outside, the ocean wind brushed against her face. She felt lighter, as if the town itself had exhaled with her. The sense of possibility stayed with her all the way home.

Five days later, the phone rang while she was folding laundry.

"Hello, this is Angela from the Women's Resource Center. We want to formally offer you the position of Director. Your background and energy are exactly what we need."

For a moment, Celeste couldn't speak. Her throat tightened, her eyes stung. "Thank you," she finally said, her voice low but full. "I accept."

When she hung up, Micah looked up from his toy cars. "Mama? You got a job?"

She laughed, a sound bright and unguarded. "Yes, baby. I did."

Micah clapped his hands. "Then we can get ice cream!"

Celeste smiled, pulling him into her arms. "Yes. Ice cream to celebrate."

On the morning of her first day, Celeste arrived early. The small office space was simple but filled with potential: sunlight through gauzy curtains, a secondhand desk, and an old filing cabinet in the corner. She unpacked her small box: a framed picture of Micah, her grandmother's worn Bible, and a notebook where she kept fragments of poetry.

Angela appeared in the doorway with two mugs of coffee. "Welcome home," she said softly.

Celeste smiled. "That's exactly what it feels like."

She spent the day walking through the center, learning names and hearing stories. Volunteers showed her the intake process, the reading room, and the pantry stocked with donated essentials. Each space hummed with quiet resilience.

By the end of the day, Celeste stood by her window, the ocean breeze threading through the slightly open pane. The sky outside blushed gold. For the first time since she left Texas, she felt something steady take root inside her: peace, purpose, and the beginning of belonging. The weight of the day settled gently rather than pressing on her.

She whispered to herself, "We made it."

That night, after putting Micah to bed, Celeste sat on the small balcony outside her bedroom. The ocean murmured beyond the dunes, the sound rhythmic and grounding. She opened her leather journal, the same one she had carried through every chapter of her life, and let her pen hover for a moment before writing.

October 7 —

First day. The women's stories remind me that survival wears many faces. Some came with bruises, others with invisible wounds. All of them are trying to rebuild from something broken. I know that language, the slow, trembling dialect of starting over.

She paused, listening to the faint laughter of children from a nearby house, the sigh of waves against the shore.

Today, one woman told me she hasn't slept through the night in years. Another said she wants to feel safe again. I tried to tell them I understand that healing isn't a straight road. It's a series of small, stubborn steps toward light. But instead, I just listened. Maybe that's enough for now.

Her hand slowed as she finished the entry:

Be the presence you wish had been there. You said that to yourself once, Celeste. Don't forget it now.

She closed the journal, set it on the small table beside her, and leaned back in the chair. The sea breeze tangled softly through her hair, cool and salt-sweet.

For the first time in a long time, she didn't feel like she was running. She felt anchored. And as the night deepened, she whispered a quiet prayer into the dark, not for strength this time, but for gratitude.

In the weeks that followed, she worked long hours helping other women get back on their feet, many of them escaping situations like hers. She wrote grants, built community programs, and organized literacy initiatives for young mothers who never had a chance to finish school. Her work became her purpose, a way to channel all the pain of her past into something meaningful. She settled into the rhythm of the work without even noticing when it became familiar.

Micah thrived in Solmere. He made friends, did well in school, and, for the first time, their home was peaceful, with no slamming doors or tension. There were just the quiet sounds of the waves at night and the laughter of a boy who finally felt safe.

One evening, Celeste and Micah stopped at the local supermarket to pick up groceries before heading home. The store buzzed softly with the rhythm of small-town life, carts rolling, children's laughter echoing down the aisles, the hum of an old radio playing a Motown tune overhead.

Micah walked beside her, clutching a box of cereal. "Mama, can we get this one? Kai says it turns the milk blue!"

Celeste smiled, her voice gentle. "Just this once."

They turned the corner near the produce section, and there he was. Kai stood on the lower rail of a cart, grinning, while a tall man and a woman inspected a row of avocados nearby.

"Kai!" Micah shouted, waving.

The boy's face lit up. "Micah!" He jumped down from the cart and ran over.

Kai's mother turned at the sound, her smile immediate and kind. "You must be Micah's mom. I'm Serena Carter-Tanaka, and this is my husband, Hiroshi."

Hiroshi extended his hand. "Good to meet you. We've heard a lot about Micah. It sounds like those two are already a team."

Celeste shook his hand, warmth rising in her chest. "I think so. Micah couldn't stop talking about Kai all the way home yesterday."

Serena laughed softly. "That makes two of them. They've been planning their superhero team. Kai's the inventor and Micah's the one who can fly."

The boys darted off toward the fruit display, arguing good-naturedly about which superpower was better. Their laughter rang through the aisle.

Serena placed a few apples into her cart. "We've lived here a while. Solmere's a good place to raise a child. Safe, close-knit, full of people who look out for one another."

Celeste nodded, feeling something ease in her shoulders. "That's exactly what I was hoping for."

"Welcome, then," Hiroshi said with a smile. "You'll find your footing here faster than you think."

As they parted, Micah and Kai exchanged a triumphant handshake, something they had clearly invented between snack time and nap time at daycare.

Outside, the evening sky was painted in streaks of pink and lavender. Micah chattered happily as they loaded groceries into the car, his voice full of stories and laughter.

Celeste looked toward the horizon, the ocean just beyond the town, the wind soft and salt-sweet. For the first time in years, the world didn't feel dangerous or small.

It felt possible.

She smiled, started the car, and whispered to herself as they pulled onto the road, "We're home, baby. We finally made it home."

Celeste, too, found a kind of peace. She spent evenings on her small balcony overlooking the ocean, reading poetry, letting words fill the spaces Marcus had once occupied. She rediscovered faith, not the kind that told her to endure suffering, but the kind that reminded her she was worth more than the life she had left behind.

Seven months later, Celeste's phone rang while she was sorting through papers at her desk. The name Elizabeth Warren lit up the screen.

"Hi, Elizabeth," Celeste answered, smiling. "It's been a while."

"Hello, Celeste," Elizabeth replied, her tone bright but businesslike. "I wanted to reach out with some news. The owners of the cottage have decided to sell the property. They're hoping for a quick sale, and they've asked me to see if you might be interested before we list it. They're pricing it below market value."

Celeste's heart lifted. She didn't need time to think. "Yes," she said, almost breathless. "Absolutely, yes. I want to buy it."

Elizabeth laughed softly. "I thought you might say that. I'll have the paperwork ready for you this week."

When Celeste ended the call, she stood for a moment, stunned by how right it felt. This little cottage by the sea, once just a temporary refuge, had become home. It felt like a promise she hadn't dared to imagine before now.

She hurried to find Micah, who was sprawled on the living room floor, building a fortress from blocks.

"Guess what, baby?" she said, kneeling beside him. "We're going to buy the cottage. It's going to be ours for good."

Micah's eyes widened, his grin spreading fast. "Ours? Really, Mama?"

"Really," she said, pulling him close. "No more moving. No more packing up. This is home now."

Micah jumped to his feet, pumping his small fist in the air. "Then I'm keeping my room forever!"

Celeste laughed, tears stinging her eyes. "Forever sounds perfect to me."

Chapter 6
Min Jisoo

Once again, Celeste started writing poems, journal entries, and letters she'd never send. Solmere had given her a quieter life, but the words inside her still pressed for release.

On a whim one evening, she logged back into an online literature forum she'd once used in college. It felt like stepping into an old library—screen names instead of faces, threads of poems instead of pages. She began posting short pieces about the ocean, about hospice, about starting over in a town that felt borrowed and then slowly became hers.

That's where she met him.

It began with poetry, comments under her posts about Neruda, Rilke, and Gibran. A user named Eun Sol replied with gentle observations, asking questions that felt more like invitations than critiques.

Their threads moved into private messages. At first, it was just two anonymous lovers of words.

He only knew her by her initials. She only knew him as Eun Sol.

But soon, their messages grew longer and more personal. She found herself looking forward to his words, to the way he saw the world, to the way he seemed to understand her without knowing the details of her past. For the first time in years,

Celeste felt something stir inside her, a longing she thought she had buried.

Months later, the literary world exploded.

An article circulated through the forum, then through social media and news sites: speculation that the mysterious poet Eun Sol was actually the actor Min Jisoo.

Celeste had seen his face before—movie posters, interviews scrolling past her feed, magazine covers at the grocery store. But she'd never connected the quiet man on screen with the one who wrote midnight replies to her poems.

Then one night, the speculation ended.

On a private social account he rarely used, a simple post appeared:

Yes. I am Eun Sol. For years, I wrote in shadows, afraid that my voice would not be enough. But if my words have brought even one person comfort, then they were never just mine to keep.

The post went viral.

Celeste stared at it, phone in hand, heartbeat unsteady. Eun Sol, the one who understood her poems, was Jisoo.

She sat with it for a long time, the cottage quiet around her, the ocean whispering outside. She didn't message him that night. She didn't know what to say.

Days passed. Their messages resumed, careful at first, almost shy. She now called him "Jisoo." He still called her by her initials.

And then came the night everything changed.

Celeste had gone to bed early. Micah was fast asleep upstairs in the bonus room, his bear tucked under his arm. The house settled into its familiar hush: the soft tick of the clock, the distant murmur of waves.

Her phone lay on the nightstand, screen dark.

While she slept, across the ocean, a man who seldom wrote anything personal sat awake in Seoul, the blue light of his phone washing over his face. He opened their chat, stared at her initials, and began to type.

Type again.
Stop. Pace the room. Delete

Finally, he let the first message go.

Eun Sol
I can't sleep.

A minute later:

Eun Sol:
That's not unusual for me.
But tonight it feels… different.
Like if I don't say this now, I'll carry it forever and regret it.

Another pause. Then a longer burst.

Eun Sol:
You once asked why my poems always feel like they're holding something back.
I didn't answer you honestly.
I said it was "style." It wasn't.

Dots blinked, disappeared, returned.

Eun Sol:
I was a quiet child in a noisy world.
Born in Busan.
Only child.
My father is an architect.
My mother is a literature professor.
People hear that and assume my childhood was full of warmth, books, and late-night conversations.
There were books, yes.
Conversations?
Not really.

Eun Sol:
My parents are intellectual.
Disciplined.
They believe love is best expressed through achievement.
Good grades.
Correct posture.
The right path.

Eun Sol:
I was the wrong kind of child for that kind of love.

He kept going, messages arriving in short and long waves.

Eun Sol:
While other kids played soccer in the street, I sat by the window with a book. My mother would leave poetry on my desk—Yeats, Rilke, Jeong Cheol. She never said, "I thought you'd like this." She just… left them. My father worried about how quiet I was. He'd say, "A man needs to be seen. How will the world know what you're capable of if you never speak?"

Eun Sol:

The only person who understood me was my grandmother. She lived in a small house with creaking floors and a garden that always smelled like wet earth. She used to tell me, "You don't have to be loud to be heard. The right people will listen to your silence."

Celeste slept on, the phone silent on her nightstand as his words crossed the sea.

Eun Sol:

My first heartbreak wasn't a woman. It was losing her. When she died, the house felt hollow. Too big for my grief. I wrote my first real poem then. "The House with No Voice." No one has ever seen it. But that poem… changed me. I realized writing was how I survived the things I couldn't say out loud.

Eun Sol:

My father didn't know what to do with that version of me. So he insisted on something "practical."

Eun Sol:

I enrolled at Yonsei for International Business. I went to class, took notes, and wore the right clothes. I looked like everyone else. Inside, I felt like a misplaced page in the wrong book.

Eun Sol:

Then fate, or accident, intervened. In my second year, a friend dragged me to a student play rehearsal. They were missing someone. They asked me to read a part. I still remember the feeling. Onstage, I could pour out everything I kept hidden and call it "acting." Emotion with permission. Controlled vulnerability. It felt like breathing for the first time.

Eun Sol:

I started acting in secret. Small plays. Student films. Until someone noticed, and suddenly there were auditions, contracts, and cameras.

Eun Sol:

My breakout role was in a small indie drama. I played a melancholic writer dealing with lost love. People said the performance felt "raw," "too real." Of course it did. I wasn't acting. I was letting all the unsaid things finally speak.

Another message—short, almost sheepish:

Eun Sol:
Fame followed.
I still don't know if that was a blessing or a punishment.

Eun Sol:

The public sees a brilliant, enigmatic actor who chooses his roles carefully, speaks in what they call "poetic riddles," then disappears when the spotlight gets too bright. They gave me nicknames: "The Poet Idol." "The Gentleman Introvert." "The Last Romantic."

Eun Sol:

I know how that sounds. Flattering. Charming, maybe. But the truth is less beautiful. I am an introvert pretending to belong to a world that drains me. Acting gives me life. Attention steals it.

He stopped there for a long moment, pacing, phone warm in his hand.

Then.

Eun Sol:

After my military service, I burned out. Silently, because public exhaustion isn't aesthetic. So I disappeared. Not officially, just… less of me everywhere. I traveled to Europe and to Japan. I walked through cities where no one knew my name. I sat in libraries and read until my eyes blurred. I rediscovered that before I was an actor, I was a boy with books and too many unwritten things inside him.

Eun Sol:

During that time, I started posting poetry again. Secretly. In forums like the one where I met you. Under a name that felt safer: Eun Sol. "Eun" for silver. "Sol" for the lone pine on a winter hill. Elegant, but alone.

Eun Sol:

Those poems were the truest version of me. Longing. Nostalgia. The beauty and ache of age and experience. I told myself no one would ever connect them to the man on screen.

Another burst:

Eun Sol:

I was wrong.

Eun Sol:

A literature professor in Paris cited "Eun Sol" in a paper. Fans started hunting for the identity behind the words. A journalist compared old autographs to scanned manuscripts. Then one day the theory appeared: "Is Eun Sol actually actor Jisoo?"

Eun Sol:

My team said to deny it. My friends said to ignore it. My heart said: You have hidden long enough.

Eun Sol:

So I posted the truth. You saw it. You didn't say anything for three days. I thought I'd lost you.

He exhaled, dropped onto his sofa, and kept going.

Eun Sol:

That reveal changed everything. The poems became a phenomenon. They gave me a book deal. *The Quiet Between Us.* They teach it in university courses now. They say I "captured the modern condition of distance and connection." But I wrote those poems because I was lonely. Because the only person who ever fully understood me, my grandmother, was gone. Because every room I walked into as "Jisoo" made me feel farther from the boy she loved.

The next series of messages came in quicker, like he'd stopped censoring himself.

Eun Sol:

There is one more thing I need to tell you.

Eun Sol:

People speculate about the woman behind my poems. They aren't entirely wrong. There was someone once.

Eun Sol:

Her name was Isabelle Laurent. A French Korean poet and literature professor. Seven years older than me. We met in Paris during my hiatus.

Eun Sol:

I was in a small Montmartre bookstore café, scribbling in my journal, trying to outrun myself. She walked up, holding Baudelaire and black coffee. "Excusez-moi… you write in Korean?" she asked.

Eun Sol:

A conversation about poetry became hours.
Then weeks.
Then late nights in hidden jazz bars,
poems read under the dim lights along the Seine.
Our love was slow.
Beautiful.
And temporary.

Eun Sol:

She had already lived a whole life before me—marriage, heartbreak, continents.
She understood something I didn't want to accept:
"Some love stories," she told me once,
"aren't meant to be lived fully.
They're meant to be written."

Eun Sol:

She was offered a position in Canada.
I had a career waiting in Korea.
Neither of us asked the other to stay.
On our last night, she gave me a handwritten letter.
She told me, "Read it when you're ready."

Eun Sol:

It took me months.
When I finally unfolded it, it said:
"You once told me you fear being forgotten.
But some people are never meant to be forgotten.
You will write about this. I know you will."

Eun Sol:
And I did.
She is in the bones of many poems.
Not all, but many.
And yet…
Even that love was a bridge I was never meant to cross all
the way.

The next message came slowly, like he had walked laps
around his apartment before sending it.

Eun Sol:
I'm telling you all of this because I need you to know what
kind of man is asking for a place in your life.

Eun Sol:
I am a man between two worlds.
Public and private.
Poet and actor.
Adored and misunderstood.
Surrounded and lonely.

Eun Sol:
The world sees a brilliant, enigmatic actor.
But privately,
I still belong to
books,
handwritten letters,
nights alone with jazz playing in the background,
and one grandmother's voice telling me
that somewhere in the world,
the right person will understand my silence.

Long pause.

Then.

Eun Sol:

For a long time, you were only initials on a screen to me.
Two letters.
A strange comfort.
A mind that met mine in Neruda and hospice and oceans and
quiet faith.

Eun Sol:

You told me once that you write poems in the sand
so you can watch the waves carry them away.
I haven't been able to stop thinking about that.
You, on a shoreline in a town I have never seen,
letting the ocean erase your pain one tide at a time.

Eun Sol:

I need you to know something.
Your messages have become the brightest part of my days.
Your words are the first thing I look for in the morning, and
the last thing I reread at night.

A shorter line:

Eun Sol:

I am afraid of saying this.
But I am more afraid of never saying it.

Eun Sol:

I am in love with you.
Several seconds passed.

Then:

Eun Sol:
I do not say that lightly.
I do not mean it as a passing warmth or a flattering phrase.
I mean:
I love the way your mind moves.
The way you speak about death with tenderness instead of fear.
The way you protect your son in every sentence, without even knowing you are doing it.
The way you carry grief and still choose compassion.
The way you make me feel less alone in a world that has misunderstood me my whole life.

Eun Sol:
I am asking something of you that I have never asked anyone:
Please consider whether you can love a man like me.
A man whose life is not simple.
Whose work is public even though his heart is private.
Who carries a past filled with unfinished loves and unspoken poems
Who is still learning that he is worthy of being loved for himself and not his image.
A final set of messages, sent slowly:

Eun Sol:
If this is too much, tell me.
Tell me and I will pull back.
I will still be grateful for every line we have shared.

Eun Sol:
But if it is not too much, if some part of you feels the same thread I do, pulling quietly between Solmere and Seoul, then let me come to you. Not as the Poet Idol. Not as the Last Romantic. Not as the man the world thinks it knows.

Eun Sol:
Let me come to you simply as Jisoo.
Just a man who is tired of being lonely
and who is daring, for the first time,
to ask someone to choose him back.

Eun Sol:
When you wake, you do not have to answer right away.
I know your mornings.
You will make coffee.
You will check on your son.
You will listen to the ocean.

Eun Sol:
If, after all that, you still want me in your life type just one
word.

Eun Sol:
Stay.

Morning light slipped through the curtains of the Solmere
cottage.

The waves murmured against the shore.

Celeste reached for her phone, expecting the usual handful
of messages.

What she found instead was a night's worth of confession,
lines stacked one after another, a man's whole life and heart laid
bare across a screen.

She read in silence, tears slipping down her cheeks, one
hand pressed to her chest as if holding something fragile in
place.

By the time she reached the last word, *Stay*, her hands were trembling.

She set the phone down, wiped her eyes, and stepped to the window, watching the water catch the early light.

This man.

This quiet child from Busan.

This actor who spent his life on stages and still felt invisible.

This poet who hid behind the name Eun Sol and finally stepped into his own name.

This man who had loved and lost and still believed in deep, old-fashioned love.

This man was asking her to be his future.

She picked up the phone, stared at the message thread for a long moment, and then, with fingers still shaking, she typed a single word:

Celeste:
Stay.

One night, Jisoo sent her this.

"You remind me of the golden hour when the world hushes in admiration. You are a quiet fire, and I, a moth drawn too close."

Celeste's heart stuttered. His words had again crossed from admiration into something more. Her fingers hesitated over the keyboard, but the response came before she could stop herself.

"And if you are the moth, then let me be the night breeze carrying your longing to the stars."

Their messages stretched across time zones, their lives unfolding in mismatched hours. When Celeste woke up in Solmere, Jisoo was ending his day in Korea. When she sat on the beach in the late afternoon, he was just beginning his morning in Seoul.

But they made it work. They found each other in stolen moments, morning messages, midnight calls, voice notes sent between meetings or while walking home. They spoke in poetry and prose, in midnight confessions and whispered dreams. Every message carried echoes of something more profound than either of them dared name.

Months passed, their bond growing with every exchange. Celeste found herself waiting for his words the way the tide waited for the moon. Jisoo confessed that her messages had become the brightest part of his days, a lighthouse guiding him through the monotony of life.

And then, one evening, a message from Jisoo changed everything.

"What if words are no longer enough? What if I long to hear your laughter, to watch your eyes light up when you speak?"

Celeste stared at the message, heart pounding.

She had been avoiding this moment. Afraid that reality would not match the dream, afraid that what they had built in ink and longing would crumble under the weight of the real world. But Jisoo's next words shattered her doubts.

"No matter the distance, I will find my way to you."

When Jisoo arrived in America, Celeste was waiting for him at the airport. She had been nervous the whole way there, palms sweating against the steering wheel. Would it be awkward? Would he look at her differently?

And then, there he was.

The same kind eyes, the same gentle smile, the same presence that had comforted her through screens and letters. For a moment, they simply stood there, taking each other in. Then Jisoo spoke, his voice soft but certain.

"Celeste."

And just like that, everything else faded away.

They spent the next few weeks together, wandering through Solmere, retracing the words they had written to each other. They sat by the shore, the wind tangling their voices together. They found a little bookstore where Celeste read him poetry, her voice trembling at first and then steady.

Days melted into nights, and their love unfolded like the verses they had shared, tentative and then bold. But love, no matter how beautifully written, is not without its trials. When the time came for Jisoo to return to Korea, reality pressed against the dream. Would distance steal what they had built?

Their love story, once whispers on a screen, had found its way into the real world. And like the tide returning to shore, they always found their way back to each other.

In this new town, Celeste sought solace, not expecting to find love again. But fate had other plans. The man she met was in another country, yet their connection defied distance. Their love story began with chance encounters, gentle conversations, and the exchange of heartfelt messages and poetry. They found comfort in each other's words, in the way their pain and longing intertwined, healing wounds neither of them thought would ever mend.

"In your words, I find peace, like waves that calm the restless sea. You speak and my world quiets, a melody only my heart can hear."

His messages brought light into her life, and she responded in kind.

"You are the warmth in winter's chill. A whisper in the night so still. With you, I am found, no longer lost, love's beacon despite the cost."

Each day, they unraveled parts of themselves that had been buried under years of pain. Love became their refuge, a story written in moments and emotions too deep to ignore. The past lingered, but together, they dared to dream of a future where love could thrive despite the scars they carried.

Jisoo knew before he even left that he could not go back to Korea without making a decision.

"I do not want this to be the end," he told her one night, fingers tracing the curve of her hand. "I want to stay."

But staying meant facing more than just love. It meant cultural adjustments, legal challenges, and the weight of Celeste's past, a past neither of them knew was about to catch up with them.

Because while Celeste and Jisoo were falling deeper into love, Marcus was already on his way.

Chapter 7

Blind Rage

For years, Marcus had tried to push Celeste from his mind, convincing himself that she had vanished, leaving their life behind like a bad dream. But deep down, the fact that she had disappeared without a trace gnawed at him. He had looked for her before, halfhearted searches fueled by wounded pride rather than real effort. But then something shifted in him. He realized he did not just want to find her; he needed to. He wanted to be with her.

His attempts had led to dead ends. No address, no listed phone number. Just a ghost of a woman who had once shared his life. But Marcus was not a man who gave up easily. One night, sitting in a dimly lit bar nursing a glass of whiskey, he overheard a conversation at the next table. A man, half drunk, was talking animatedly to his friend.

"Yeah, I ran into her a couple weeks ago in Solmere. Still got that same quiet grace about her. You remember Celeste Monroe, right?"

Marcus's entire body went still. His grip tightened around the glass. He turned toward the man, keeping his expression neutral.

"Excuse me. Did you say Celeste Monroe?"

The man blinked, then grinned in recognition.

"Marcus? Man, it has been years. You used to be married to her, didn't you?"

Marcus forced a casual nod, though his pulse pounded in his ears.

"Yeah. Just surprised to hear her name."

The man shrugged.

"Saw her in Solmere not long ago. She looked good, serene, you know?"

Marcus muttered a thank you, threw some cash on the bar, and walked out. Solmere. That was all he needed to know.

When Marcus arrived in Solmere, it did not take long to find her. Small towns had a way of keeping track of people, and Celeste, despite her attempts to live quietly, had established a presence here. He spotted her through the window of a café, sitting at a corner table, sipping tea and reading.

For a moment, he just watched her. She looked different, more relaxed, maybe. But she was still Celeste. His Celeste. His jaw tightened as he pushed the door open.

Celeste sensed him before she saw him. The moment she looked up, her entire body tensed. The fear in her eyes sent a rush of something dark through Marcus, but he smothered it.

"Celeste," he said, his voice low.

She did not speak, just set her cup down with careful precision. Marcus leaned in slightly, his voice steady but firm.

"We need to talk."

Before Celeste could respond, another presence emerged beside her, Jisoo.

He moved with quiet confidence, his gaze calm yet unwavering. He set his hand lightly on the back of Celeste's chair, a subtle but unmistakable act of protection.

Marcus exhaled sharply.

"This is between my wife and me."

Jisoo tilted his head slightly, his voice even but cold.

"She is not your wife."

Marcus's fingers curled into fists at his sides.

"That is not for you to say."

Jisoo's expression did not change, but there was something immovable about him.

"Celeste has already said it."

For a long moment, the two men held each other's gaze. The tension in the air was thick, but Jisoo did not back down.

Marcus turned to Celeste.

"We need to talk. Alone."

Celeste, her voice steadier than she felt, finally spoke.

"I have nothing to say to you, Marcus. Please leave."

Marcus let out a sharp breath, his jaw clenched, but he saw the resolve in her eyes. And standing beside her, Jisoo did not move an inch.

After a beat, Marcus stepped back.

"This is not over."

He turned and walked out of the café.

Celeste let out a shaky breath. Jisoo did not say anything at first, just gently touched her hand. "Are you alright?" Jisoo, he asked softly.

Celeste looked up at him, her heart still racing, but in his presence she felt something stronger than fear. She felt safe.

"I am now."

Jisoo had never liked leaving Celeste behind when he returned to Korea. But, this time, his concern was more serious. The incident with Marcus at the café had left an uneasiness in his chest that would not settle.

"Come with me to Korea," Jisoo urged, brushing his thumb over Celeste's knuckles as they sat on her porch one evening.

"I do not feel right leaving you alone."

Celeste sighed, squeezing his hand in return.

"I wish I could, but there is too much happening at work. The literacy initiative is launching, and I need to be here for it. I will be okay, Jisoo."

He studied her carefully. His dark eyes filled with concern. He did not argue. Celeste was independent, and he respected that. But as he prepared to leave, he could not shake the unease gnawing at him.

"Call me the moment you need anything," Jisoo told her before he left.

"Promise me."

Celeste smiled, pressing a kiss to his cheek.

"I promise."

But even as Jisoo's plane touched down in Seoul, he could not shake the feeling that something was about to go wrong.

Days later, Jisoo was in a meeting with his agents, discussing potential scripts and endorsement deals, when his phone rang. It was Celeste. Relief flooded him until he answered.

All he could hear were muffled shouts.

"Celeste?"

Jisoo sat upright. A loud bang came through the line, followed by Celeste's terrified voice.

"Marcus, stop!"

Jisoo's blood ran cold.

"Celeste, what is happening? Talk to me!"

But she could not answer. The sound of fists pounding against a door filled the silence, followed by Marcus's drunken, slurred rage.

"Open the door, Celeste. I swear I will break it down."

Jisoo's heart pounded against his ribs.

"Celeste, listen to me. Call the police. Now."

"I am trying," Celeste's voice shook.

Then came the sickening sound of splintering wood, a crash.

Jisoo shot to his feet, knocking his chair over. His agents looked at him in alarm, but he barely noticed.

"Celeste!" Jisoo shouted

The sound of the phone hitting the floor, Celeste's terrified screams, and Marcus's furious shouting made Jisoo feel utterly helpless.

He clenched his fists, his breath coming in rapid gasps. Celeste! Celeste!

"Celeste, stay with me. The police are coming," Jisoo pleaded.

A scuffle. A loud thud.

Then, Celeste's strangled gasp.

Jisoo's world narrowed to that sound. He heard Marcus's voice, close, too close.

"You think you can run from me? You think you get to be happy without me?"

Jisoo's entire body went rigid with fury.

"Marcus, if you hurt her, I swear…"

Then, finally, sirens.

A commotion. Angry shouts.

A strangled sob from Celeste.

Jisoo gripped the phone so tightly his knuckles turned white.

"Celeste? Celeste, are you there?"

A shaky breath. Then her voice, small and trembling.

"Jisoo, he is gone. The police took him."

Jisoo exhaled sharply, pressing a hand to his forehead. He felt his entire body unclench, only to be flooded with a new urgency.

"I am coming home."

"Jisoo, you do not have to"

"I am coming home," he repeated, already signaling for his assistant to book the earliest private flight back.

Nothing else mattered. He was going back to Celeste. And this time, he was not going to let Marcus anywhere near her again.

Chapter 8

Silent Rebellion

Jisoo had spent years carefully curating what parts of his life the world could see. Even his family knew only fragments, enough to satisfy their curiosity but never enough to invite scrutiny. As he sat across from his mother in their family's Seoul apartment, he knew there was no more room for secrecy.

His mother, Park Jiyeon, was a woman of quiet elegance. Though she rarely pried, Jisoo knew she had sensed something different about him lately, how often he checked his phone, how his gaze softened when he spoke about Solmere.

"There is someone I need to tell you about," Jisoo finally said, setting down his tea.

His mother arched a brow, waiting. His father, a man of few words, remained focused on his newspaper, although Jisoo could tell he was listening.

"Her name is Celeste," Jisoo continued. "I met her through poetry."

His mother tilted her head slightly. "Through poetry?"

He smiled. "It started that way. But she is more than that to me."

Jiyeon set her cup down with precision. "You mean to tell me that after all these years, you have fallen in love and I am only just hearing about it?"

Jisoo chuckled, rubbing the back of his neck. "It was not something I planned, Mother. It just happened."

His father finally spoke. "Is she Korean?"

"No."

A pause. His father folded his newspaper, regarding him with the same critical stare he had given Jisoo when he first chose acting over business.

"Then she will never understand what it means to be with someone like you."

Jisoo stiffened. "She understands me better than anyone ever has."

Jiyeon studied him carefully. "How serious is this?"

Jisoo met her gaze without hesitation. "I intend to marry her."

For the first time, his mother looked genuinely surprised. She had watched him drift in and out of relationships, always distant, never fully invested. To hear him speak with such conviction was unexpected.

"And she feels the same?"

"Yes."

His mother asked, "Who is this woman? What is her background?"

"She is a college graduate with three degrees. She is divorced and has a son. She is two years older than I am, and she is African American."

His father sighed, setting his paper aside. "This life you lead, Jisoo, it is not normal. It is not quiet. You cannot disappear into love and expect the world to leave you in peace."

Jisoo's jaw tightened. "I have never wanted the world, Father. I only want her."

His mother exhaled, shaking her head. "This will not be easy, Jisoo. Have you considered what it means for her? For you?"

He nodded. "I have. And I do not care."

Jiyeon studied him for a long moment, then sighed, a small, knowing smile tugging at the corners of her lips.

Jisoo had expected resistance. But he had not expected outright refusal. His mother's face, usually composed, was taut with disapproval. His father, who rarely displayed strong emotions, sat rigidly in his chair, the weight of his silence heavier than words.

His father's voice was firm and final.

"No."

"Excuse me?" Jisoo asked, although he had heard him clearly.

"We do not approve of this," his mother said, her voice measured but unwavering. "And we forbid it."

Jisoo let out a breath, gripping the edge of the dining table. "I am not a child. You do not get to forbid anything."

His mother narrowed her eyes. "You may be a grown man, but you are still our son. And this woman, this Celeste, she is not right for you."

"You do not even know her," Jisoo shot back.

"We know enough," his father said. "She is older than you. She is a foreigner. A divorcee. And she has a child. Do you think that kind of woman fits into our family? Into your life?"

Jisoo clenched his jaw. "She is not that kind of woman. She is the woman I love."

His mother exhaled sharply, folding her hands in her lap as if to contain her frustration. "Jisoo, think rationally. Do you know what people will say? What the industry will say? Your career has survived because you have been careful and private. Do you think they will stay silent about this?"

Jisoo shook his head. "I do not care about the industry."

His father scoffed.

"Then what about her? Have you considered how difficult this will be for her? If you marry her, the media will devour her. She will be scrutinized, picked apart, and insulted. And you," he said, leaning forward, his eyes sharp, "you will regret it."

Jisoo inhaled slowly, trying to keep his temper in check. "I will never regret loving her."

His mother's expression softened for a fraction of a second, but then she steeled herself.

"And when it becomes too hard? When the pressure is unbearable? When your life, your reputation, your entire world begins to unravel, will she still be enough?"

Jisoo stood abruptly, his chair scraping against the floor.

"She has always been enough."

His mother flinched at the edge in his voice. His father, however, remained unmoved.

"You are being foolish," his father said. "You will realize that soon enough."

Jisoo met his father's gaze, something cold settling in his chest.

"I thought you wanted me to find happiness."

"We want you to be wise," his father corrected. "And this is not wisdom."

His mother reached out as if to reason with him one last time.

"Jisoo, please. You do not have to do this."

Jisoo swallowed hard, his heart aching with the weight of their rejection.

"Yes, I do."

And with that, he turned and walked away.

Jisoo had always been a respectful son. He had spent his life honoring his parents' wishes, following the path they laid out for him, even when it went against his own desires. But this time, he could not obey.

He did not argue. He did not plead his case further. Instead, he listened in silence as his mother and father made their position clear. Celeste was not the woman for him.

"We forbid it."

The words echoed in his mind long after he left the conversation. There had been no need to fight, no need to convince them. They had made up their minds, and Jisoo knew that nothing he said would change that.

So he made his decision.

That night, while the house was quiet, Jisoo packed a single bag. He moved through his childhood home without a sound, the weight of unspoken words settling over him like an unbearable fog. His parents would wake up to find him gone, his absence a silent rebellion.

His driver took him to the airport without question. There was no public flight, no scheduled departure, just a private jet ready to take him back to the only place he wanted to be.

Back to Celeste.

As he settled into his seat, exhaustion pulled at him, but sleep refused to come. His mind was filled with the sound of her voice, frantic and terrified, calling his name as Marcus shattered her safety. He had been powerless to protect her then, trapped halfway across the world, listening to her fear through the phone.

Never again.

The jet took off, and Jisoo exhaled, his hands clenched into fists. His parents had asked him if Celeste would be enough. If love would be enough. He already knew the answer.

Yes. It had always been yes.

Jisoo stepped off the private jet, his body weary from the long flight but his heart full of urgency. The moment he landed, he called Celeste.

"I am here," he said, his voice a quiet promise.

She was waiting for him at the small private terminal in Solmere, arms wrapped around herself as the cool coastal air swept around her. The moment their eyes met, she exhaled a breath she had not realized she was holding.

Jisoo did not hesitate. He crossed the space between them and pulled her into his arms, holding her tightly, feeling the way her body relaxed into his.

"You are here," she whispered.

"I will always come back to you," he murmured into her hair. "But next time, I am not leaving without you."

Celeste pulled back just enough to look at him, concern flickering in her eyes.

"Jisoo"

"No." He cut in gently, shaking his head.

"I will not leave you alone again, not after what happened."

His fingers traced the side of her face, his touch both reverent and protective.

"We travel together from now on. No matter where I need to go, you are coming with me."

Celeste hesitated, but she saw the determination in his gaze. He was not making a request. He was making a vow.

"I cannot always drop everything for a trip," she admitted softly. "My work, my commitments…"

"Then we will plan around them," Jisoo assured her.

"But I refuse to be an ocean away the next time you need me."

His voice dipped lower, raw with emotion.

"When I heard you scream, when I could not reach you, Celeste, I have never felt so helpless. I will not let that happen again."

She reached up and held his face, as though confirming he was solid. "You were with me," she whispered. "Even an ocean away, I wasn't alone."

Jisoo leaned into her touch, closing his eyes for a brief moment before pressing a soft kiss to her forehead.

"And now I am never leaving your side."

Later that evening, as they sat together in Celeste's cozy home, Jisoo stretched out his long legs, glancing around the small but warm space she had made for herself. He smiled at the books stacked on the coffee table, the soft throw blankets draped over the armchair, and the faint scent of lavender lingering in the air.

"This place is you," he said, looking at her with quiet admiration.

Celeste chuckled. "It is small, but it is home."

Jisoo hesitated before speaking again, his voice thoughtful. "I was thinking that we should find something bigger."

She blinked. "Bigger?"

He nodded.

"I will be moving everything here, my books, my piano, my work equipment. I need a proper office, a library, and a space for my workouts. We will also need rooms for when my family or your family comes to visit."

He looked at her with gentle intensity.

"We need a home, Celeste. A place that is ours."

The realization hit her fully then. He was not just staying temporarily. He was settling.

With her.

She exhaled softly; the weight of his words settled into her chest.

"Jisoo, are you sure?"

Jisoo reached for her hand, his fingers lacing with hers.

"Celeste, I did not just come back for you," he said, his voice steady. "I came back to build a life with you."

He turned her hand over, tracing soft circles against her palm.

"I know my parents disapprove. I know there are challenges ahead. But none of that changes the way I feel."

He lifted his gaze, meeting hers with quiet certainty.

"I want to marry you."

Celeste's breath caught.

Jisoo continued, his voice unwavering.

"I do not want to love you from a distance anymore. I want to wake up next to you every morning. I want to come home to you, no matter where life takes us."

He brought her hand to his lips, pressing a tender kiss to her fingers.

"I want you to be my wife, Celeste."

Tears welled in her eyes as she let his words settle.

Jisoo, the man who had once lived between two worlds, had finally chosen his.

And it was her.

Chapter 9

The Cost of Rebellion

Celeste sat in silence, her fingers resting lightly against her lips as she absorbed Jisoo's words. I want you to be my wife.

She had dreamed of this, of hearing him say those words, of the quiet certainty in his voice as he asked her to build a life with him. And yet, beneath the overwhelming love she felt for him, there was an ache. A hesitation.

Jisoo's parents.

She swallowed hard and pulled her hand from his, standing slowly. Jisoo watched her, his brows furrowing in concern.

"Celeste?"

She turned away, wrapping her arms around herself as she walked toward the window. Outside, the night stretched vast and endless, the waves lapping softly against the shore. She had come to Solmere to rebuild, to start fresh. She had never imagined she would find a love like this in the process.

But love wasn't just about two people. It was about the lives entwined with theirs.

Finally, she spoke, her voice quiet but firm.

"Jisoo… I can't marry you."

The silence that followed was heavy.

Jisoo rose slowly, his expression unreadable.

"You don't mean that."

She turned to face him, her eyes filled with sorrow.

"I do."

Jisoo took a step closer, searching her gaze.

"Celeste, if this is about Marcus, if you're afraid"

She shook her head.

"This isn't about Marcus. This is about your family."

A flicker of understanding passed through Jisoo's eyes, but he remained silent, allowing her to speak.

"I know how much your family means to you," she continued. "I know how deeply you respect your parents. And I know that they disapprove of me." Her voice wavered slightly, but she steadied herself. "I won't be the reason you lose them."

Jisoo's jaw tightened. "You wouldn't be."

She gave him a sad smile.

"Maybe not in your eyes. But in theirs?" She exhaled, her hands clasping together. "Jisoo, if I marry you knowing that your parents don't accept me, I'll always feel like an intruder in your life. Like a wedge between you and the people who raised you."

Jisoo ran a hand through his hair, frustration flickering across his face.

"Celeste, I love you. This is our life, not theirs."

"And yet, they are your family," Celeste whispered. "The people who shaped you, who stood by you long before I ever did." She stepped forward, placing a hand against his chest. "I would never forgive myself if I took that away from you."

His heart pounded beneath her touch, but he didn't pull away.

Celeste's voice softened.

"You've always been a respectful son, Jisoo. You didn't argue with them when they forbade our relationship. You didn't try to convince them because you honor them. I love that about you." She swallowed hard. "But if you marry me against their wishes, you'll be forced to choose, and I can't let you do that."

Jisoo shook his head. "You're asking me to wait for something that may never happen."

Tears burned at the back of her eyes, but she nodded. "I know."

"Celeste…" His voice cracked slightly. "Don't do this."

She reached up, cupping his face in her hands. "I love you. But I need to know that we can have a future without resentment, without pain, without looking over our shoulders, wondering if we've broken something that can't be repaired."

Jisoo's hands tightened into fists at his sides.

"So what? I go back to Korea and ask for their permission like a child?"

His voice wasn't angry, but there was deep hurt laced within it.

She shook her head.

"I just want you to talk to them. To try." She inhaled shakily. "And if they still refuse to accept me, then I need to know you are at peace with your decision."

Jisoo was silent for a long time.

Then he exhaled sharply, closing his eyes. When he opened them again, there was something resolute in his gaze.

"Alright," he said softly. "I'll talk to them."

Celeste's lips trembled as she nodded.

He took her hand, bringing it to his lips.

"But know this," he whispered. "No matter what they say, I will not let them take you from me."

Celeste closed her eyes, leaning into his touch. She prayed that love would be enough.

The night was quiet. Outside, the waves whispered against the shore, their rhythmic lull a familiar comfort in Solmere. Inside, Celeste sat curled up on the couch, her bare feet tucked beneath her, flipping through a book of poetry. The lamp beside her cast a soft glow, painting her in warm, golden shadows.

Jisoo watched her from across the room, pretending to read but not absorbing a single word. She was humming under her breath, some melody she must have picked up in passing. The sound was light and effortless, like the quiet happiness that had settled between them since his return.

He should feel at peace.

Instead, his mother's voice echoed in his mind.

"This is not the life we wanted for you."

"A woman like her… divorced, older, American. Do you think she understands what it means to be part of our family?"

"If you marry her, you are turning your back on everything, your name, your duty, us."

Jisoo closed his eyes for a brief moment, inhaling deeply. He had not argued with them and had not begged or pleaded for mercy. That wasn't his way. He had only listened in silence as his father's disappointment and his mother's heartbreak settled over him like a weight he couldn't shake.

Even now, in this moment, watching Celeste's lips curve into a soft smile as she read, feeling the warmth of her presence so near, he still felt the weight of it pressing down on his chest.

If I'm this happy, why does it feel like I've lost something?

His hands clenched slightly against the book in his lap. His parents had always been his anchor. He had spent a lifetime making them proud, doing what was expected, what was honorable. Their rejection felt like an unraveling, as though the thread that had bound him to his past had been severed.

"Jisoo?" Celeste's voice was gentle, pulling him back to the present. She looked up from her book, her brow furrowed in quiet concern. "You're a million miles away."

He exhaled slowly, offering a small smile. "Just thinking."

She tilted her head, studying him. She always saw more than he wanted her to.

"Good thoughts?" she asked softly.

Jisoo hesitated. The truth sat heavy on his tongue, but he couldn't bring himself to place that burden on her. Not yet.

Instead, he reached across the space between them, threading his fingers through hers.

"I'm here," he said, as much a reassurance to himself as it was to her.

She gave his hand a gentle squeeze, seeming to accept his answer. But as she went back to reading, Jisoo stared at their joined hands, knowing that sooner or later, he would have to tell her the truth.

That loving her had come at a cost.

And he wasn't sure if he would ever stop mourning it.

Jisoo and Celeste spent the next few weeks searching for a home, their days filled with quiet excitement and the warmth of shared dreams.

Jisoo, ever the planner, had a list of requirements: an office where he could write and work in solitude, a library filled with natural light, a dedicated space for his workouts, and enough room for family and friends when they visited. Most importantly, a private, secure location. Celeste, on the other hand, wanted a place that felt like them, something warm, something peaceful, something that whispered home the moment they stepped inside.

They toured houses along Solmere's quiet streets, from charming cottages to sleek modern homes, but none of them felt quite right. Jisoo would walk through each space, running his fingers along the bookshelves or standing before large windows, imagining the life they would build within the walls. But Celeste could always tell when he wasn't convinced.

One afternoon, as they stepped into yet another house, Celeste let out a small sigh.

"Are we being too picky?" she mused.

Jisoo turned to her, a small smile playing at his lips.

"Isn't that the point? We're not just looking for a house. We're looking for our home."

She nodded, squeezing his hand. "You're right."

Then, they found it.

A breathtaking coastal estate situated on a private, two-acre property, offering both luxury and seclusion. The residence, accessible via a private paved road, ensured privacy and exclusivity. A gated entrance provided security, and guests could be seen and granted access remotely from inside the home.

Upon entering, Jisoo and Celeste were greeted by cathedral ceilings in the large foyer. The moment they walked inside, Celeste could feel it; this was the one.

Jisoo stood in the open living room, turning to her with a look of certainty.

"This is it," he murmured.

Floor-to-ceiling windows throughout the house flooded the space with natural light, providing panoramic views of the ocean and creating a tranquil atmosphere.

The open floor plan facilitated effortless movement between spaces, complemented by solid wood cabinets and stone counters that lent an air of sophistication to the kitchen. A wet bar with built-in features, along with an eating space in the kitchen, made it both functional and perfect for entertaining.

At the heart of the home, a striking floor-to-ceiling fireplace anchored the formal living room, offering a cozy yet elegant space to unwind. The formal dining room was ideal for hosting special occasions, while the large sun porch extended the living space outdoors, providing an idyllic spot to take in the ocean breeze and breathtaking sunsets.

For work and study, the home featured a combined large office and library, providing a quiet and inspiring space with an ocean view, as well as a medium-sized office for additional workspace.

The primary suite was a true retreat, featuring tray ceilings, two walk-in closets, and an en-suite bathroom with solid-surface countertops and spa-like amenities. In addition to Micah's bedroom and bathroom, there were four generously sized guest bedrooms, each with its own private bath, offering a peaceful escape with expansive windows overlooking the water or the surrounding landscape. There were two separate half baths for visitors, one near the home's entrance and the other near the pool.

Outside, the patio led to a swimming pool and an adjacent pool room, creating a private oasis perfect for relaxation and entertainment. A fully equipped gym ensured that fitness could be an integral part of daily life without requiring a trip to the gym.

With its floor-to-ceiling windows, breathtaking ocean views, and a design that balances luxury with warmth, this home was not just a place to live; it was a sanctuary where the beauty of nature meets the comforts of modern living.

Celeste smiled, her heart swelling. "Yes," she whispered.

Jisoo reached for her hand, threading his fingers through hers. "Then let's make it ours."

Chapter 10

Min Jisso's Citizenship

Jisoo's decision to become an American citizen was not easy. It was driven by his desire to build a life with Celeste and secure his place in her world. But his journey to citizenship was far from straightforward.

The first hurdle was the immigration process itself. Jisoo's legal team explained that becoming a citizen was a long, meticulous process. As a high-profile figure, Jisoo had to navigate both personal and public scrutiny while handling a labyrinth of legal paperwork. From visa applications to background checks, the process felt like a never-ending cycle of waiting and uncertainty.

Jisoo couldn't help but feel overwhelmed at times. The legal jargon was alien to him, and while his team was efficient, it didn't stop the frustration from creeping in. Each form he signed reminded him that, despite his fame, he was still a foreigner in the land he was trying to call home.

To further complicate matters, Jisoo's celebrity status added another layer of complexity. His public life made him more visible than the average applicant, and that scrutiny seemed to heighten every challenge. He had to be mindful of every move, knowing the press was always watching.

Living in Solmere with Celeste, Jisoo had come to love the quiet beauty of the town, but it wasn't always easy. He often found himself reflecting on his cultural differences, things he'd previously brushed off as minor but that now felt magnified in the context of his new life.

For example, Jisoo was used to the social structure and familial ties in Korea, where respect for elders was paramount and a sense of obligation often defined relationships. In America, however, he encountered a much more individualistic culture, one that sometimes left him feeling isolated or uncertain of his place. He was used to the concept of community but found that he had to work harder to build his own in this new country.

There were also the small but significant everyday cultural differences that added up over time. He had to adjust to American slang and colloquialisms, sometimes misinterpreting casual phrases or coming off as stiff when he didn't understand the context of certain expressions. At the same time, his natural politeness, deeply ingrained by his upbringing, was occasionally misinterpreted as aloofness or distance, especially in more informal American social settings.

And then there was food. As much as he loved American cuisine, including burgers, pizza, and all the deliciously unhealthy options, he also missed Korean comfort food. At times, the lack of familiar flavors left him feeling a little out of sync with the world around him. He found solace in cooking his own dishes, which also helped him feel closer to his roots.

Although Jisoo had studied English for years, the language barrier sometimes became more evident in moments of emotional weight. During his citizenship interviews, he had to express not only legal facts but also personal experiences. There were moments when he struggled to fully convey his thoughts or feelings in English, leaving him feeling as if a part of his identity was lost in translation.

The most challenging part wasn't necessarily understanding the language. It was understanding how to express his evolving sense of self. As he moved closer to American citizenship, Jisoo found himself at a crossroads in his identity. In Korea, he had always been the celebrated actor, the beloved son. In America, he was becoming something else, someone who belonged to a quieter, more intimate world with Celeste. This feeling of duality, being both an outsider and someone who was starting to feel at home, was a challenge he often pondered.

Jisoo knew that his family still valued tradition above all else, and the thought of him becoming fully integrated into American society was yet another obstacle he faced, as he balanced his love for his family with his desire to build a life with Celeste.

They had always envisioned him living in Korea, representing their family's legacy in the Korean entertainment industry. The thought of him leaving his country for good was difficult for them to accept.

But when they learned that he was now actively pursuing American citizenship, their disappointment turned to outright indignation.

During a conversation with his father on a rare phone call, Jisoo's father asked, "Jisoo, are you sure this is what you want? To be an American citizen? You'll be giving up your roots." His father's voice was tinged with concern, and Jisoo could hear the weight of his worries.

"This is how you repay everything we have given you?" his father's voice was sharp over the phone, the weight of his disapproval cutting through the distance. "You are turning your back on your country, your heritage?"

Jisoo stood by the window of his home in Solmere, staring out at the ocean, his grip on the phone tightening. He had expected resistance, but the sheer depth of their anger still struck a painful chord.

His mother's voice came next, softer but no less heavy with sorrow. "You would give up everything for this woman? You would throw away your name, your place in our family?"

Jisoo closed his eyes and inhaled deeply. "I am not throwing anything away. I will always be your son, and I will always honor my roots. But my life is here now. I need to do this for my future."

His father scoffed. "Your future? What future? You have no family there, no roots. Just her."

And there it was again. The blame was always placed on Celeste. To them, she was the reason for everything: his departure, his choices, his supposed betrayal.

His mother's voice wavered. "Jisoo, come home. We can fix this. Whatever hold she has on you."

"No," Jisoo cut in gently but firmly. "Celeste hasn't done anything to me. I love her, but this decision is mine. Becoming an American citizen doesn't erase who I am. It only strengthens my ability to build a future here."

But they would not hear it. His father muttered bitterly in Korean, and his mother, unable to continue, hung up first. The silence after the call was deafening.

Jisoo set his phone down slowly, his chest tight. He had spent his whole life trying to be the son they wanted him to be.

But for the first time, he was learning that living for their approval would only leave him empty.

He had chosen his path even if it meant walking it without them.

Despite his outwardly calm demeanor, the pressure of it all began to take a toll on Jisoo's mental health. The constant juggling of cultural identity, legal challenges, and family expectations weighed heavily on him. At times, he found himself questioning whether he was doing the right thing, whether he was genuinely ready to give up a part of his old life in Korea to create a new one in America.

But there was one thing he knew for sure: Celeste. Their relationship had given him the strength to continue moving forward, to push through the setbacks and doubts. He realized that even though the process of becoming an American citizen was complex, his love for her and the life they were building together made it worthwhile.

As Jisoo prepared for his American citizenship exam, Celeste became his unofficial tutor, guiding him through the complexities of U.S. history, government, and culture. Their study sessions became more than lessons; they became moments of connection, of understanding each other's worlds, of exploring what it truly meant to call a place home.

One evening, as they sat at their dining table, Jisoo flipped through his study guide. He tapped a passage about the Founding Fathers and their vision for the country.

"This idea of freedom," he mused, "it's different. In Korea, we have democracy, but there is still a deep sense of duty to society and to family. Here, it seems more individual."

Celeste nodded. "That's true. America prides itself on personal freedom. It can be a beautiful thing, but sometimes people forget that freedom comes with responsibility. It's not just about doing what you want; it's about making choices that don't harm others."

Jisoo looked thoughtful. "So, in a way, freedom here is like poetry. There are rules, but within them, you have endless ways to express yourself."

She smiled. "Exactly."

One afternoon, Jisoo sprawled on the couch, flipping between channels on the television. A political debate flashed across the screen. He shook his head.

"America is full of contradictions," he said. "It calls itself the land of opportunity, yet there are so many who struggle. It values hard work, yet people are drowning in jobs that don't pay enough."

Celeste sighed. "You're not wrong. America is a place of contradictions. There is a lot of inequality, and many problems people avoid addressing because they believe hard work alone should be enough. But at the same time, it is a country where change can happen. It is messy and flawed, but always evolving."

Jisoo nodded. "That is what makes it so fascinating to me. In Korea, tradition is deeply ingrained. Change occurs, but slowly. Here, people fight for what they believe in, even when the system resists."

Celeste leaned against him. "So, does that make you want to be a part of it?"

Jisoo glanced at her, a small smile playing on his lips. "I think I already am."

One night, they took a walk along the beach, the waves rolling in gently. Jisoo had been quiet for most of the evening. Finally, he stopped and looked at Celeste.

"Do you think I'll ever feel American?" he asked.

She studied him for a moment. "What does being American mean to you?"

He exhaled. "I don't know. I've spent my whole life being Korean. My parents made sure I never forgot my roots. But now I'm choosing this place. Choosing us. Will I ever stop feeling like an outsider?"

Celeste reached for his hand. "Being American isn't about erasing who you are. It's about adding to it. You don't have to stop being Korean. You just get to be something more."

Jisoo squeezed her fingers. "Something more." He repeated the words as if testing them. After a moment, he smiled.

"You should write that down," he teased. "It's almost poetic."

Celeste laughed. "You're rubbing off on me."

As they continued walking, Jisoo knew the answers would not come overnight. But in that moment, he also knew something else. Home was not a place on a map. It was wherever Celeste was. And no matter what, he was exactly where he was meant to be.

Chapter 11

Celeste Nightmares

It started with little things. Celeste had always been good at keeping her emotions in check, at burying the past so deeply that even she could pretend it had no hold on her. But lately, the ghosts of what she had endured had begun to slip through the cracks.

The first time Jisoo noticed, they had been walking home from dinner. It was late, the streets mostly empty, the soft glow of streetlights flickering as they passed. He reached for her hand, as he always did, but the moment his fingers brushed against her wrist, she flinched. It was small, barely perceptible, but he felt it.

She covered it quickly, lacing her fingers through his and offering a smile. But Jisoo knew what he had felt.

Then there were the nights.

Jisoo had always been a light sleeper, but now he woke to the sound of Celeste gasping in her sleep, her body rigid with tension. Once, he found her curled up on the farthest edge of the bed, as if she were trying to disappear.

She never spoke of the nightmares, and Jisoo never pressed. But when he pulled her into his arms, she never resisted, only buried her face against his chest, her breathing shaky but slowly evening out.

One evening, as they sat on the porch watching the waves roll in, he decided he could not keep ignoring it.

"Celeste," he said gently, "do you want to talk about it?"

She tensed beside him. "About what?"

Jisoo turned slightly, watching her profile. "The nightmares. The way you flinch when I touch your wrist. The way you look over your shoulder when we walk home at night."

Her fingers tightened around the blanket draped over her lap. "It's nothing."

"It's nothing." His voice was quiet and patient. "You don't have to pretend with me."

She exhaled slowly, staring out at the horizon. "It's been years, Jisoo," she murmured. "You would think I would be over it by now."

Jisoo reached for her hand, this time moving slowly, giving her the chance to pull away. She did not.

"Pain doesn't follow a timeline," he said softly. "Neither does fear."

Celeste closed her eyes for a long moment. When she opened them again, they shone with unshed tears.

"I thought I was free of him," she admitted.

"But after what happened, after he showed up again, I feel like he's everywhere. Even when I know he's not."

Her voice trembled, frustration creeping into her tone. "I hate it. I hate that he still has this power over me."

Jisoo's grip on her hand tightened slightly. "He doesn't."

She let out a small, humorless laugh. "Doesn't he?"

Jisoo shifted, turning fully toward her. "No," he said firmly.

"Because he is not the one you come home to. He is not the one who holds you when you cannot sleep. He is not the one sitting beside you right now, loving you through every moment, even the hard ones."

Celeste's breath hitched. She looked at him then, truly looked at him, and something in her gaze softened.

Jisoo lifted their joined hands and brushed his lips against her knuckles. "You don't have to fight this alone," he whispered. "Not anymore."

For the first time in a long while, Celeste let herself believe that was true.

It was late when the phone rang. Far too late for it to be anything good. Celeste sat on the couch, curled beneath a knitted blanket, a half-read book in her lap. Jisoo had gone to bed earlier, exhausted from a long day of studying, and the house was still. Peaceful. Or at least it had been.

When the shrill ring cut through the quiet, her heart stuttered. For a moment, she stared at the screen, dread curling in her stomach. The caller ID read Unknown, but somehow, she already knew.

With a deep breath, she answered. "Hello?"

There was silence. And then, "Celeste."

Her grip tightened on the phone. His voice was calm, too calm, as if nothing had happened, as if he had not shattered her peace time and time again.

She closed her eyes and inhaled slowly. "Marcus."

"Yeah, Celeste, I need you to come get me."

His voice had that old, familiar edge, demanding and expectant, as if he were telling her what to do rather than asking.

"They have got me in here for some nonsense. Drunk in public, a little fight, nothing serious." A chuckle. "You know how it is."

She felt sick. "Marcus, you are in jail," she stated flatly.

He sighed, exasperated. "Yeah. And you are my wife."

"I am not your wife," Celeste exclaimed. The words came out sharp before she could stop them.

A pause. The casual act slipped for a second.

"Celeste," Marcus said, slower now, his voice lowering into something more familiar.

"Come on. You do not want me in here, do you?"

She clenched her jaw, forcing herself to stay calm.

"Marcus, I am not bailing you out."

Silence.

And then, the shift.

"You think you are better than me now?"

His voice turned venomous so quickly it made her skin crawl. "Because you have got some fancy new life? Some actor playing house with you?" He let out a humorless laugh. "You think he is going to save you, Celeste?"

Her pulse thundered in her ears.

"You owe me," Marcus spat. "After everything I did for you."

She hung up.

Her hands were shaking. Her breath came fast and uneven.

She set the phone down on the coffee table and pressed the heels of her hands into her eyes, forcing herself to take a deep breath.

It took less than a minute for the phone to start ringing again.

She did not pick up. She knew what would come next: the voicemails, the texts, the apologies laced with manipulation, the anger simmering just beneath the surface.

But she would not answer. Not this time.

A few minutes later, she felt the warmth of Jisoo's presence before she heard him speak.

"Celeste?" His voice was thick with sleep but laced with concern. "Who was that?"

She turned toward him, swallowing hard. "It was Marcus."

Jisoo's expression darkened. He did not ask if she was okay. He could already see the answer in her face. Instead, he walked over and sat beside her, taking her hand in his without a word.

Celeste let out a slow breath, leaning into his touch.

She was not alone in this anymore.

Chapter 12
Cold Hard Truth

Marcus sat on the hard bench in the dimly lit holding cell, elbows on his knees, head in his hands. The stench of sweat and stale alcohol clung to him, a reminder of how far he had fallen. The fight at the bar had been stupid. He barely even remembered how it started.

What he did remember was Celeste's voice when she told him no.

No, she would not bail him out.

No, she was not his wife anymore.

His jaw tightened.

A guard walked past, then stopped. "You got a visitor."

Marcus frowned. He was not expecting anyone. He was not even sure who would care enough to come.

A few minutes later, he was led into a small visitation room. When he saw who was waiting for him, a strange mix of shame and frustration settled in his gut.

Coach Rivers.

The man had not changed much since high school. A little grayer. A little slower getting up from the chair. But the sharp eyes were the same. The same ones that used to watch Marcus tear down the football field, the same ones that once told him he could be somebody.

Marcus sat down across from him. "Didn't expect to see you here, Coach."

Coach Rivers leaned back in his chair, studying him. "Didn't expect to find you here, son."

Marcus exhaled through his nose, running a hand over his face. "You come to lecture me?"

"No," the older man said. "I came to ask you what the hell you're doing."

Marcus let out a bitter laugh. "What does it look like?"

Rivers shook his head. "It looks like you're wasting your life." He leaned forward, folding his hands on the table. "You were always driven, Marcus. You had direction. You had a family who wanted better for you." A beat of silence. "If your father could see you now, what do you think he would say?"

Marcus's stomach twisted. He stared at the floor.

"I'll tell you what he would say," Rivers continued. "He would say, get your damn head on straight."

Marcus clenched his jaw. "Yeah? And how am I supposed to do that?" He looked up, his eyes flashing. "I lost everything, Coach. Celeste, she was my wife. And now she's with…" He cut himself off, jaw tightening. "What am I supposed to do, just accept it?"

"Yes," Rivers said.

Marcus flinched as if he had been slapped.

"You think throwing punches and getting locked up is gonna bring her back?" Rivers asked. "You think scaring her is gonna fix things?" He shook his head. "She's moved on, son. And whether you like it or not, it's time you did too."

Marcus swallowed hard.

"You've got a son out there," Rivers reminded him. "You still have a life to live, Marcus. But if you keep going down this road, you're gonna end up with nothing."

Silence stretched between them.

Finally, Marcus let out a slow breath. "I don't know how to fix it," he admitted, his voice quieter than before.

Rivers studied him for a long time. Then he said, "Start by fixing yourself."

Marcus looked away.

The guard tapped on the door. "Time's up."

Rivers stood, adjusting his jacket. "You get out of here, you come find me," he said. "We'll talk."

Marcus didn't reply.

But as the guard led him back to his cell, Rivers's words echoed in his head.

Start by fixing yourself.

Coach Rivers didn't leave Marcus alone after that night in jail. He showed up the day Marcus was released, waiting outside with crossed arms and a no-nonsense expression.

"Come on," he said, tossing Marcus a bottle of water. "You're dehydrated, and you smell like bad decisions."

Marcus smirked despite himself. "Where are we going?"

"To talk."

They drove to a quiet diner on the outskirts of town. Rivers ordered coffee, black, just as he always had. Marcus, still reeling from the hangover, asked for a glass of water.

The conversation started slowly. Football talk. Memories of the past. Then Rivers got to the point.

"You need help, Marcus."

Marcus stiffened. "I don't need"

"You do," Rivers cut him off. "And you know it."

Marcus exhaled sharply, rubbing a hand over his face.

"You're hurting. This started when your parents died," Rivers said quietly, leaning forward and clasping his hands on the table. "And I don't just mean the grief knowing they're gone. I saw how everything changed in you. The focused Marcus, the disciplined son, he was gone. In his place, you became someone desperate, someone angry."

Rivers paused, letting the words hang in the air.

"You channeled that anger onto the field. You played recklessly. You charged in without looking, you risked hits you didn't need to make. You weren't trying to win so much as you were trying to punish someone, maybe yourself."

Rivers's voice hardened.

"And now look where that has got you. The knee injury was the culmination. Not just a physical break, but a marker. All that pain and rage finally caught up with you. And this? This isn't just anger anymore. This is self-destruction."

Marcus didn't respond.

Rivers leaned in.

"You've got a choice, son. Keep spiraling until you lose everything, including yourself, or put in the work to fix it."

Marcus looked down at his hands. His knuckles were still bruised from the fight.

"You don't have to figure it out alone," Rivers continued. "I know a guy. Runs an anger management group. You should go."

Marcus scoffed. "What, sit around in a circle and talk about my feelings?"

Rivers didn't smile. "You think you're too good for it?"

Marcus hesitated. Then, reluctantly, he muttered, "I don't know how to start."

"Then let this be the first step."

The first meeting was the hardest. Marcus walked into the small community center, feeling like every set of eyes in the room was sizing him up. A few people sat in a circle, men and women of different ages, backgrounds, and stories.

The facilitator, a man in his late fifties named Greg, greeted him with a firm handshake. "Welcome, Marcus. No pressure. Just listen if that's all you can do today."

So he did.

A woman spoke first about how her temper cost her a job she loved. Then a man spoke about how he pushed away his family because he couldn't control his outbursts. Each story hit Marcus harder than he expected.

Then Greg looked at him. "What about you?"

Marcus hesitated. His instinct was to deflect, to downplay. But then he thought about Celeste's face the night he cornered her in Solmere. The fear in her eyes. The sound of her voice when she told him no.

"I lost someone," he admitted, voice low. "And I handled it the wrong way."

Greg nodded. "Loss can turn into anger if you don't face it."

Marcus clenched his fists. "I don't know how not to be angry."

"That's why you're here," Greg said.

The meetings became a routine.

At first, Marcus just listened. Then he started talking more. He learned how to recognize his triggers, how to stop himself before he spiraled.

He connected with another member, Ray, a former soldier who had lost his marriage to his temper. Ray didn't sugarcoat anything.

"Took me years to admit my anger was the problem. Don't waste that kind of time, man."

Slowly, Marcus started changing. He began writing things down instead of lashing out. He hit the gym instead of hitting walls.

One night, after a session, he found himself sitting in his truck, staring at his phone.

He typed a message. Deleted it. Typed it again. Finally, he sent it.

Message: Celeste, I don't expect anything from you. But I wanted you to know I'm trying.

He didn't know if she would respond. But for the first time in a long time, he wasn't acting out of anger. And that was something.

Coach Rivers didn't just push Marcus into anger management; he made sure he had something to do with his time.

"You need structure," Rivers told him one evening after a group session. "Something to keep you steady. I made a few calls."

Marcus raised an eyebrow. "To whom?"

Rivers tossed him a piece of paper with a name and an address.

"Dan Carter. Runs a construction business. He needs workers. I told him you're strong, you work hard, and you need a chance."

Marcus stared at the paper. "You didn't have to do that."

"Yeah, I did," Rivers said firmly. "Because I believe you can turn this around. But it's on you to show up."

Marcus arrived at the construction site early. The foreman, Dan Carter, a gruff but fair man in his fifties, sized him up.

"Coach Rivers speaks highly of you," Dan said. "Don't make me regret giving you this shot."

Marcus nodded. "I won't."

The work was tough, long hours, heavy lifting, but it was exactly what Marcus needed. It kept his hands busy, his mind focused. He found that the physical labor helped channel his frustration in a way that didn't destroy things.

He was quieter than most of the crew, but over time, they began to warm up to him. Ray, one of his fellow workers, clapped him on the back after a long day.

"You're a beast, man. Ever done this kind of work before?"

Marcus shook his head. "No, but I like it."

"Good. Means you're not afraid to get your hands dirty."

A few weeks into the job, Coach Rivers stopped by the site to check on Marcus. He watched as Marcus worked, noticed how he interacted with the crew, how he carried himself.

When Marcus took a break, Rivers walked over.

"You look different," he said.

Marcus smirked. "What, less angry?"

"Something like that."

Marcus exhaled, wiping sweat from his brow. "I still have my moments. But this helps."

Rivers nodded. "Proud of you, kid."

Marcus looked at him, the man who had never given up on him, even when he had given up on himself.

"Thanks, Coach."

For the first time in a long time, Marcus felt like he was moving forward instead of looking back.

Marcus kept attending anger management. At first, he sat not sharing much, arms crossed, listening more than talking. But over time, he started to open up.

One evening, during a session, the group leader asked, "What's one thing you've learned since starting this journey?"

Marcus exhaled. "That anger isn't the problem. It's what you do with it. I used to let it control me. Now, I'm trying to control it."

There were nods around the circle.

"You're making progress," the leader said. "Keep going."

By day, Marcus worked construction, pouring sweat into every task. He started picking up overtime shifts, determined to save money and prove to himself more than anyone that he could build a life on his own terms.

On payday, instead of wasting his check at the bar, he deposited it into a savings account. He wanted stability, not just for himself, but for the son he had neglected for too long.

One night, as he counted his savings, he realized something. He had enough for a small apartment. It wasn't much, but it was his.

One afternoon, Coach Rivers called him.

"Come by the high school," Rivers said. "I need to talk to you."

Marcus arrived to find Rivers waiting in the gym.

"They need an assistant football coach," Rivers said. "I put your name in."

Marcus hesitated. "Why me?"

"Because I see something in you. And those kids? They need someone who's been where they are. You could be that guy."

Marcus swallowed hard. He thought about his own high school days, how football had given him structure, how Rivers had never let him fail.

"Think I can handle it?" he asked.

"I wouldn't have made the call if I didn't."

The first time Marcus stood in front of the team, he felt the weight of it. These kids were looking up to him, expecting something from him.

He took a deep breath.

"I know what it's like to screw up," he said. "I also know what it's like to get back up. That's what this game is about. That's what life is about. So let's get to work."

As the weeks passed, he found himself investing in the players, pushing them, mentoring them, being there in ways someone had been for him.

And when one of the kids, a troubled boy with a temper, pulled him aside after practice and asked, "Coach, how'd you turn things around?"

Marcus said, "One step at a time."

For the first time in years, he felt like he was truly living not as the man he used to be, but as the man he was trying to become.

Chapter 13

Intimacy

As the months passed, Jisoo and Celeste's relationship deepened, woven together by shared moments of joy, laughter, and the quiet comfort of simply being together. Their bond grew stronger not only through their challenges but through the peaceful, everyday joys that often went unnoticed.

Solmere, with its peaceful shorelines and gentle breezes, became their sanctuary, a place where they could be in each other's presence. Most mornings, Jisoo would rise early, drawn to the soft hum of the ocean outside their window. Celeste, a morning person by nature, would often already be up, her notebook in hand as she scribbled thoughts in her journal.

On these mornings, Jisoo would sit beside her, coffee in hand, watching as the sky gradually lightened, transforming the world into shades of orange and pink. There was something magical about these quiet hours, as the world slowly came to life. They rarely spoke, sometimes exchanging only glances, their fingers brushing as a shared understanding passed between them.

It was in these moments that Jisoo realized how much he cherished the simplicity of their life together. He had never known such contentment, no grand gestures, no demands, just the serenity of being in her presence. Celeste often read poetry aloud during these mornings, her voice carrying over the waves, and Jisoo would sit quietly, lost in the beauty of her words.

Cooking became another cherished ritual. Jisoo, who had always been accustomed to elaborate meals prepared for him in his native Korea, discovered the joy of cooking with Celeste in their cozy kitchen. They often tried out new recipes, sometimes succeeding with delicious results, other times laughing at their culinary failures.

Jisoo would carefully chop vegetables, his movements steady but still learning the nuances of American cooking styles, while Celeste, a gifted cook, guided him with patience and humor. Their conversations flowed freely in the kitchen, a perfect balance of laughter, shared stories, and learning about each other's tastes and preferences.

On one particular evening, they attempted a complicated seafood dish that Jisoo had always loved but never tried making himself. As they prepared the dish together, there was a sense of pride in their teamwork. Celeste playfully teased Jisoo about his habit of overcooking the rice, while Jisoo insisted on showing off his knife skills, which, to Celeste's surprise, had improved over the months. When the meal was finally ready, they sat down at their dining table, their faces lighting up with joy over the shared accomplishment.

Another joy they found in their life together was the little celebrations, the small victories that brought them closer. Jisoo often surprised Celeste with thoughtful gestures, like bringing home flowers after a long day or setting up a small picnic for her by the ocean, knowing how much she loved to feel the sand beneath her feet.

Celeste, in turn, made sure to honor Jisoo's moments of success, especially as he made strides toward his citizenship. After Jisoo had taken a significant step in his immigration process, Celeste threw a small celebration for him at their home, inviting a few close friends and family. Jisoo had been so focused on the legalities and logistics, but that evening, he allowed himself to enjoy the moment. His smile never left his face as Celeste hugged him, her heart full of pride and love for the man who had become so much a part of her life.

While Solmere was their peaceful escape, Jisoo and Celeste also enjoyed trips to the city, where they explored new places together. They loved wandering through museums, bookstores, and hidden coffee shops, reveling in the city's vibrancy and energy. They would laugh over silly things, like Jisoo's struggle to understand certain American slang or Celeste's knack for getting lost in the city's labyrinthine streets.

One particular adventure stood out in their memory, a spontaneous trip to a jazz club. Jisoo had always been drawn to jazz music, and he introduced Celeste to the smoky, soulful tunes that had been his comfort growing up. That night, they found themselves in a dimly lit, cozy jazz bar, where Jisoo tapped his fingers to the rhythm while Celeste leaned against him, captivated by the music. There was a sense of joy in being in each other's company, a feeling that no amount of external distractions could overshadow.

One of the most memorable aspects of their relationship was how they made each other laugh. Jisoo, often serious and reserved in public, let his guard down completely when he was with Celeste. His dry wit and occasional playful banter came out in full force. He would tease her about her love of poetry, calling her a hopeless romantic, while she would respond with mock indignation, calling him too logical for his own good.

One evening, Celeste and Jisoo decided to try painting together. Neither of them had any real artistic skill, but they spent hours laughing at their clumsy attempts to create something beautiful. Celeste's attempt at painting a simple landscape turned into a blur of colors, while Jisoo's abstract piece looked more like a chaotic mess than anything resembling art. They both laughed until their sides ached, and as they stepped back to admire their "masterpieces," they couldn't help but feel a deep, unspoken connection, one that was painted in laughter, not perfection.

Late nights, when the world had quieted, Jisoo and Celeste would walk down to the beach, lying side by side under a blanket, gazing up at the stars. Celeste had always been fond of stargazing, and Jisoo, in turn, found comfort in her fascination with the night sky. It was during these quiet moments that they spoke about their dreams and the future, often in hushed tones as if the world around them didn't matter in those precious minutes of peace.

There was something serene about the way the stars seemed to twinkle just for them, as if the universe itself was celebrating their love. They would share their hopes for the future, with Celeste discussing her nonprofit work and Jisoo discussing his desire to focus more on acting roles that meant something to him. But in the end, both of them knew that whatever came next would be easier as long as they faced it together.

These moments, simple yet profound, reminded both Jisoo and Celeste of the quiet joys of life, the love that grew not just in grand gestures but in the everyday, ordinary acts of kindness and understanding. It was in these moments that they truly found peace with each other, and it was in these moments that their relationship flourished.

Celeste had always known that Jisoo was sacrificing more than just a location by choosing to stay in America. He rarely spoke about what he missed, but she could see it in the way his fingers lingered over books written in Korean, in the way he paused when he heard someone speaking his native language in passing. She knew it in the quiet moments, when he would sit by the window, lost in thought, his gaze distant as if he were somewhere else entirely.

She wanted to help, but how could she? She couldn't bring Korea to Solmere. But maybe, just maybe, she could find a piece of it.

One afternoon, while Jisoo was studying lines for his next film, Celeste took a trip to the nearby city. She had heard whispers of an Asian district there but had never visited. Now, as she walked down streets lined with Korean, Chinese, and Vietnamese storefronts, the scent of familiar spices in the air, she felt a surge of hope.

She wandered through a Korean bookstore, running her fingers over the spines of novels Jisoo had mentioned reading in his youth. She stopped by a café where the menu was written in Hangul and ordered a traditional tea, taking in the warmth and comfort of the space. She listened as people spoke in Jisoo's language, their conversations fast and lively, a sound she knew he must miss more than he admitted.

Then she found the restaurant. A small, family-owned place tucked between a grocery store and a bakery. Inside, an older woman greeted her warmly, and Celeste explained, hesitantly, with the few Korean words she knew, that her partner was from Korea and missed home. The woman smiled, understanding instantly.

"You bring him here," she said, her accent soft but firm. "He will feel at home."

Celeste returned to Solmere that evening, excitement bubbling beneath her exhaustion. She waited until they were curled up together on the couch before she spoke.

"I found something today," she said, tracing small circles on the back of his hand.

Jisoo looked at her, amused. "Should I be concerned?"

She laughed softly. "No. I just, I know you miss home, and I can't change that. But there's a place in the city: a bookstore, a café, a whole community. I found a restaurant too. We could go together?"

For a moment, Jisoo didn't speak. Then he exhaled, his eyes warm with something she couldn't quite put a name to. Gratitude, maybe. Or something deeper.

"You went looking for that? For me?"

She nodded. "I just wanted you to have a piece of home."

Jisoo pulled her into his arms, holding her close. "You don't know how much this means to me."

The following weekend, they went together. And for the first time since leaving Korea, Jisoo felt a little less like a man between two worlds and a little more like he had found a way to exist in both.

The Asian community in the nearby city is known as Little Hanseong, named after Seoul's historical name, reflecting its deep cultural ties to Korea while embracing its presence in America.

The restaurant owner was Mr. Park, a kind but no-nonsense man in his late sixties who had immigrated to America decades earlier. Park Dae-jung had built Seojin's Kitchen from the ground up, naming it after his late wife, who had been the heart of both their home and their business.

His granddaughter, Hana Park, is a college student studying literature and creative writing. She grew up helping in the restaurant but dreams of becoming a novelist. She has a deep appreciation for poetry and admires Eun Sol's work, though she never expected to meet him in person.

The bookstore, Haneul Pages, was run by Mrs. Moon, an old friend of Mr. Park's who had always encouraged young Korean Americans to stay connected to their heritage through literature. Moon Ji-won had built the shop into a quiet refuge, one that smelled of paper and tea.

On Jisoo and Celeste's third visit to Little Hanseong, they returned to Seojin's Kitchen for dinner. As they sat down, Hana walked by their table to refill their tea, then froze midstep, her eyes widening.

"You're," she gasped, nearly dropping the teapot. "You're…Min Jisoo."

Celeste blinked in surprise, but Jisoo only smiled, used to occasional recognition. "I am," he admitted gently.

Hana turned toward her grandfather, her voice almost frantic. "Grandfather, do you know who this is?"

Mr. Park glanced over and shrugged. "Some actor?"

"Not just any actor," Hana said, her voice breathless. "He's Eun Sol. The poet. The one I told you about."

Mr. Park raised an eyebrow, looking Jisoo up and down. Then, with a grunt, he muttered, "I thought you'd be older."

Celeste stifled a laugh as Jisoo chuckled, unfazed.

"I get that a lot."

Hana, still wide-eyed, practically bounced with excitement. "Would you, would you consider doing a reading at Haneul Pages? Mrs. Moon would be honored. We do poetry nights, and if people knew you were coming, it would mean so much to the community."

Jisoo hesitated, glancing at Celeste. She gave him an encouraging nod.

"I'd be happy to," he finally said.

Hana squealed, clapping her hands together before quickly composing herself.

"Sorry. Sorry, I just, this is amazing. Thank you so much."

That night, as they walked hand in hand through Little Hanseong, Jisoo squeezed Celeste's fingers.

"This place is starting to feel like home."

Celeste smiled up at him. "Then we'll keep coming back."

Chapter 14

New home

Celeste and Jisoo stood in front of their new home, keys in hand, the weight of the moment settling in. It was theirs, a fresh chapter, a space that belonged to them both. The house was larger than Celeste's cozy cottage, with room for Jisoo's office and library, a gym for his workouts, a room for Micah and four guest rooms for visiting friends and family. It was nestled in a quiet part of Solmere, close enough to the ocean for them to hear the waves when the wind was right.

Jisoo's shipment from Korea arrived the following week, boxes of books, artwork, personal belongings, and a few pieces of furniture he had insisted on keeping. Together, they sorted through everything, arranging Jisoo's office just the way he liked and blending their styles as they furnished the rest of the house. Celeste found joy in the process, watching Jisoo settle into their shared space.

Once they had their home in order, they turned their attention to Celeste's cottage. Rather than sell it, they decided to rent it out. After careful screening, they found the perfect tenant, Elliot Graves, a freelance travel photographer who had spent years abroad but wanted a quiet place to call home between assignments. He was in his early forties, easygoing, and appreciative of the cottage's charm.

On move-in day, Celeste and Jisoo handed him the keys, giving him a warm welcome.

"You'll love it here," Celeste assured him. "It's a peaceful place."

Elliot grinned. "That's exactly what I need. And if you ever need travel photos, I owe you a discount."

As they left the cottage behind, Jisoo reached for Celeste's hand. "Everything is falling into place," he said softly.

Celeste squeezed his fingers, looking up at him with a smile. "Yes. It really is."

Despite the coldness he had felt from his parents in their last exchange, Jisoo knew he had to try again. Their disapproval weighed on him, but their absence in his life weighed even more. Late that night, after staring at his phone for too long, he finally made the call.

His mother answered first, her voice distant yet composed.

"Min Jisoo," she said, his full name laced with quiet disappointment. "You finally remembered to call?"

His father's voice followed, rough and unforgiving.

"If you missed us, you wouldn't have abandoned everything for this decision."

Jisoo closed his eyes briefly, steadying himself.

"Father, I haven't abandoned anything. I will always be your son. I will always be Korean. But my life is here now, and I need you to understand that."

There was silence, thick with unspoken emotions. His mother spoke first.

"You are choosing another country, another life. One without us."

Jisoo shook his head, even though they couldn't see him.

"That's not true. I'm applying for dual citizenship. I'm not erasing my identity. I'm expanding it. I belong in both places."

His father scoffed, but his mother hesitated. "And what kind of life do you think you will have there?" she asked.

He exhaled, choosing his words carefully.

"Celeste knew I missed home, so she searched for a Korean community nearby. It's called Little Hanseong. Restaurants, bookstores, people who share our culture. It feels familiar. She made sure I had a piece of home."

There was another pause. His mother's voice softened just slightly.

"She did this for you?"

"Yes," Jisoo said without hesitation. "Because she loves me. Because she respects where I come from."

His father remained silent, but Jisoo could tell he was listening. Pressing forward, he added,

"I want you to meet her. I want you to meet her parents. Her mother is a literature professor, like you, Mother. And her dad is a physician, Father."

He gave a short chuckle, hoping to lighten the tension. "If things had gone your way, I might have been a doctor too."

His mother inhaled sharply at the mention of Celeste's mother's profession. A literature professor. That was a connection she couldn't ignore.

His father finally spoke. "And why should we meet them?"

Jisoo's voice was steady. "Because Celeste and I want to talk about wedding plans. And I want my family to be a part of that."

For a long time, there was silence. It stretched between them, filled with the weight of everything unspoken. Then his mother exhaled, her voice quiet but laced with emotion.

"You are really going to marry her?"

"Yes," Jisoo said firmly. "And I want you to be there."

His father let out a deep sigh, the sound more exhausted than angry. "We will think about it."

His mother hesitated, then finally said, "Take care of yourself, Jisoo."

The call ended, leaving Jisoo staring at the phone in his hand. They weren't ready to accept it yet. But they hadn't said no.

And for now, that was enough.

The dim glow of the fireplace cast long shadows as Celeste sat on the couch, knees tucked under her. Jisoo sat beside her, his fingers absentmindedly tracing circles on her hand. They had been discussing his family, their disapproval, and his desire to move forward without them. But Celeste couldn't shake the weight of her own thoughts. She exhaled, her voice quiet but firm.

"Jisoo, I need you to hear me on this. I know your parents have made things difficult. And I know how much they've hurt you. But I also know what it's like to have no connection to where you come from, to have questions about your roots that may never be answered. And I don't want that for you."

"Celeste, I'm not cutting them off forever. But they made it clear."

"Honey, I get it. They disapprove of me. They disapprove of us. But Jisoo, family isn't just about approval. It's about history, about belonging. I don't have that, not in the way you do. And as much as I love who I am, there's always this hole. This unknown. A past that was taken from my ancestors and, by extension, from me."

Jisoo studied her, the weight of her words settling into his chest. He had seen Celeste confident, resilient, and strong, but this was a vulnerability she rarely let show.

"Baby, do you know what it's like not to know your real last name? Not knowing what country your people came from. To have a history that was erased. I don't have stories passed down through generations. I don't have old letters, family heirlooms, or records that tell me who I am beyond what I see in the mirror. All I have are fragments, DNA test guesses, old census records that list my great-great-grandmother as property before she was a person in the eyes of this country."

Her voice broke, and Jisoo felt his own heart tighten. He knew Celeste carried this, but hearing it this way, raw and unfiltered, makes it so much more real.

"You have a homeland, Jisoo. A language, traditions, a lineage that traces back for centuries. Your parents, as much as they disapprove, are still there. Your culture is alive. It is something you can pass down to your children, something they will never have to wonder about. And you want to throw that away because they hurt you? I understand the pain, I do. But Jisoo, once you cut that cord, once you let go of where you come from, you cannot get it back."

Jisoo looks away for a moment, jaw tightening. He had not thought of it like that. He had been so consumed by the sting of rejection, the shame of disappointing his family, that he had not considered the irreversible loss that could come with turning away completely.

"Okay, honey. You are right."

Celeste exhales, her shoulders slumping slightly.

"I don't want to lose them, Celeste. But I also don't want to keep chasing after people who refuse to see me for who I am. Who refuse to see us."

"And, Jisoo, I will not ask you to. But I will ask you to keep the door open. Even if they never walk through it, even if they never change, at least you will know you did not erase your past in the process of building your future."

Jisoo nods, his hand tightening around hers. Silence stretches between them, thick with emotion. Then he pulls her close, pressing a kiss to her forehead.

"I will not lose myself, Celeste. And I will not let you feel like you are in this alone. We will build something new together. And if my parents ever choose to be part of it, the door will be open."

Celeste lets out a shaky breath and nods. For the first time in a long time, the weight on her chest feels just a little lighter.

Jisoo sat in his study, staring at his laptop screen, his fingers hovering over the keyboard. The conversation with Celeste had stayed with him, weighed on him in a way he couldn't ignore. He had always known that identity and ancestry were important, but hearing Celeste's pain, the absence of a tangible past, made him realize how much of a privilege it was to know where you came from.

He wanted to give her something real, something that connected her to the history she had always longed to know. And so, he decided to take action.

After hours of research, Jisoo found someone who specialized in African American genealogy: Dr. Olivia Bennett, a highly respected genealogist known for uncovering lost histories, particularly those obscured by slavery and migration. He sent an email detailing Celeste's background as best he could, emphasizing that she knew very little beyond a few family names.

Within a day, Dr. Bennett responded.

Dear Mr. Min:

Thank you for reaching out. I would be honored to assist in tracing Ms. Monroe's ancestry. African American genealogy can be complex due to historical erasures; however, with persistence and access to records, significant information can be uncovered.

To begin, I will need any available names, birthplaces, and dates of Celeste's parents, grandparents, or great-grandparents. I also recommend a DNA test, which can provide connections to distant relatives and potential ethnic origins. Let us set up a consultation to discuss the next steps.

Looking forward to working together.

Best,

Dr. Olivia Bennett:

Jisoo immediately scheduled a call. When the time came, he spoke with Dr. Bennett, explaining that he wanted this to be a surprise for Celeste. He provided the names of Celeste's parents, Diana and Charles Monroe, and what little Celeste had mentioned about her grandparents.

Dr. Bennett reassured him that while challenges existed, she had helped many African Americans reconnect with their pasts, even when historical records were scarce. She would start by examining census records, Freedmen's Bureau documents, and, if necessary, plantation records.

Weeks passed, and Jisoo kept in touch with Dr. Bennett, who provided updates on her progress.

- ❖ DNA Testing: Celeste's DNA results, which Jisoo had secretly arranged, showed a mix of West African ancestry, primarily from Nigeria, Ghana, and Senegal. It was a revelation that would give Celeste a more profound sense of connection to her ancestral homeland.
- ❖ Census and Marriage Records: Dr. Bennett traced Celeste's paternal lineage to the late 1800s in Louisiana, where her great-great-grandfather, Micah Monroe, was listed as a free Black man who had worked as a carpenter after emancipation.
- ❖ Slave Records: On Celeste's maternal side, they found a painful but significant discovery: a record from Mississippi

in the 1850s listing her ancestor, Mariah, as a child enslaved on a plantation. But further research revealed something incredible: after emancipation, Mariah had moved to Tennessee and founded a small school for Black children.

Jisoo felt overwhelmed with emotion as he pieced together the information, imagining how Celeste would react. One evening, as they sat together in their living room, he reached for her hand.

"Sweetheart, I have something for you. Something I hope will give you some of the answers you have always wanted."

She looked at him curiously as he handed her a folder. She opened it slowly, her eyes scanning the pages. First, the DNA results. Then, census records. Old documents with handwritten names she had never seen before, but names that belonged to her bloodline.

Her hands trembled as she read about Micah Monroe. Then, about Mariah. When she reached the part about Mariah founding a school, her breath caught.

"Jisoo, baby… she was an educator. Jisoo, she was an educator. Just like my mother."

Tears welled in her eyes as the weight of history settled in her heart.

"You come from people who survived, who built something even after everything was taken from them. Celeste, you have a history. You have names. You have a legacy."

Celeste let out a choked laugh, wiping her eyes.

"Jisoo baby, I can't believe you did this."

"Honey, you made me realize how important it is to stay connected to where we come from. I never want you to feel lost, Celeste. You deserve to know your roots."

She threw her arms around him, holding him tightly, overwhelmed with gratitude and emotion.

For the first time in her life, the question of where I come from had an answer.

Chapter 15

Poetry Reading

Jisoo and Celeste arrived at Haneul Pages, the quaint bookstore in Little Hanseong, for Jisoo's much-anticipated poetry reading. The shop, owned by Mrs. Moon, had become a cultural hub for the community. Moon Ji-won had built it into a space where stories, language, and memories were kept alive. The intimate space was lined with wooden bookshelves filled with both Korean and English literature, its walls adorned with handwritten poetry and vintage calligraphy scrolls.

As soon as they stepped inside, they were warmly welcomed by familiar faces, shopkeepers, restaurant owners, and families who had embraced them on their earlier visits. The evening carried an air of excitement, and when Jisoo took the small stage, the crowd hushed in anticipation. He held Celeste's hand briefly before stepping up, giving her a reassuring squeeze. He began with a poem about longing and belonging:

Between Two Shores,
I stand between two shores,
one shaped by the voice of my mother,
one softened by the whisper of love.
The tide pulls, the wind calls.
Yet, in your steady hands,
I am not lost,
but home.

The audience remained still for a moment, the weight of his words settling over them, before breaking into applause.

Celeste watched as Jisoo met her gaze, a soft smile playing on his lips.

For his second poem, he read one about finding unexpected love:

At the Edge of Winter
I thought love was spring,
the bloom of cherry blossoms,
petals carried by the wind.
But love found me in winter,
wrapped in the quiet hush of snow,
a hand reaching through the frost,
warm, certain, unwavering.

When he finished, the room erupted in applause, and Mrs. Moon stepped forward. "You have a gift, young man," she said warmly. "You speak to the soul."

As the night went on, the community members approached them, extending invitations to upcoming cultural festivals, tea ceremonies, and holiday gatherings. Mrs. Kim, who ran a nearby tea shop, insisted on adding Celeste's email to the community newsletter—The Hanseong Chronicle—so they wouldn't miss a single event.

Walking back to their car under the glow of lanterns, Jisoo looked over at Celeste.

"I never thought I'd find a piece of home here."

Celeste leaned against his arm. "That's what love does. It makes home wherever we are."

News of Jisoo's life in America finally made its way back to Korea, sending shockwaves through the media. The revelation that the beloved actor was not only residing in the U.S. but also applying for American citizenship and planning to marry a Black woman, who is older than him, divorced and has a child, sparked an immediate media frenzy.

Entertainment outlets and social media platforms were flooded with headlines:

"Actor Min Jisoo Abandoning Korea?"

"Beloved Actor Chooses a Life in America Over His Homeland!"

"Mystery Woman Revealed—Older, Divorced, and a mother!"

The reaction from fans was deeply divided.

Some were supportive, leaving messages of encouragement.

"If he's happy, that's all that matters!"

"Love is love. Min Jisoo deserves to follow his heart."

"Celeste must be an incredible woman for him to choose this path."

But the backlash was loud and relentless. Some couldn't understand why Jisoo had made such an unconventional choice:

"Why would he throw everything away for this woman?"

"He could have had anyone! A younger, more traditional partner!"

"He's betraying his heritage. How can he turn his back on Korea?"

Celeste became an easy target. Strangers picked apart her life, scrutinizing every aspect of her identity.

"She's too old for him."

"A divorced woman? Does she even respect marriage?"

"She has a child—what does she expect from Min Jisoo? To play daddy?"

Reporters dug into Jisoo's past, analyzing his past relationships, searching for any possible scandal, and questioning whether this decision was a phase or a rebellion. Jisoo's management team was overwhelmed, scrambling to contain the media firestorm. His family was humiliated, further solidifying their disapproval. His agents and producers were bombarded with calls—was this the end of his career in Korea?

Amidst it all, Jisoo remained silent, refusing to justify his love to anyone. But as the noise grew louder, the pressure became impossible to ignore.

The afternoon was peaceful, the sun's warmth making the air feel gentle as Jisoo and Celeste sat outside their favorite coffee shop, sipping their drinks. It had become their ritual— these small, quiet moments together, sharing stories, laughter, and simple companionship.

Celeste was mid-sentence when she suddenly went still. Her fingers tightened slightly around her coffee cup.

Jisoo followed her gaze, his body tensing as he saw who had caught her attention. Marcus.

He stood across the street, looking different. Not as ragged as before. His stance lacked its usual aggression. Instead, there was something hesitant about the way he stood there, hands in his pockets, shoulders squared yet not confrontational.

For a moment, time seemed suspended, the hum of the street fading into the background. Celeste's heart ticked a little faster, a mix of caution and curiosity pulling at her. Memories she had tried to block away nudged the edges of her mind—past arguments, harsh words, the sting of betrayal—but they softened under the strange calm she now saw in him. The Marcus before her was familiar, yet subtly changed, like a storm that had passed and left the air lighter, the world quieter.

For a long moment, no one moved.

Then, slowly, Marcus crossed the street.

Jisoo placed his cup down, his posture calm but alert. Celeste exhaled softly, bracing herself.

Marcus stopped a few steps away. "Celeste." His voice was quieter than she remembered. Lacking the sharp edge she had come to expect.

She studied him carefully. His eyes, once clouded with anger and alcohol, were clearer. There were signs of wear, yes—lines deeper on his face, shadows under his eyes—but also a kind of stillness she had never associated with him.

"I came to apologize," Marcus said, looking directly at her.

"For everything. The way I treated you. The way I showed up here and made a mess of things. I had no right."

Celeste let out a slow breath. "No, you didn't."

Marcus nodded, accepting that without argument.

"I've been working on myself. Anger management. Got a steady job coaching now. I'm not the same man I was." He paused. "But I know that doesn't erase what I did."

There was silence—a weight between them.

"I don't expect you to forgive me, Celeste," Marcus admitted. "I just needed to say it."

She studied him for a moment before her gaze softened, ever so slightly.

"I hope you're telling the truth. Not for my sake, but for yours."

Marcus glanced at Jisoo and gave a brief nod, acknowledging him for the first time.

Jisoo gave a slight nod, his expression unreadable. "Marcus."

Marcus exhaled, glancing between them.

"I know I've caused nothing but problems, and I don't intend to anymore. I came back to Solmere to see my son."

At that, Celeste's lips pressed together.

"Micah doesn't know you like that, Marcus."

"I know." His voice was steady, not defensive. "I don't expect him to welcome me with open arms. But I need to try."

Silence stretched between them again before Marcus took a step back.

"I'll leave you both to your coffee."

Jisoo, ever composed, studied Marcus before saying,

"Good luck, Marcus."

Marcus met his gaze. There was a hint of respect in his eyes. Maybe for Jisoo's quiet strength. Maybe because he had been there when Marcus hadn't.

Marcus nodded once before walking away, leaving Celeste and Jisoo sitting in the golden afternoon light, coffee cooling in their cups, hearts just a little heavier than before.

The silence that followed Marcus's departure lingered in the air, a quiet pause that seemed to stretch longer than it should. Celeste's hand brushed against Jisoo's, a small reminder of their shared calm before the next wave of reality settled in.

Jisoo sat at the dining table in their new home, the soft hum of the afternoon quiet around him. His phone buzzed on the table, and he glanced at it. His manager's name flashed on the screen. He hesitated for a moment before answering, already sensing the urgency in the message.

"Jisoo, we need to talk," his manager's voice came through the phone, clipped and tense.

"The media's been going wild."

Jisoo straightened, setting the phone against his ear, trying to steady himself.

"What about?"

"The fact that you've applied for American citizenship," the manager continued.

"And, well… your relationship with Celeste. The fans are fuming, Jisoo."

Jisoo's hand tightened around the phone. He had anticipated something like this. The public's reaction had always been unpredictable, and with his decision to marry Celeste—a Black divorcee, older than him, and with a child—it was bound to stir controversy. He had hoped the media would give them time, but it seemed like the storm was already brewing.

"They're calling it a scandal," his manager added, frustration leaking into his voice.

"The age difference, the divorce… It's hitting a nerve with your fanbase. Some of them are defending you, but there's a lot of backlash."

Jisoo's mind raced. He knew the media was ruthless. He had experienced it before, the spotlight scorching and unforgiving. But this was different. This was Celeste, and he wasn't about to let her be dragged into this fire.

"I'm not backing down," Jisoo said, his voice low but firm.

"I'm marrying Celeste. We're building our life together. I don't care about the noise."

His manager sighed heavily.

"I get it. But you need to understand, Jisoo—this could have long-term effects on your career. We need to prepare for the backlash. Media outlets are already digging into your past, questioning your judgment, your image. They want to know why you're doing this, why her, why now…"

Jisoo leaned back in his chair, his jaw set. He glanced toward the window where Celeste was outside, tending to their small garden, the soft breeze lifting strands of her hair. He loved her. He didn't owe anyone an explanation. But he understood his manager's concern.

"I don't want Celeste hurt by this," Jisoo said quietly.

"I don't want anyone to think I'm hiding her or trying to avoid the truth."

"You're not hiding anything," his manager responded quickly.

"But you have to be ready to handle what comes next. We can't control the media, Jisoo. You have to decide how you want to play this."

Jisoo's eyes shifted to Celeste again, watching her smile as she planted a new flower in the garden. He had never been so certain of anything in his life.

"I'm not playing anything," Jisoo replied, the resolve clear in his voice. "I'll face whatever comes my way. But I'm not backing down."

There was a long pause on the other end of the line.

"Alright… keep us in the loop. And Jisoo… be careful."

Jisoo ended the call, his fingers lingering on the screen for a moment. He exhaled slowly, gathering his thoughts. It was going to be a rough road ahead, but he was ready. They were ready.

He stood up, walking toward the door to join Celeste outside. She looked up at him as he approached, her eyes warm, her smile unshaken by the storm that was beginning to brew.

Jisoo leaned down, brushing his lips against her cheek, and when he pulled back, he whispered softly, "I love you, Celeste. And nothing is going to change that."

Celeste's smile grew, and she nodded, her hand resting on his. "I know. We'll face it together."

Chapter 16

Little Hanseong Rises Up

Jisoo was finishing a cup of coffee at the small café near Little Hanseong when the phone call came through. It was his manager again, but this time the tone was different—less urgent, more cautious.

"Jisoo," his manager's voice crackled through the line.

"I need to warn you. The media has escalated things. They're not just questioning your choices—they're attacking your relationship, and now it's spreading into your heritage, your identity as a Korean actor."

Jisoo felt his pulse quicken, but he stayed calm. The storm had been brewing for days. The attacks were no surprise, but hearing it so bluntly from his manager made the weight of it more real.

"Do you want me to make a statement?" Jisoo asked, keeping his voice even.

"No, the community is already responding," his manager said.

"What you might not know is that Little Hanseong—the community you're a part of now—they're stepping up in your defense. They're having discussions, sending letters to media outlets, even getting involved in a few online forums where your fans are arguing with the critics. They're reminding people that your decision isn't just personal; it's about who you are and where you come from."

Jisoo's heart warmed a little, though he knew the struggle wasn't over. He still had a long road ahead.

"They've brought up something I think you'll appreciate," the manager continued.

"They're comparing your situation to the stories of other Asian celebrities who've faced similar scrutiny. It's not just about you anymore. The narrative is shifting, people are starting to see this as an issue of cultural identity and generational expectations."

Jisoo sat back in his chair, listening intently. He had spent time in Little Hanseong, and he had felt the tight-knit warmth of the community, but this felt different.

"What are they saying exactly?"

"Some members of the community are pointing out the hypocrisy in how some fans treat their own heritage," the manager explained.

"They're talking about how many Korean parents send their children abroad to study in the U.S., and then those same children build their lives there, just like you have. They're bringing up the fact that many of these children end up marrying outside of their race and culture, and it's no different from what you're doing now. But you're under a spotlight, so the scrutiny is more intense."

Jisoo felt a pang of relief, hearing his community support him so openly. They had become a second family to him in ways he hadn't expected. The emotional ties he had formed with the people of Little Hanseong were deeper than he realized.

"There's more," his manager continued. "Some of them are also sharing their thoughts on how the older generation of Koreans has viewed their children marrying outsiders for years. They're pointing out that it's about time the community starts supporting these choices, especially when the love is genuine. They're not just defending you; they're making it a broader statement about acceptance and breaking down barriers within their own culture."

As he pictured the streets and faces, a quiet pride settled in him. These weren't just neighbors or acquaintances; they were people who had seen him, understood him, and stood by him. Their support wasn't just words; it was a living reminder of the connections he had built and the home he had found here.

Jisoo's mind drifted back to the first time he and Celeste had visited Little Hanseong together. The vibrant street lined with Korean restaurants, the chatter in both Korean and English, the smells of kimchi and grilled meats wafting from the eateries, and the old bookshop where he had done a poetry reading—it was all a reminder of how important this community had become to him.

A few moments later, Jisoo felt a tap on his shoulder, pulling him from his thoughts. It was one of the shop owners from Little Hanseong, Mr. Park, who had become a close friend since Jisoo and Celeste first visited. His wife, Mrs. Park, was with him, both wearing kind smiles.

"We heard about the media," Mr. Park said in Korean, his tone serious yet warm. "We wanted to let you know that we're with you, Jisoo-ya. Don't let them tear you down. You've found something beautiful with Celeste. That's all that matters."

Mrs. Park nodded, her gentle face lined with the wisdom of years. "It's not just about your love, Jisoo-ya. It's about breaking old walls. The younger generation is different. We understand that, and we stand with you. Your choices reflect the future, not the past."

Jisoo felt the weight of their words settle in his chest. The support from this community — these people who had become his family — was what he needed to hear. He looked at Mr. and Mrs. Park, his heart swelling.

"We're proud of you," Mrs. Park said, her voice soft but firm.

"And we're proud of Celeste, too. You've shown that love knows no borders, and that's something we should all embrace."

Jisoo smiled, feeling a warmth spread through him. "Thank you," he said, his voice sincere. "Your words mean a lot to me."

As they spoke, a few more familiar faces from the community gathered around, joining in the support. Jisoo realized that while the media might try to tear him down, his community—his true family—was lifting him. They weren't just defending his relationship with Celeste; they were defending a future where love and acceptance went beyond boundaries.

And in that moment, Jisoo knew that no matter how difficult things became, he wasn't facing this alone. He had Celeste, his new family, and a community that saw him for who he truly was.

Chapter 17

Celeste Family

Jisoo was both nervous and excited as he sat in the living room of Celeste's parents' home, waiting for her family to gather. He had met Celeste's parents a few times before, but today was different. Today, he would meet her siblings, their spouses, and their children. It was a pivotal moment in his relationship with Celeste—one where he would also gain a deeper understanding of the woman he loved and her family, which were just as important to her as her own heart.

Celeste had reassured him countless times that her family would be welcoming, but Jisoo couldn't help but feel a knot in his stomach. His parents' disapproval was still fresh in his mind, and the thought of navigating through Celeste's family's expectations made him a little anxious.

Celeste's parents, Ronald and Diane Monroe, were chatting in the kitchen while Jisoo waited for her siblings to arrive.

First to arrive was Celeste's older brother, Elijah Monroe, a tall, broad-shouldered man who exuded confidence. He had a quick smile and an air of protectiveness toward his family. Elijah was married to Angela, a gentle and compassionate woman with an infectious laugh. Together, they had two children: Amara, a lively, inquisitive daughter and Xavier, a quiet but observant child who spent most of his time sketching in his notebook.

"Jisoo, it's good to meet you finally," Elijah said, extending his hand with a firm grip. "Celeste has told me a lot about you. I'm glad to see you're a man who appreciates the quieter things in life. I think you'll fit in here."

Angela smiled warmly at Jisoo. "It's nice to meet you, Jisoo. Celeste has always been so reserved, but it's clear she's happy with you. That's all we could ask for."

Jisoo felt a soft warmth spread through him as he looked around the room. The kindness in Elijah and Angela's expressions eased some of the nervousness he had carried since arriving. For a moment, he allowed himself to relax, noticing the gentle way the family interacted and the genuine curiosity shining in the children's eyes.

Amara and Xavier, though shy at first, were both curious and excited to meet the man who made their aunt so happy. Amara had a habit of questioning everyone, her large brown eyes wide with curiosity. She immediately asked Jisoo, "Do you like poetry? Aunt Celeste said you write poems. Can I read one?"

Xavier, on the other hand, was quieter and more reserved, but his gaze never left Jisoo as he observed him. He had a quiet intensity that made Jisoo smile, knowing that children often saw things adults missed.

Soon, Celeste's sister, Nadia, arrived with her husband, Kofi, and their two children, Elena and Julian. Nadia was the more outgoing of the siblings, always quick with a joke or a story to keep everyone laughing. Her husband, Kofi, a soft-spoken man, was supportive of Nadia's bubbly personality and always had a quiet strength. Their children, Elena and Julian, were both athletic and boisterous, frequently competing with each other in games and jokes.

Elijah and Kofi had a playful rivalry, teasing each other about their favorite sports teams, while Nadia and Angela chatted animatedly, sharing stories of their childhoods with Celeste. Jisoo listened in, occasionally chuckling at the stories, but he also felt a bit overwhelmed by the energy in the room. It was a lively household, full of love and playful banter. He could sense how much Celeste valued her family and how deep their bond was.

After a while, the group gathered around the dining table, and Jisoo found himself seated next to Celeste's parents, while the siblings and their families settled around him. The conversation flowed easily, with everyone catching up on life events. When the subject turned to Celeste's childhood, her parents shared anecdotes about her early years—her love of reading, her independent nature, and her tendency to put others before herself.

Celeste, sitting next to Jisoo, flushed slightly as her family teased her good-naturedly.

"I can't believe you all remember that," she said, smiling with a hint of embarrassment.

Elijah laughed. "You were always the one who could recite whole books by the time you were ten. We could never get away with anything around you; you knew exactly what was going on."

Jisoo smiled, feeling a deeper connection to Celeste as he learned more about her upbringing. He saw the tight-knit bond between her and her siblings, the way they supported each other and teased each other without malice. It was a family full of love, despite their quirks.

At one point, Nadia asked,

"So, Jisoo, we've heard a lot about your acting career. What made you decide to settle down in Solmere, of all places?"

Jisoo looked at Celeste, who gave him an encouraging smile. He took a deep breath before answering.

"I wanted peace, a place where I could be myself. I had been living in the chaos of my career for so long, and when I met Celeste, I realized that I wanted to build something real, something grounded. Solmere felt like home."

Nadia nodded, her expression softening.

"I get that. Solmere's peaceful, but it's also full of character. You've made a good choice."

As the evening wore on, Jisoo felt more at ease, especially as he bonded with the children. Amara continued asking him questions about his poetry, and Julian insisted on showing off his soccer skills in the backyard. Jisoo felt an overwhelming sense of warmth and acceptance, even though the day had been filled with nerves.

Later that night, after everyone had left, Celeste took Jisoo's hand and smiled at him.

"I'm happy you got to meet everyone," she said softly. "I know it was a lot, but I think they really liked you."

Jisoo squeezed her hand, feeling deeply grateful. "I liked them too. They're just like you—kind, supportive, and full of love. I'm happy to be a part of your world, Celeste. I'm happy to be here."

As they walked out into the cool evening air, Jisoo couldn't help but reflect on the importance of family—both his and

Celeste's. They had created a life together, and now, it was time to build it with the love and support of the people who mattered most.

143

Before Jisoo and Celeste returned home, Celeste's mother told Jisoo that her class was currently studying his poetry and asked if he would come and speak to them.

Chapter 18

Military Service

Jisoo stood alone in the kitchen. The house was wrapped in rare quiet. The kettle clicked off behind him, but he barely heard it. Lately, whenever the world felt too loud with headlines, opinions, strangers clawing at his life, his mind slipped somewhere else.

Back to the barracks.

He thought of the day he enlisted in the Republic of Korea Armed Forces, fulfilling his mandatory military service requirement. At the time, he was already a rising figure in the entertainment industry, recognized for his literary work and growing public presence. However, the call to serve was unavoidable as it is mandatory for all able-bodied South Korean men and despite his success, he knew he had to put everything on hold for nearly two years.

The contrast between the life he had left behind and the one awaiting him was almost dizzying. Jisoo could still remember the quiet mornings filled with poetry and thought, the freedom to linger over small joys, and the gentle rhythm of his civilian days. Stepping into the barracks wasn't just a change of location, it was a leap into an entirely different world, one that demanded every ounce of his discipline and resilience.

He recalled that reality hit him harder than he had expected the day he stepped onto the training base. The rigid structure, early morning drills, grueling physical training, and absolute loss of personal freedom were stark contrasts to his previous life. Gone were the days of coffee shop musings, poetry readings, and deep literary discussions—commands, schedules, and endurance tests now dictated his world.

He went in knowing that at six feet one inch and one hundred eighty-five pounds, he was in good physical shape. However, military training demanded more than physical fitness. It required mental resilience, discipline, and complete subordination to authority, —something that deeply challenged him as a creative thinker accustomed to questioning the world rather than simply following orders.

His first weeks were a blur of:

- Early morning calls at 5:30 AM
- Endless push-ups, running drills, and combat training
- Firing range exercises and field survival training
- Teamwork exercises that forced him to rely on and trust his fellow soldiers

Despite the hardships, he remembered he was determined to prove himself. He refused to be seen as the "celebrity recruit" who couldn't handle the real world.

The fact that by the third month, something had changed stood out in his memory. It was when he realized that military service wasn't just about endurance—it was about brotherhood. He forged deep bonds with his fellow soldiers, many of whom came from vastly different backgrounds. Some men had grown up in rural villages, others in wealthy business families, and others had barely graduated from high school. Yet, in the military, status disappeared. They were all equals in the same uniform, facing the same challenges.

One soldier, Sergeant Park, became an unexpected mentor. A seasoned officer with a sharp mind and a past filled with hardship, Park recognized Jisoo's intellect and encouraged him to apply his talents.

Sergeant Park said "You may not see it now, but everything you're learning here—the discipline, the patience, the ability to push through discomfort—will make you stronger in the real world."

He found himself writing again, but this time, his poetry was about the stark beauty of struggle—about exhaustion, camaraderie, and resilience. In the quiet moments before lights-out, he scribbled verses in a small notebook, capturing the raw emotions of his experiences.

Halfway through his service, he was assigned to a peacekeeping unit near the DMZ (Demilitarized Zone). The tension was palpable; soldiers were constantly reminded that at any moment, the fragile peace between North and South Korea could shatter. It was here that Jisoo truly understood the weight of duty.

His mind flashed back to an evening, during an unexpected security drill near the border, when he and his unit were stationed at an observation post. He watched as North Korean soldiers moved on the other side, their presence a stark reminder of the unresolved conflict. In that moment, he realized that his service was part of something much larger than himself.

When he returned to the barracks that night, he wrote a poem titled "Between Two Worlds", reflecting on the divide that had shaped his homeland for generations.

He was honorably discharged. He returned to civilian life with a new sense of discipline, purpose, and mental strength. His military experience had changed him—he was no longer just a dreamer lost in literature but a man who had endured hardship, learned perseverance, and understood the true meaning of responsibility.

As he reintegrated into the literary and entertainment world, he carried those lessons with him, shaping his future works and personal philosophy. His poetry became deeper, more profound, infused with the understanding that suffering and growth were two sides of the same coin.

And years later, when facing personal and public scrutiny for his choices—his decision to move to America, to love Celeste despite societal backlash—he leaned on that inner strength forged in the military.

Because he had already learned how to stand firm.

As soon as he entered the base, his head was shaved—something he knew was coming but still felt strange. The moment the clippers buzzed over his scalp, he caught a glimpse of himself in the mirror. It was the first time he truly saw himself as just another soldier: no celebrity, no artist—just another young man about to serve his country.

The brown bag collecting his hair was unnerving. He had heard the stories that it would be sent home in case of death, along with the official military photo taken that same day. A picture meant for funerals. It was a sobering thought, but he didn't dwell on it.

Along with his fellow recruits, Jisoo underwent grueling five-week basic training. The physical exertion was unlike anything he had ever experienced:

- Daily marches under the weight of full gear
- Endless push-ups and running drills
- Firing weapons for the first time
- Speech training, where every sentence had to end in formal, authoritative military expressions

Then there was the gas chamber training, a moment he would never forget. Wearing a mask, he felt fine—until the trainers ordered them to remove it. Instantly, his eyes burned, his throat constricted, and his lungs screamed for air. By the time they stumbled out, Jisoo and his fellow soldiers were covered in sweat, snot, and drool—an utterly humiliating but necessary experience.

The red hat and black hat trainers were relentless. No-questions-asked orders were to be followed immediately. And if one recruit messed up? The entire unit suffered. The idea of collective punishment was harsh, but it instilled a sense of unity among them. He learned quickly to take responsibility —not just for himself, but for the team.

He heard stories about bullying, the dark underbelly of military life, but he was lucky. His unit was disciplined, and the camaraderie was strong. They all wanted to prove themselves especially Jisoo, who knew some people assumed a celebrity like him wouldn't last.

After 100 days of active duty, he was granted his first leave a short four-day break. Going home, seeing his family, and stepping back into civilian life even for a brief moment was surreal. He knew he was changing.

Jisoo's military service was more than an obligation—it was a transformation. It hardened him, disciplined him, and gave him a different perspective on life. He was no longer just an actor or a poet. He had been trained to endure, to lead, and to protect.

Those memories, etched into his mind, gave him a quiet strength. Even as the world pressed in with headlines and opinions, he could anchor himself in the lessons learned through hardship. The discipline, resilience, and clarity forged in those long, grueling days of service became his refuge, reminding him that no challenge, public or personal, was insurmountable.

Years later, when facing adversity—whether from media scrutiny, family pressure, or personal struggles—he would often reflect on those days. The sleepless nights, the physical exhaustion, the moments of doubt. And he would remind himself: If I survived that, I can survive anything.

Jisoo's phone buzzed on the kitchen counter, bringing him back to reality, the caller ID flashing Mother. He took a deep breath before answering.

"Mother," he said, his voice steady but cautious.

"Jisoo," his mother's voice was gentle but laced with worry.

"Your father and I have been watching the news. We've seen everything—the articles, the interviews, the speculation."

Jisoo closed his eyes, rubbing his forehead. "I figured you would. I was going to call you soon."

His father's voice cut in, firm yet restrained. "Are you all right, son? This kind of attention… It's not easy to handle. People dig into your life, your choices. We worry about how this might affect you, your work, and your reputation."

Jisoo glanced at Celeste, who was watching him from across the kitchen with quiet concern. He took a breath before responding.

"I won't lie—it's been overwhelming. But I'm handling it. And Celeste... she's handling it too."

There was a pause on the other end. Then, his mother spoke again.

"Jisoo-ya, we also wanted to say… we've heard about the people in Little Hanseong. The way they've supported you. That means a lot to us."

His father cleared his throat. "You have represented us well among them. We are grateful for their kindness."

Jisoo felt a slight weight lift from his chest. His parents weren't just worried about the scandal—they were seeing the support he had, the community standing beside him. That meant something.

His mother hesitated before continuing. "We've talked, your father and me. We've decided… It's time we came to America. To see you. To meet Celeste properly."

Jisoo blinked, taken aback. "You're serious?"

"We are," his father confirmed. "We need to see for ourselves. To understand your life there."

Jisoo exhaled slowly, glancing at Celeste, who was now watching him with wide, questioning eyes. He gave her a slight nod.

"Okay," he said, his voice steady. "Then come. See for yourselves."

Jisoo hung up the phone, still processing the conversation. He turned to Celeste, who had been watching him closely, her hands resting on the kitchen counter.

"They're coming," he said, his voice carrying a mix of disbelief and relief.

Celeste blinked. "Your parents?"

He nodded. "They've decided to come to America. To meet you. To see my life here."

For a moment, she just stared at him, absorbing the weight of his words. Then, she let out a slow breath. "Wow. That's… big."

"It is," Jisoo admitted. He stepped closer, searching her face. "They're still worried. About the media, about how this might affect my career. But they're also grateful for the support we've had in Little Hanseong. I think they need to see for themselves."

Celeste crossed her arms, chewing on her bottom lip. "And what do you think? Are you ready for that?" Jisoo took her hands and squeezed them gently. "I don't know if I'm ready. But I want them to meet you. To understand why I chose this life, why I chose *us*."

Celeste exhaled, a small smile tugging at her lips. "Then we'll make sure they see the truth."

Jisoo pulled her into his arms, holding her close. "Thank you," he murmured.

"For what?"

"For being you."

Chapter 19

The Parents

That evening, as they sat together on the couch, Celeste shifted nervously. "Jisoo, I need you to teach me the proper way to greet your parents."

Jisoo looked at her with soft amusement. "You don't have to worry. Just being yourself is enough."

"Jisoo," she said firmly, giving him a pointed look. "I want to do this right. I want to show them I respect them and your culture."

He smiled, brushing a strand of hair from her face. "Alright. Let's start with bowing." He stood up, motioning for her to follow. "Bowing is very important in Korean culture. It's a sign of respect, especially when greeting elders."

Celeste got to her feet, watching him closely.

"For my parents, a polite bow should be about 30 degrees," he demonstrated, tilting forward smoothly. "Not too deep, not too casual."

Celeste mimicked his movement. "Like this?"

Jisoo tilted his head, assessing. "A little slower. And keep your hands at your sides, not clasped."

She adjusted, bowing again.

"That's better," he said, nodding approvingly.

Celeste straightened, a satisfied smile on her lips. "What's next?"

Jisoo chuckled. "Handshakes. In Korea, it's not always expected, but if they offer one, take it with both hands to show respect. Never just one." He demonstrated by extending his right hand and lightly placing his left under his forearm.

Celeste mimicked him again. "This feels very formal."

"It is, but it's polite," he said. "Now, let's talk about pouring drinks."

He grabbed two glasses and a bottle of water from the table. "In Korean culture, when pouring alcohol or tea, you never pour your own drink. You pour for others, and they pour for you. And when receiving a drink, always hold the cup with both hands—one supporting the bottom."

Celeste took the bottle and carefully poured it into Jisoo's glass using both hands.

He smiled. "Good. And if you're drinking in front of elders, turn your head slightly to the side when you sip."

"Like this?" She turned her head and took an imaginary sip.

Jisoo grinned. "Perfect."

Celeste sighed, rolling her shoulders. "Okay, this isn't too bad. Just a lot to remember."

"You'll be fine," Jisoo assured her, wrapping his arms around her waist. "They'll appreciate the effort. And even if you forget something, they'll see how much you care."

Celeste leaned into him, feeling more confident. "Alright. Let's hope I don't accidentally insult anyone."

Jisoo chuckled. "I promise, I won't let that happen."

That evening, as Jisoo and Celeste sat together, she gently placed her hand on his.

"Jisoo, we need to figure out when your parents are arriving and how long they'll be staying."

Jisoo nodded. "You're right. I'll call them tomorrow to finalize their plans. My guess is they'll stay for at least a couple of weeks, maybe longer depending on how things go."

Celeste took a deep breath. "I want to take them to Little Hanseong while they're here. I think it would be good for them to see the kind of support we have, and I want them to feel comfortable in this space."

Jisoo smiled. "They'll appreciate that. They need to see that I have a community here, even away from Korea."

She hesitated before continuing. "I'd also like to spend some time alone with them before my family arrives. I want to talk about the wedding, about us—to make sure we have that time together before things get hectic."

Celeste took a deep breath, letting the thought settle. The idea of having a quiet moment with Jisoo's parents, away from schedules and expectations, felt like a small sanctuary amid the whirlwind of preparations. She imagined them sitting together, talking openly, sharing hopes and concerns, and finding reassurance in each other's presence before the flurry of visits and family gatherings began. Jisoo's eyes softened, and he squeezed her hand. "I think that's a great idea. It'll give them time to get to know you more, without the added pressure of everyone being here at once."

Celeste smiled, relieved. "Good. I want to make sure we do this right, for both of our families."

Jisoo leaned in, kissing her forehead. "We will. I'll make the call, and we'll plan everything together."

That evening, Celeste sat beside Jisoo, her laptop open on the coffee table. Her expression was one of quiet intensity, her fingers hovering over the keyboard.

"Jisoo, I've been doing some research," she began, looking up at him. "I found something exciting."

Jisoo leaned in, curious. "What is it?"

She turned the screen toward him, showing an old book from The Project Gutenberg titled *Corea or Cho-sen: The Land of the Morning Calm* by Arnold Henry Savage Landor. "This book provides evidence that during the Cho-sen period, there were 'men as Black as Africans' living in Korea. And there are even pictures of Black Koreans."

Jisoo frowned slightly, his interest piqued. "Black Koreans? I've never heard of this before."

"Exactly," Celeste said, her voice gaining an edge of frustration. "Where did they all go? Why isn't this talked about? It makes me wonder—what happened to them?"

Jisoo exhaled slowly, scanning the text. "Korean history is so focused on the struggles with China and Japan, colonization, war… Maybe their existence just got buried under everything else."

Celeste shook her head. "But buried by who? And why? It's the same pattern I see everywhere—history gets rewritten, people disappear, and then no one talks about it."

Jisoo nodded thoughtfully. "I want to help you dig into this more. Maybe we can find historians or records that can tell us more."

Celeste smiled, reaching for his hand. "I'd love that. Because the more I think about it, the more I feel like knowing our histories—yours and mine—is even more important. Maybe we'll never have all the answers, but at least we can try."

Jisoo squeezed her hand gently. "Then we'll do it together."

Jisoo adjusted the strap of his messenger bag as he walked through the grand stone archway of the university, his breath visible in the crisp autumn air. Professor Diane Malone had invited him to speak to her literature class about poetry—his poetry, specifically. It was a strange feeling, standing on the threshold of academia in a place that was not his own, knowing that students were waiting inside to hear his words, to analyze his emotions, to dissect the meaning behind his carefully crafted lines.

The classroom was already full when he entered. A group of students sat in a semi-circle, some holding printed copies of his translated work, others poised with notebooks and pens. Professor Malone, a woman with an air of quiet authority, greeted him with a warm nod.

"Everyone, this is Min Jisoo," she announced. "He's been kind enough to share his time with us today. As you know, we've been studying contemporary poetry that explores themes of displacement, identity, and love across cultural lines. His work speaks to all of those themes and more."

Jisoo offered a polite bow before speaking. "Thank you, Professor Malone, and thank you all for having me. Poetry has always been a way for me to navigate the complexities of my identity—between two cultures, between expectation and desire, between love and fear. It's personal, but I think that's what makes it universal."

A student with thick glasses raised his hand. "Your poem 'Paper Bridges,' it seems to be about loss, but also about connection. What inspired it?"

Jisoo smiled faintly. "That poem was written when I was struggling with my place between two worlds—Korea and America. It was about building something fragile — something that might collapse — but still trying anyway. Sometimes the most delicate things—words, relationships—are the ones that carry us the farthest."

Another student, a young woman with curly hair, leaned forward. "Your work has a lot of themes about longing. Would you say that comes from your personal experiences or something more philosophical?"

Jisoo considered her words carefully. "Both. I think longing is a fundamental human experience. Whether it's for a person, a place, or even a version of ourselves that no longer exists. My poetry often comes from a place of searching—for understanding, for belonging, for love."

As the discussion went on, Jisoo was surprised by how deeply the students connected with his work. Their interpretations brought new perspectives, and their questions encouraged him to express emotions he had long felt but never fully voiced.

After class, Professor Malone walked him to the building's entrance. "You have a gift, Jisoo," she said. "Not just with words, but with connection. I think your poetry resonates because it's honest."

Jisoo glanced back at the lecture hall, where students were still gathering their belongings, some lingering in conversation. He thought of Celeste, his parents, and the life he was creating in a country that was still becoming his home.

"Thank you," he said softly. "Maybe poetry is my way of finding my place in all of this."

Later that evening, Jisoo sat on the couch with his phone in his hand, debating whether to call his parents. The past few weeks had been a lot—his growing media presence, his poetry reaching more people, and his relationship with Celeste getting deeper. Yet, his parents' agreeing to visit the U.S. gave him hope, like a bridge to something he feared was slipping away: their understanding.

Taking a deep breath, he dialed the number. The familiar ringtone echoed, and after a few moments, his mother answered.

"Jisoo-ya," she said, her voice warm but cautious. "Are you well?"

"Yes, Mother. And you? Father?"

"We are well," she assured him. "Your father is here."

A slight rustling, and then his father's voice came through, firm but not unkind. "Jisoo, have you been taking care of yourself?"

"I have," Jisoo said, pressing his fingers to his temple. "And I wanted to thank you both again for agreeing to come. It means a lot."

There was a pause, then his mother spoke. "We have been thinking about everything. About you. About Celeste."

His heart clenched. "I know this hasn't been easy for you. I know you worry about me—about what people say."

His father sighed. "It is not just what people say. It is about family. Legacy. We raised you with expectations, Jisoo. Not out of control, but out of love. And… this path you are walking, it is different from what we imagined."

Jisoo nodded, even though they couldn't see him. "I understand. But this is my life. And Celeste—she is my future."

His mother exhaled softly. "You love her very much."

"Yes," Jisoo said without hesitation. "More than anything."

There was another pause, then his father said, "We will come. We will meet her. And we will see for ourselves."

Jisoo's grip on the phone tightened. This wasn't a declaration of full support, but it was something.

"Thank you," he said, his voice thick with emotion.

His mother's voice softened. "Jisoo-ya, we raised you to be strong. To stand by what you believe in. We may not fully understand, but we will try."

Jisoo closed his eyes. That was all he could ask for. "That's all I need."

The next morning, Jisoo sat at the kitchen table, sipping his coffee as he scrolled through his phone. He had promised Celeste he would finalize the details of his parents' trip, and after their last conversation, he felt hopeful. With a deep breath, he tapped his father's number and placed the call.

Jisoo paused for a moment, setting his phone down as he thought through the conversation he was about to have. He wanted to make sure everything was clear, dates, plans, and expectations, without adding any unnecessary stress for his parents. The quiet morning around him, the soft hum of the refrigerator, and the lingering aroma of coffee seemed to give him a small sense of calm before the call. Taking another slow breath, he picked up the phone again, ready to speak with them.

His mother answered first. "Jisoo-ya," she greeted. "Are you well?"

"I am, Mother," he said warmly. "I wanted to check in about your travel plans. Have you booked your flights yet?"

There was a short pause before she responded. "We have been discussing it. Your father has been checking flights, but we need to confirm the best time to come."

Celeste and I would love to take you to Little Hanseong first, " Jisoo explained. "I want you to see the community here before things get too hectic. We also want some time with you before her family arrives so we can talk about the wedding."

His mother hummed in thought before Jisoo heard his father's voice in the background. A few muffled words passed between them before his father got on the line.

His father said, "We were thinking of arriving in three weeks." "We can stay for two weeks, but we will need to return before the end of the month."

Jisoo nodded. "That works. I'll help you with anything you need for the trip."

His mother spoke once more, her voice gentler. "This is important to you."

"It is," Jisoo admitted. "And I want you both to feel welcome, to see our life here."

His father exhaled, then said, "Then we will come with open minds."

Jisoo smiled. "That's all I ask."

Chapter 20

Jisoo's Parents Arrive

Jisoo was in the middle of reading a script when his phone buzzed with an unknown number. He hesitated before answering, but something told him to pick up.

"Hello?"

A familiar voice came through the line. " Jisoo-ya," it's been a long time.

Jisoo's brow furrowed before the realization hit him. "Sang-ho?"

"That's right," the man chuckled. "It's been years, but I've been following your story. You've been making waves, my friend."

Jisoo stiffened slightly. He knew exactly what Sang-ho meant. The media in Korea had been relentless ever since his relationship with Celeste became public knowledge. Some praised him, others questioned him, and many indulged in wild speculation.

"I can imagine what you've heard," Jisoo said cautiously. "That's why I'm calling," Sang-ho admitted. "As a journalist, I've seen how rumors spread. I don't like the way people are talking about you. We served together, and I know the kind of man you are. I'd rather people hear your story straight from you instead of tabloids twisting it."

Jisoo exhaled. "So you want to do a story?"

"Yes," Sang-ho said. "A real one. Not just about your relationship, but about your life there, your poetry, and the choices you've made. If you're open to it, I'd like to come to America, meet Celeste, and spend a few days with you both. Let people see the truth, not just the gossip."

Jisoo was silent for a moment, weighing the offer. He had always respected Sang-ho. They had endured tough times together in the military, and if there was one journalist he could trust to tell an honest story, it was him.

"I'll need to talk to Celeste about it," Jisoo finally said.

"Of course," Sang-ho replied. "I want both of you to be comfortable with this."

Jisoo nodded to himself. "Alright. I'll let you know soon."

"Good," Sang-ho said. "And Jisoo—it's good to hear your voice again."

"You too, my friend," Jisoo said before ending the call.

Now, he just had to figure out how to bring this up to Celeste.

Celeste stood in the cozy kitchen of her friend's restaurant in Little Hanseong, her sleeves rolled up as she carefully arranged colorful vegetables over a bed of steaming rice.

"Good, good," her friend, Mrs. Park, encouraged, nodding approvingly. "Bibimbap is about balance—not just in flavor, but in how it looks."

Celeste paused for a moment, taking in the vibrant colors in the bowl. She had always loved cooking, but preparing a dish with such cultural significance made her more mindful of every detail. The responsibility of honoring Jisoo's heritage, while also showing her own care and effort, added a quiet intensity to the task.

Celeste bit her lip in concentration, carefully placing the julienned carrots next to the sautéed spinach, ensuring the colors complemented each other. "Like this?" she asked.

Mrs. Park peered over her shoulder and grinned. "Perfect. Now, don't forget the gochujang. Just enough to give it the right heat, but not too much."

Celeste reached for the red pepper paste, mixing it with sesame oil just as Mrs. Park had taught her. She had already mastered tteokbokki—the spicy, chewy rice cakes Jisoo loved—and had even learned to make bulgogi, though she was still perfecting the marinade.

"You're learning quickly," Mrs. Park said as she watched Celeste work. "Jisoo must be proud."

Celeste smiled, thinking of the nights spent in the kitchen with him, his hands guiding hers as she kneaded dough for mandu or flipped pancakes for pajeon. "He's been teaching me a few things, too," she admitted. "But he's better at eating than cooking."

Mrs. Park laughed. "That sounds about right."

As Celeste finished plating the bibimbap, she felt a growing sense of confidence. She had come a long way from struggling to handle a wok properly. Now, she was creating dishes that

Jisoo and his family would enjoy—dishes that carried history and meaning.

"You're doing well," Mrs. Park said warmly. "And trust me, his parents will see the effort you're making. That matters more than anything."

Celeste exhaled, relieved. "I hope so."

Mrs. Park patted her arm. "Now, let's eat. You can't serve something you haven't tasted."

Celeste laughed and picked up her chopsticks. She was getting the hang of this, one dish at a time.

Jisoo stepped into the kitchen, inhaling the rich aroma of simmering broth and sizzling oil. Celeste stood at the counter, expertly flipping pieces of golden-brown fried chicken, her face a mask of concentration.

"Smells amazing," Jisoo said, slipping his arms around her waist from behind. "You've been working hard."

Celeste let out a breathy laugh. "Your friends in Little Hanseong have been putting me through a culinary boot camp. Mrs. Park made me redo the japchae three times before she was satisfied."

Jisoo chuckled. "That sounds like her." He peeked over her shoulder at the spread on the counter—perfectly arranged banchan, a steaming pot of doenjang jjigae, and of course, her famous fried chicken.

"You really made all of this?" he asked, clearly impressed.

"Yep," Celeste said with a hint of pride. "And before you ask, yes, I can actually eat kimchi now without tearing up."

Jisoo grinned. "I'm so proud of you."

She smirked. "You better be. Your parents are going to get the best fusion of Southern and Korean home cooking they've ever had."

Jisoo reached for a piece of chicken, but she swatted his hand away.

"Not until dinner," she scolded playfully.

He laughed, then grew a little more serious. "I know you're putting so much effort into this, and I appreciate it more than I can say. But Celeste, you don't have to prove anything to my parents. They're coming here to know you, not judge you."

Celeste sighed, turning to face him. "I know. But this is important to me, Jisoo. I know what it's like to feel disconnected from your roots. Cooking is such a big part of your culture, your family… I just want to show them that I respect where you come from. That I respect them."

Jisoo cupped her face gently. "They're going to love you, Celeste. Just like I do."

She smiled, leaning into his touch. "I hope so. But just in case, I made an extra batch of fried chicken. No one can resist that."

Jisoo laughed. "Now that's a flawless strategy."

Jisoo stood at the arrival gate, shifting his weight slightly as he scanned the crowd of passengers disembarking from the plane. His heart pounded—not out of nervousness, but anticipation. It had been too long since he last saw his parents in person.

Then, he spotted them. His father, tall and dignified despite the weariness of travel, and his mother, her sharp eyes scanning the airport before landing on him. Their faces softened instantly.

"Mother! Father!" Jisoo called, waving.

His mother, Park Jiyeon, broke into a warm smile, and his father gave him a nod of approval. As they approached, Jisoo immediately took their luggage and bowed respectfully.

"You must be tired," he said in Korean. "How was the flight?"

"It was good," his father Min Si-woo replied, adjusting his suit jacket. "Long, but comfortable. The service was excellent."

His mother touched his arm, looking him over. "You look well, Jisoo." Her eyes held a quiet warmth. "And America… it is different from what I expected."

Jisoo tilted his head. "Different how?"

His father exhaled, looking around. "The people, Jisoo. They are polite. More respectful than I imagined."

Jisoo chuckled. "Not all the time, but yes, people try to be courteous here."

His mother nodded. "The airport staff were kind. A young man even offered to help with my bag." She looked at Jisoo with a hint of amusement. "I expected more… chaos."

Jisoo laughed. "Well, you haven't been here long enough yet."

His father's gaze settled on him more seriously. "You have changed, Jisoo."

Jisoo straightened slightly. "Is that a bad thing?"

His father hesitated, then shook his head. "No. You seem happy."

Jisoo smiled. "I am."

His mother squeezed his hand. "Then that is all that matters."

Jisoo felt a swell of emotion in his chest. Maybe this visit would go better than he had feared.

"Come on," he said, leading them toward the exit. "There's a whole new world for you to see."

As they made their way through the airport, Jisoo's mother adjusted the strap of her handbag and glanced at him.

"And Celeste?" she asked. "How is she?"

Jisoo smiled. "She's at home, preparing a feast for your arrival. She's really excited to meet you both. Maybe a little nervous, too."

His father raised an eyebrow. "Nervous?"

"She wants to make a good impression," Jisoo explained. "She's been practicing Korean customs, learning to cook

Korean dishes—she even asked our friends in Little Hanseong for help."

His mother's lips curled into a smile. "That is very thoughtful of her. It means a lot that she is making the effort."

Jisoo nodded. "She knows how much family means to me, and she wants you to feel welcome."

His father let out a small grunt of approval. "And her son?"

"Micah is doing well," Jisoo replied. "He's a good kid—smart, kind. He's been curious about you both. He even asked me how to say 'hello' properly in Korean."

His mother chuckled. "It sounds like we will have much to talk about."

They walked in comfortable silence for a moment before his father spoke again. "I assume the news coverage has been a problem?"

Jisoo exhaled. "It's been… intense. A lot of rumors, a lot of speculation."

His father frowned. "Your mother and I have seen some of it. Reporters trying to paint you as someone you are not."

Jisoo clenched his jaw but kept his voice steady. "Yes. That's why I agreed to let an old military friend interview me. He wants to set the record straight."

His father nodded thoughtfully. "Good. You should control your own story before others do it for you."

They stepped outside, and his father's gaze lifted to the cityscape before them. He studied the surrounding architecture, his keen eyes scanning the buildings.

"Interesting," he murmured. "The structures here are bold, yet practical. The lines are sharp, but there is a certain warmth to them."

Jisoo followed his father's gaze and smiled. "I never thought about it that way, but I suppose you're right. American cities feel different, don't they?"

His father nodded. "Yes. Very different from home, yet there is something familiar in the way people move through them. Cities have their own language, no matter where they are."

Jisoo glanced at his mother. "And what do you think?"

She gave a small, knowing smile. "I think I am eager to see the home you have built for yourself. And I look forward to meeting the woman who holds your heart."

Jisoo felt a wave of warmth and relief wash over him. "Then let's not keep her waiting."

As they drove through Solmere, Jisoo's mother gazed out the window, her eyes lighting up with familiarity. "It reminds me of Jeju Island," she murmured. "The way the shops line the streets, the ocean just beyond them… it feels nostalgic."

Jisoo glanced at his parents, noticing how the small details of Solmere—the gentle sway of the trees, the distant hum of the harbor, even the sunlight glinting off the rooftops—seemed to awaken memories and emotions he hadn't expected. He felt a quiet pride, knowing this was the life he had built, a place where his past and present could coexist, and a home where he hoped his parents would feel welcome and at ease.

His father nodded in agreement. "Yes, the air is different, but there is something comforting about a town by the water."

Jisoo smiled as they continued toward his and Celeste's home. When they finally arrived, he parked the car, stepped out, and gestured toward the house. His father looked at the structure with a quiet, unreadable expression, but said nothing. His mother, however, smiled softly, taking in the warm, inviting exterior.

As the front door opened, a gentle breeze carried in the faint scent of the ocean, mingling with the warm aromas from the kitchen. Jisoo's heart quickened slightly. They stepped inside, and Jisoo called out, "Celeste, we're here."

A moment later, Celeste emerged from the kitchen, wiping her hands on a towel before tucking it neatly aside. She took a breath, then bowed respectfully and greeted them in carefully practiced Korean.

Jisoo's mother's eyes brightened with delight, and she returned the bow graciously. His father gave a slow, approving nod.

"Welcome," Celeste said warmly. "I hope your trip was good. Jisoo will show you to your room so you can rest before dinner."

His mother gently touched Celeste's arm. "Thank you. We are happy to be here."

Jisoo gathered their luggage and led them to the guest room. He set their things down, making sure they had everything they needed before stepping back. His mother glanced around the space and gave an approving nod, while his father remained contemplative but respectful.

"We will freshen up," his mother said. "Thank you, Jisoo."

Jisoo nodded and left them to settle in, heading back to the kitchen.

Chapter 21

Blessings Given

Celeste was stirring a pot, her movements steady but her expression slightly tense. "Everything okay?" Jisoo asked.

She exhaled, nodding. "Yeah, I just want everything to be perfect."

Jisoo reached for her hand and squeezed it gently. "It already is."

She smiled at him before returning to her cooking.

Jisoo leaned against the counter. "I wanted to mention something before we get too caught up in dinner. My friend, the reporter, wants to come after my parents leave to do a story about me. About us."

Celeste's hand stilled on the spoon, and she turned to him. "Jisoo, we can't talk about that right now."

"I know," he said gently. "But I think we should discuss it with my parents. In my culture, what impacts me also impacts them. They understand the cultural implications of my choices in ways that we might not. They can offer guidance."

Celeste considered his words, her expression softening. She knew how much family meant to him, and she respected that.

"Okay," she said finally. "We'll talk about it after dinner."

Jisoo smiled, pressing a quick kiss to her forehead. "Thank you."

She exhaled, shaking off her nerves. "Now, go set the table before your parents think I'm making you do all the work."

He chuckled and got to work, feeling a deep sense of gratitude that they were in this together.

As the evening settled, the soft hum of conversation and clinking of dishes filled the dining room. Micah had helped set the table, placing the carefully arranged centerpieces with precision, eager to contribute to the special occasion. He wanted everything to be perfect for Celeste and Jisoo.

Micah straightened his back, sensing the moment's importance. The chatter in the dining room softened as all three of them paused, anticipation settling over the space like a quiet, expectant hush. When Jisoo's parents entered the living room, Jisoo stood up, placing a hand on Micah's shoulder. "Mother, Father, this is Micah," he said warmly.

Micah, with practiced ease, bowed deeply and greeted them in Korean. "Hello," he said, his pronunciation careful and deliberate.

Jisoo's mother smiled approvingly, and his father gave a slight nod, his expression unreadable but not unkind.

Jisoo gestured toward the dining room. "Shall we eat?"

Everyone took their seats, and as the meal began, conversation flowed easily. Jisoo's parents complimented the food, and Celeste, slightly nervous but pleased, explained that she had been learning from friends in Little Hanseong.

"You've done well," Jisoo's mother said, tasting the bibimbap. "This is very good."

Celeste beamed, grateful for the kind words. Jisoo, catching her eye, gave her an encouraging smile.

Micah, knowing this was a special night for Celeste and Jisoo, ate quietly, only speaking when asked a question. He wanted them to have this time. After dinner, he excused himself and retreated to his room, leaving the adults to their conversation.

In the great room, the gentle sound of the ocean waves drifted through the open windows as Jisoo poured tea for everyone. His parents sat comfortably on the couch, their expressions calm but attentive.

Jisoo cleared his throat. "There's something I wanted to discuss with you." He glanced at Celeste before continuing. "An old friend of mine from the military—he's a journalist now—wants to do a story about me. About us."

His father set his teacup down, considering his words. "A story?"

Jisoo nodded. "There's been a lot of speculation in the media. He wants to put the rumors to rest, to tell the truth."

His mother exchanged a glance with his father before looking at Jisoo. "And you think this will help?"

Celeste leaned forward slightly. "Jisoo thought it would be good to get your perspective before making a decision. He values your advice."

Jisoo's father exhaled slowly, his gaze shifting between Jisoo and Celeste. "We will need to consider this carefully."

Jisoo nodded. "I know. That's why I wanted to talk to you first."

The conversation was beginning, and there was much to discuss. But as they sat in the warm glow of the great room, the ocean stretching out beyond them, Jisoo felt a sense of peace. Whatever decision they made, he knew he wasn't facing it alone.

Jisoo took a slow breath, letting the sound of the waves outside fill the quiet room. He felt the weight of the moment; his parents' visit was not just about sharing a meal, but about bridging worlds: the home he had built with Celeste in America and the heritage he carried from Korea. Whatever discussion lay ahead, he knew their guidance and perspective would be invaluable.

Jisoo's father sat upright, his expression calm yet firm as he addressed his son. His mother listened silently beside him, nodding in agreement as he spoke.

"Korea must understand that you are not abandoning your homeland," his father began, his deep voice steady and measured. "You are still a Korean citizen. You have responsibilities there, but that does not mean you cannot also build a life in America. You will live and work in both places, and that must be clear."

Jisoo nodded, taking in his father's words carefully. Celeste sat beside him, listening intently, her hands resting in her lap.

His father continued, "Your love for Celeste and your upcoming marriage—this must come from you. It must be honest and forthright. If people believe this is anything other than your decision, there will always be doubt." He looked between his son and Celeste. "You do not need to justify your love, but you must stand firm in it."

Jisoo swallowed, feeling a mix of relief and gratitude. His father offered his full support, but he also guided him toward the right way to present it.

"As far as our family is concerned, you have our full support," his father said firmly. "We will stand by you. And of course, when you speak, you must mention your friends in Little Hanseong. They have supported you, and they are part of your story."

Celeste exhaled softly, glancing at Jisoo. He met her gaze, his lips pressing into a small, grateful smile.

Jisoo's mother finally spoke, her voice softer but no less resolute. "Whatever you say, say it with confidence. Let them see that you are not uncertain about your path."

Jisoo nodded. "Thank you, both of you. Your support means everything."

His father gave a slight nod of approval, and his mother reached for her tea, taking a quiet sip. The conversation had been serious, but the weight on Jisoo's shoulders felt lighter. He wasn't facing this alone his family was with him, and that made all the difference.

His parents' support meant everything to him—she could see it in the way his shoulders relaxed, in the way his eyes softened with gratitude.

Jisoo cleared his throat, glancing between his mother and father. "Then… you think I should do the interview?"

His father exhaled, setting his teacup down on the small table in front of him. "I think it could be a good thing. If done correctly." He met his son's gaze, his expression unwavering. "This is not just about you, Jisoo. It's about all of us—our family name, our reputation, and yes, our country. Whether you like it or not, you are a public figure. People will have opinions, and many will judge you without ever knowing the truth. This interview is an opportunity to ensure that truth is told."

Jisoo nodded slowly, considering his father's words. "And what if they twist my words? What if they use it to fuel more rumors?"

Jisoo ran a hand through his hair, the weight of his father's words pressing on him. He understood the importance, but a knot of anxiety tightened in his chest. The thought of his life and his relationship with Celeste being scrutinized so publicly made him uneasy. He glanced at Celeste, drawing strength from her calm presence, and realized that any decision they made needed to honor both truth and privacy.

His mother finally spoke again, her voice gentle but firm. "That is always a possibility. The media can be ruthless, but that is why you must be careful. Speak from your heart, but be mindful of your words. Do not let them corner you."

Celeste, who had been listening carefully, finally spoke. "I think we should set boundaries with this interview. We can't let them dig too deeply into our personal lives. Some things are ours alone to keep." She looked at Jisoo. "This should be about you, about your choices, your future. Not about tearing us apart for headlines."

Jisoo's father gave a slight nod of approval. "She is right. And you must make sure this journalist understands that before agreeing to anything."

Jisoo exhaled deeply, rubbing the back of his neck. "I trust him. He served with me—he's a friend. He says he wants to help clear up all the rumors."

His father leaned back slightly, folding his hands over his lap. "Then speak with him. Set the terms. If he truly wants to help, he will respect your conditions."

Jisoo turned to Celeste, searching her face. "Are you okay with this?"

She hesitated for only a moment before nodding. "Yes. If it means protecting you—and us—then I'll stand by your side."

A small, appreciative smile touched Jisoo's lips. His parents watched them both, silent for a moment, before his mother spoke once more. "Then it is decided."

The room grew quiet again, the only sound the distant crash of waves against the shore outside. The conversation had been serious, weighty, but necessary. Jisoo had always known that every decision he made carried weight—not just for himself, but for his family and those connected to him. But with their support, and Celeste by his side, he felt ready to face whatever came next.

"Thank you," Jisoo finally said, looking at his parents. "For trusting me. For supporting me."

His father gave a slight nod, while his mother reached out and gently patted his hand. "You are our son, Jisoo. That will never change."

A sense of peace settled over Jisoo, even as he knew the real challenge was still ahead. But for the first time in a long while, he felt ready to face it.

Jisoo's parents sat in the quiet of their guest suite, the sound of the ocean faint through the floor-to-ceiling windows. His mother sighed as she removed her jewelry, glancing at her husband.

"Celeste is stunning," she said softly. "I can see why he chose her. She carries herself with such grace."

Jisoo's father nodded, but his expression remained troubled. "Yes," he admitted, "but the problems this relationship is creating for our family…" He let out a weary sigh, his voice heavy with concern. "I'm not sure he won't regret it."

Jisoo's mother turned to face him fully. "I've told you before—I will not lose my son." Her voice was firm, unwavering. "He is our only child. I will not have him build a life in America while we remain distant. If this is the path he has chosen, then so be it. We must find a way to be a part of it."

Jisoo's father exhaled deeply, rubbing his temples. "I worry about how our family back home will react, how the people will talk. This is not an easy road."

She reached for his hand and squeezed it gently. "No, it isn't. But Jisoo has made his choice. And if we push too hard, if we let our fears dictate our actions, we may lose him altogether. I won't let that happen."

Jisoo's father was silent for a long moment before finally nodding. "Then we will stand by him," he said, though there was still hesitation in his voice. "Even if it is difficult."

His mother smiled faintly. "That is what it means to be a family."

Jiyeon and Si-woo make their way to the family room, where they find their son, Jisoo, and Celeste making breakfast. Jisoo asks whether they would like coffee or tea while they wait for breakfast. Jisoo's father gives him a disapproving look and says, "I didn't know you cooked." Jisoo responds, "I have been cooking since I was 18." I taught Celeste how to cook some dishes, and she has taught me how to cook some. His father clears his throat.

Chapter 22

The Tour

The next morning, Jisoo and Celeste set the table with a thoughtfully prepared breakfast—fried eggs, ham, toast, rice, kimchi pancakes, and an assortment of beverages, ensuring a blend of both Korean and Western flavors. The aroma filled the house as they put the finishing touches on the meal.

When Jisoo's parents entered the dining room, he greeted them warmly. "Good morning, Mother, Father. Did you sleep well?"

His mother nodded with a small smile. "Yes, the bed was comfortable. And the sound of the ocean is very soothing."

Jisoo gestured toward the table. "Celeste and I prepared breakfast. Please, sit and eat."

His father sat down, surveying the meal before him. "You've done well, Jisoo." He glanced at Celeste. "Thank you for preparing this."

Celeste smiled. "It was our pleasure." She took a seat next to Jisoo as they all began to eat.

As they ate, Jisoo set down his chopsticks and looked at his parents. "Mother, Father, we would like to take you on a tour of Solmere today. There are a few places we want you to see, including Celeste's workplace. After that, we'll head to Little

Hanseong. The community there has been very supportive, and they're looking forward to meeting you."

Celeste reached across the table, giving Jisoo's hand a reassuring squeeze. "I think you'll really enjoy it," she said softly. "Little Hanseong is full of warmth—people who have welcomed us both and supported everything we do. It'll give your parents a glimpse of the life we've built here, the friends who have become like family." Jisoo smiled, feeling a quiet sense of pride at how far their little community had come, and at the thought of sharing it with the people who mattered most to him.

His mother looked intrigued. "Little Hanseong?"

Jisoo nodded. "Yes, it's a Korean enclave within Solmere. Many of the people there have become like family to us."

His father considered this before giving a slow nod. "That sounds like a good plan."

Jisoo exchanged a glance with Celeste before continuing, "And tomorrow evening, Celeste's parents will be arriving. We'll have dinner together as a family."

Jisoo's mother placed her teacup down gently. "It will be good to meet them."

Celeste smiled, relieved that things were moving smoothly. She wanted Jisoo's parents to feel welcome, to see the life she and Jisoo were building, and to understand that they were truly a family—one that, despite cultural differences, would stand strong together.

Jisoo and Celeste had carefully planned the day's itinerary, selecting highlights of Solmere that would appeal to Jisoo's parents. They wanted them to experience the city's beauty while also introducing them to the life Jisoo and Celeste were building together.

As they were having breakfast, Jisoo smiled at his parents. "Mother, Father, we've planned a special day for you."

Jiyeon, looked up with interest. "Oh?"

"Yes," Jisoo said. "We've chosen some places we think you'll enjoy. Mother, knowing your love of literature, we're taking you to the Solmere Literary Museum. They have a collection of rare books and exhibits on both Western and Eastern literary traditions."

His mother's expression softened with interest. "That does sound lovely."

Jisoo turned to his father. "And Father, since you appreciate architecture, we'll visit some of Solmere's most iconic buildings. There's a mix of historical and modern designs that I think you'll find fascinating."

Si-woo nodded approvingly. "That sounds promising."

After the city tour, they would visit New Beginnings, where Celeste served as the Director. The project had grown immensely under her leadership—from a small nonprofit helping 50 women to a full-scale operation that now provides live-in crisis support for 150 women and emergency services to over 100 women per week.

Jisoo glanced at Celeste, admiration evident in his eyes. "They're going to see not just the city, but the heart of what we do," he said softly. Celeste nodded, feeling a mix of pride and anticipation. She wanted Jisoo's parents to understand the depth of her work and the impact it had on the women she served, as well as the community that had embraced them both. This tour was more than sightseeing—it was a bridge between their worlds, a way to show that their lives in Solmere were built on connection, purpose, and care. Celeste spoke up, "I'd love to show you the work we do there. It's something I'm deeply passionate about."

Jiyeon gave her an appraising look, nodding. "It must be rewarding to help so many women."

Celeste smiled. "It truly is."

Finally, the day would end in Little Hanseong, where they would enjoy an evening filled with food, fun, and poetry. The close-knit community was eager to meet Jisoo's parents, and Celeste wanted them to see the level of support Jisoo had within the community.

"It will be a good way for you to see the people who have been by our side," Jisoo added.

His father leaned back slightly. "It seems you've thought of everything."

Jisoo glanced at Celeste before turning back to his parents. "We just want you to experience our life here, to understand that we are building something strong together."

His mother gave him a small smile. "Then let's see it."

With that, they finished their breakfast and prepared for the day ahead, ready to share their world with Jisoo's parents.

The morning sun cast a warm glow over Solmere as Jisoo and Celeste prepared to take Jisoo's parents on a carefully planned tour of the city. The day was more than just sightseeing—it was about sharing their lives, their passions, and the community that had embraced them. Jisoo and Celeste hoped that by the end of the day, Jisoo's parents would truly understand why their son had chosen this path.

The first stop of the day was the Solmere Literary Museum, a perfect choice for Jisoo's mother, Park Jiyeon, who had always found solace in books. The museum housed an impressive collection of rare manuscripts, both Korean and Western, and celebrated the art of storytelling across cultures. Mrs. Park's eyes lit up as she walked through the exhibits, stopping to admire beautifully preserved texts.

Jisoo watched her with quiet satisfaction. "I thought you would like this, Mother."

She turned to him, her expression softening. "It's beautiful. You chose well."

Next, they visited Solmere's architectural landmarks, an experience tailored for Jisoo's father, Min Si-woo. The contrast of historic stone buildings alongside sleek, modern skyscrapers fascinated him. They walked through old cobblestone streets, past restored colonial-era structures, and finally arrived at a newly designed cultural center, where his father admired the intricate glasswork and sharp geometric designs.

"This city is not without its charm," he finally admitted, his keen eye analyzing every detail of the buildings.

Jisoo exchanged a look with Celeste, sensing a small victory. His father, who had been so skeptical about this place, was starting to appreciate its beauty.

Their next destination was New Beginnings, the nonprofit organization that Celeste had poured her heart and soul into. What had started as a small initiative serving 50 women had flourished under her leadership. Now, it provides live-in crisis support to 150 women and emergency services to over 100 women per week.

As they walked through the facility, Si-woo and Jiyeon observed the women and staff moving with purpose. The atmosphere was warm but structured, offering both refuge and empowerment.

One of Celeste's staff members approached with a grateful smile. "Director Celeste, I just wanted to say thank you again for what you've done for us."

Celeste responded with a modest nod. "This place belongs to all of us. I'm just here to help guide it."

Jiyeon who had remained quiet for most of the visit, finally spoke. "You have built something meaningful."

Celeste met her gaze, understanding the weight of those words. "It's something I believe in."

Jisoo's father, who had been skeptical of everything, nodded. He did not fully understand this world, but he could see the impact Celeste had made.

As the sun began to set, they made their way to Little Hanseong, the heart of the Korean community in Solmere. The streets were lined with traditional hanok-inspired shops, colorful Hangul signs, and the scent of sizzling meat from street vendors. Jisoo's parents seemed more at ease here, surrounded by familiar sights and sounds.

Their first stop was Seojin's Kitchen, a beloved restaurant owned by their friend Park Dae-jung. The air was filled with the mouthwatering aroma of bulgogi, kimchi stew, and freshly made tteokbokki.

"Ah, you must be Jisoo's parents," Mr. Park greeted them warmly. "We've heard so much about you."

The meal was a feast of both flavors and conversation. Celeste, having learned how to prepare traditional Korean dishes, Jiyeon nodded approvingly at Celeste's efforts. "You've been learning well."

Celeste smiled. "Jisoo and our friends here have been great teachers."

After dinner, they made their way to Haneul Pages Bookstore , where Jisoo was set to read poetry. The cozy space was packed with community members, all eager to hear him speak. As he stepped up to the front, a hush fell over the room.

Jisoo took a breath and began to read:

"Love is not bound by borders,
nor caged by expectations.
It is a whisper in the wind,
a promise in the quiet dawn.
It does not ask for permission to exist—
It simply does."

The words flowed effortlessly, carrying a weight that resonated with everyone in the room. Celeste watched as Jisoo's parents absorbed his poetry, seeing their son not just as the man they raised, but as the artist he had become.

For a moment, the room seemed suspended in quiet reflection, the weight of Jisoo's words lingering in the air. Faces softened, eyes glistened, and even those who had come expecting formality felt the warmth of sincerity. Celeste felt a swell of pride not just for the poetry itself, but for the way it revealed the depth of Jisoo's heart to the parents who had shaped him. She realized that tonight was more than a reading; it was a bridge being built, a gentle weaving together of love, family, and understanding.

When he finished, the room erupted in applause. Jiyeon. reached for her son's hand and squeezed it. "You speak from the heart."

Jisoo's father, ever reserved, nodded. "It was well done."

Jisoo turned to Celeste and saw the pride in her eyes. Tonight, they had taken an important step toward bridging the gap between their two worlds.

As they left the bookstore and walked under the glowing street lanterns of Little Hanseong, Jiyeon finally said, "tomorrow, we will meet Celeste's family."

Celeste nodded. "Yes. And we hope you will see that just as I have embraced Jisoo's world, he has embraced mine."

Si-woo looked at the city around him, then back at his son and Celeste. He still had concerns, but tonight, he saw something undeniable—his son was happy.

And for now, that was enough.

As the clock ticked past 10:00 PM, Celeste, Jisoo, and his parents finally stepped through the front door of their home. The day had been long and filled with new experiences, laughter, and deep conversations, but exhaustion was beginning to set in. With quiet goodnights exchanged, they each retreated to their rooms, the house soon falling into a peaceful silence.

Lying in bed, Si-woo stared at the ceiling, his mind replaying the events of the day. With a sigh, he finally spoke. "It is not at all what I expected."

Beside him, Jiyeon turned to face him in the dim light. "No, it is not," she agreed. "And this woman—Celeste—she is impressive. She carries herself with confidence, she is kind, and she seems to love our Jisoo truly."

Si-woo nodded slowly, but a furrow remained between his brows. "Yes… But love is not always enough. There is so much at stake. We need to speak with Jisoo once more. We need to be sure this is truly what he wants before we give him our full blessing."

Jiyeon reached for her husband's hand and squeezed it gently. "Tomorrow, then," she said softly. "We will talk with him tomorrow."

With that, they both settled into their pillows, though sleep did not come easily. There was still much to discuss, much to understand—but for now, they would rest.

The following morning, after a quiet but pleasant breakfast, Si-woo and Jiyeon asked to speak with Jisoo in their room. The request was expected, but as Jisoo stepped inside and closed the door behind him, he could feel the tension in the air. His parents sat side by side on the small couch near the window, their expressions unreadable.

His father, was the first to speak.

"Jisoo," he began, his voice steady but serious. "First, we want to say that we truly enjoyed ourselves yesterday. Your home is beautiful, and we can see how much effort Celeste put into making us feel welcome. She and her son are wonderful people." He paused, exchanging a glance with Jiyeon before continuing. "And we can see how much she loves you. That is clear."

Jisoo remained silent, knowing there was more to come.

His mother sighed and folded her hands in her lap. "But love alone is not always enough," she added gently. "We need to know that you fully understand the challenges ahead. Not just here, but in Korea as well. Even in America, there will be people who disapprove of your relationship. We have seen the media frenzy already."

His father nodded, his brows furrowed. "And what about children?" he asked. "Celeste already has a son, but you do not have any children of your own. Have you truly thought about what that means? Will you regret it later if you never have your own biological child?"

Jisoo opened his mouth to respond, but his father raised a hand, signaling that he wasn't finished.

"Then there is your career," his father continued. "You know how your industry works. You rely on public support. You will surely lose fans over this. How does your agency feel about it? Have they warned you? What if the disapproval is too great? What if you have to give up acting altogether?"

The room fell into silence, the weight of his parents' concerns settling over Jisoo like a heavy blanket. He had anticipated these questions, but hearing them spoken aloud made them feel more real. His parents weren't trying to hurt him—they were trying to protect him.

Jisoo paused for a moment, letting the weight of their questions settle, his hands clasped loosely in his lap. He felt the familiar pull of tension and love intertwining, the protective instinct of his parents pressing down, yet beneath it, a trust that had been built over the years. He knew that whatever he said next would not only reflect his feelings for Celeste but also his readiness to take responsibility for the life he was choosing.

He took a deep breath, gathering his thoughts before he responded.

Jisoo took a deep breath, meeting his parents' concerned gazes with steady determination.

"Father, Mother," he began, his voice calm but firm, "I know you are asking these things because you are worried about me, because you love me and want to protect me. I don't take that for granted. But please, let me ask you something—do you ever recall me introducing you to a woman before?"

His parents exchanged glances, unsure where he was going with this.

"Yes, you knew I dated from time to time, but never once have I ever told you that I was serious about someone. Never once have I brought someone into our family's life like this."

He let that sink in before continuing.

"There was a woman once, part Korean. I cared for her deeply, but in the end, we were on different paths. Neither of us was willing to give up what we were doing to be together. I let that love go."

He paused, his expression resolute.

"But with Celeste, it's different. I would give up acting to be with her. If my studio no longer wants me because of her, then fine. If my fans want me to choose between my career and the woman I love, I choose Celeste."

His mother let out a quiet breath, while his father's face remained unreadable.

"Father, Mother, you have always told me that above all else, you want me to be happy," Jisoo said, his voice softening. "Well, I am happier than I have ever been in my life. Celeste completes me. I cannot imagine a life without her. I love her, and I will stand by her—no matter what."

Silence stretched between them, thick with unspoken emotions. His parents had spent their entire lives preparing him for a particular kind of future, one they believed was best for him. Now, he was asking them to trust that he had found something even better.

Si-woo leaned back, studying his son in silence for a long moment. The sternness in his expression slowly gave way to something gentler, understanding, perhaps even pride. "You are your own man now, Jisoo," he said at last. "Your mother and I… we may not have understood at first, but we see now what this love means to you. We see how it has changed you—for the better. If Celeste makes you this certain, this alive, then she is the right one. You have our blessing, son. Live your life without regret."

Jisoo exhaled in relief at his father's words. His parents' approval meant everything to him, and knowing they supported him and Celeste filled him with gratitude. He nodded and stood.

"I'll get Celeste," he said before leaving the room.

A few minutes later, he returned with Celeste by his side. She looked composed, though Jisoo could tell she was slightly nervous. They both took seats across from his parents, their hands lightly intertwined for reassurance.

Jiyeon offered Celeste a small but warm smile. "Celeste, I want to say how happy I am that Jisoo has found someone who loves him and wants to spend her life with him." She paused, glancing at her husband before continuing. "That being said, Si-woo and I have concerns. You and Jisoo have already faced scrutiny, and that will only continue. The media frenzy surrounding both of you will not disappear, and as an interracial couple, even in the United States, you will face challenges."

Si-woo nodded, his expression serious but not unkind. "We have seen the way the world reacts to things they do not understand. You will need to be strong, both of you, to withstand the pressures that will come."

Celeste took a deep breath and nodded. "I understand your concerns, and I appreciate your honesty," she said sincerely. "I know the media will always find something to talk about, and I know there will be people who disapprove of us. But the truth is, Jisoo and I have already faced challenges, and we've come out stronger every time. We are prepared for whatever comes our way." She glanced at Jisoo, squeezing his hand gently before looking back at his parents. "As long as we stand together, we can handle any storm."

Jiyeon studied Celeste carefully for a moment before nodding. "That is good to hear. Marriage is not just about love; it is about partnership, about being there for one another no matter what."

Si-woo leaned back in his chair, a thoughtful expression on his face. "Then we trust that you will take care of each other."

Celeste smiled warmly. "Always."

Jisoo squeezed her hand, his heart swelling with pride and love. This was the family he had always dreamed of—a family that would stand together, no matter what the world threw at them.

Si-woo and Jiyeon , still feeling the effects of jet lag, decided to take a well-needed nap before Celeste's parents arrived. Jisoo retreated to his office to study lines for his next movie, while Celeste took the opportunity to rest in their bedroom, knowing it would be a long evening ahead.

By 1 p.m., Celeste woke up, stretched, and glanced at the clock. With her parents expected to arrive at 6 p.m., she knew it was time to start preparing dinner. She made her way to the kitchen, only to be met with an unexpected but heartwarming sight—Jisoo and his mother were already hard at work.

Jisoo stood at the stove, focused as he stirred a pot, the rich aroma of spices filling the air. His mother moved gracefully through the kitchen, effortlessly preparing ingredients, her presence commanding yet nurturing.

Jisoo looked up and smiled when he saw Celeste. "You can relax," he said, waving her off with the wooden spoon in his hand. "Mother and I have everything under control."

Celeste raised an eyebrow but couldn't help smiling. She leaned against the counter, watching them work. Jisoo was carefully making the dishes she had taught him, while Jiyeon prepared traditional Korean dishes with expert precision. It was a beautiful blend of cultures—her recipes interwoven with his mother's, creating a meal that represented their unity.

Jisoo's father walked into the kitchen, inhaling deeply as the rich aromas of spices, simmering broth, and sizzling meat filled the air. He folded his arms across his chest, nodding in quiet approval.

"Something smells good," he remarked.

Without missing a beat, Jisoo grinned and responded, "Father, what you're smelling is the love language of the world—great food."

Laughter filled the room as Celeste chuckled, and Jisoo's mother shook her head with an amused smile.

Just then, Micah walked in, nodding respectfully to Jisoo's parents before turning to Celeste and Jisoo. "Hey, need help with anything?"

"You can set the table," Celeste said, handing him the neatly folded napkins.

As he started his task, he glanced at them casually. "So, I was thinking… after I see Grandma and Grandpa and finish dinner, could I go out with my friends for a bit?"

Jisoo looked at Celeste. Celeste looked at Jisoo. Without a word, they both nodded at the same time.

Micah smirked. "Y'all have been spending way too much time together."

Jisoo leaned against the counter, arms crossed. "Alright, same curfew."

Micah rolled his eyes playfully. "I know, I know. No drinking, no drugs, no girls."

Jisoo raised an eyebrow. "And?"

Micah sighed, grinning. "And if my friends start doing any of those things, I'll call you, and you'll come pick me up."

Jisoo nodded. "And what's the password?"

Micah sighed dramatically. "Did Grandpa get there?"

"Okay then," Jisoo said with satisfaction.

Celeste chimed in, raising an eyebrow at Micah. "And no speeding, no taking rides from people we don't know, and no going anywhere that wasn't on the original plan."

Micah groaned. "Yes, ma'am. Anything else? Want me to submit a full itinerary in writing?"

Celeste smirked. "Not necessary. Just don't make me have to come looking for you."

Micah laughed. "Noted."

Si-woo and Jiyeon watched the interaction with interest, exchanging a glance. Jiyeon leaned slightly toward her husband and whispered, "They really are a family."

Si-woo exhaled, nodding slowly. "Yes. They are."

As the evening sun cast a golden glow over the house, Celeste's parents, Ronald and Diane, finally arrived. The moment their car pulled into the driveway, Micah was already out the door, running to greet his grandparents with an excited grin. Diane embraced him warmly, ruffling his hair as Ronald clapped a firm hand on his grandson's shoulder.

After warm greetings were exchanged, Si-woo stepped forward with a respectful bow, introducing himself formally. Diane and Ronald, though initially unfamiliar with Korean customs, returned his greeting with warm smiles, immediately sensing his sincerity. Jisoo then took their luggage, and he and Micah led them to their room, ensuring they had everything they needed to freshen up before dinner.

A short while later, everyone reconvened in the family room before moving to the dining room, where the table was set with a beautiful array of dishes. As they settled in, Diane and Ronald turned their attention to Micah, asking about his school, grades, and how he was adjusting. Micah, though slightly exasperated by the routine questioning, answered honestly, assuring them he was doing well.

The conversation shifted to their flight, with Diane mentioning how smooth it was overall, except for a brief moment when Ronald had to step in and assist with a minor medical emergency. "Nothing serious," Ronald assured, "just someone who felt lightheaded. They were fine by the time we landed."

As dinner continued, Diane and Jiyeon found themselves discussing poetry, quickly discovering a shared appreciation for the craft. Their discussion soon expanded to include Celeste and Jisoo, who both contributed enthusiastically, exchanging thoughts on various poets and their works.

Then, unexpectedly, Ronald steered the conversation toward architecture, a topic that caught everyone's interest. The biggest surprise, however, came when Micah joined in. His insights and knowledge on architectural design left everyone momentarily stunned. "You've been studying?" Ronald asked, clearly impressed.

Micah shrugged, looking a little embarrassed at the sudden attention. "I just think it's interesting," he admitted.

As dinner came to a close, Micah excused himself to call his friends, eager to confirm his plans for the evening. Jisoo, always mindful, asked, "Who are you riding with?" making sure Micah's transportation was safe.

Meanwhile, in the kitchen, Diane and Jiyeon insisted on helping Celeste with the dishes despite her protests. The three women worked together in comfortable harmony, sharing stories and laughter.

In the adjacent family room, the men settled in, enjoying the warmth of good company. Ronald, Si-woo , and Jisoo found themselves discussing a range of topics, from travel to culture, bridging gaps in their experiences.

As the conversation flowed, laughter and stories weaving through the room, each man felt the unspoken bond strengthening between them. Differences in background and experience seemed to fade, replaced by mutual respect and genuine curiosity. In that moment, the evening became more than just a gathering—it was a quiet celebration of connection, understanding, and the shared threads that tied their families together. The evening had unfolded seamlessly, blending traditions, perspectives, and relationships into something more profound-family.

Chapter 23

The Wedding

As the house settled into quiet stillness around 10:30 p.m., everyone except Jisoo retired for the night. The warmth of the evening's conversations still lingered, but Jisoo had unfinished business to attend to. He retreated to his office, the soft glow of his desk lamp casting long shadows across the room.

He dialed his manager first, knowing this was a conversation he couldn't put off. The news was what he had expected, but not necessarily what he wanted to hear—his next film was scheduled to begin shooting at the start of June. A typical production cycle would keep him away for three months. Micah would be out of school by then, which was a relief, but Celeste…

Jisoo sighed, rubbing the back of his neck. He couldn't imagine being away from her for that long, not after what happened the last time. The thought of leaving her behind, even temporarily, felt impossible. They would have to find a solution—one that worked for both of them.

Shaking off his worries for the moment, he made another call, this time to Sang-ho. "I'll do the interview," Jisoo said.

Sang-ho's response was immediate. "Good. I'll get in touch with a date." There was a pause before he added, "It's the right decision, Jisoo. Let's set the record straight."

Jisoo nodded, though his friend couldn't see him. "I hope so."

Just as he ended the call, the sound of the front door opening reached his ears. He glanced at the time—right on schedule.

Micah stepped inside, looking relaxed from his evening out. "Hey," he greeted, setting his keys on the counter.

Jisoo met him in the hallway, arms crossed. "Have a good time?"

Micah grinned. "Yeah, it was fun. We just hung out and got food. Nothing crazy."

Jisoo studied him for a moment, then nodded. "Good. I trust you."

Micah smirked. "I know."

With that, their nightly routine was complete. They exchanged simple goodnights before heading to their respective rooms.

As Jisoo lay in bed, staring at the ceiling, his mind raced with the weight of his commitments: the interview, the film, his life with Celeste. Changes were coming—he just had to figure out how to navigate them without losing what mattered most.

The next morning, the house was filled with the hum of conversation and the comforting sounds of breakfast being prepared. The scent of freshly brewed coffee and sizzling eggs wafted through the air as Jiyeon and Diane worked seamlessly in the kitchen, exchanging stories and recipes. Meanwhile, Si-woo and Ronald sat in the family room, deep in conversation about architecture, while Jisoo helped Micah gather his things for school.

Amid the morning bustle, laughter and light conversation floated through the rooms, weaving a sense of warmth and togetherness. Jisoo paused for a moment in the hallway, watching his parents and Celeste's mother move gracefully around the kitchen, their ease with one another a comforting sight. Even Micah, darting between rooms with his usual energy, added to the lively rhythm of the household. It was a simple morning, yet it carried the quiet satisfaction of family and the anticipation of the important discussions yet to come.

Celeste, already dressed for work, entered the kitchen to grab a quick bite before heading out. "I should be back by noon," she said, taking a sip of her coffee. "Then we can all sit down and talk about the wedding."

Jisoo walked over and placed a gentle hand on her lower back. "I'll be waiting," he said with a warm smile.

Micah, stuffing his last piece of toast in his mouth, waved as he headed toward the door. "See you later!"

With that, the morning settled into its routine.

By noon, Celeste returned from work, stepping into the house to find everyone already gathered in the family room. The atmosphere was warm, yet an unspoken anticipation hung in the air. She took a seat next to Jisoo, who reached for her hand before turning to address the group.

"I know this might come as a surprise," Jisoo began, his voice steady, "but Celeste and I would like to get married next week, before my parents leave for Korea."

A wave of stunned silence filled the room, quickly giving way to murmurs of surprise and excitement. Celeste's parents exchanged glances, while Jisoo's parents sat quietly, listening intently.

Jisoo continued, his grip on Celeste's hand tightening. "We don't want anything extravagant—just a small ceremony on our private beach or somewhere on the property. Our parents, Celeste's siblings, people from New Beginnings, and our friends from Little Hanseong—that's all. Nothing fancy, just something intimate and meaningful."

He took a breath before adding, "When I return to Korea for my next project, Celeste will be coming with me. I want her to be my wife before that happens, so there is no doubt in anyone's mind—this is my decision, and it is final."

The room remained quiet for a moment before Mrs. Park finally spoke. "Are you absolutely sure about this, Jisoo?"

Jisoo met his mother's gaze without hesitation. "Yes, Mother. I have never been surer of anything in my life."

Celeste turned to her parents, waiting for their reaction. Diane smiled softly, reaching for her daughter's hand. "If this is what you both want, then we support you."

Ronald, ever the practical one, nodded. "We just want to make sure everything is in place. A week isn't a lot of time to prepare."

Celeste chuckled. "With all of us working together, I think we can pull it off."

Si-woo finally spoke, his voice thoughtful. "If this is truly what you want, then we will support you. But Jisoo understand, that your life will change even more after this. There is no going back."

Jisoo smiled, glancing at Celeste. "I don't want to go back. I only want to move forward—with Celeste."

A quiet agreement settled over the room, and soon, excitement took over. Plans started forming, tasks were assigned, and the realization sank in—by next week, Celeste and Jisoo would be husband and wife.

Jisoo wanted everything to be perfect. He had told Celeste not to worry about anything except finding the dress she wanted to wear. "I remember everything you said you wanted," he had assured her. "Just focus on your dress and relax—I'll take care of the rest."

With that, Celeste, her mother Diane, and Jisoo's mother, Jiyseon spent the next few days searching for the perfect wedding dress. Meanwhile, Jisoo handled logistics, ensuring every detail was in place.

He reached out to Celeste's assistant, Clara, at New Beginnings to coordinate with the women from the organization who would be attending. Then, he met with Park Dae-jung at his Little Hanseong restaurant to finalize the catering and ensure the community was involved in the celebration.

For photography, he contacted their tenant, Elliot Graves, who was more than happy to capture the day's special moments. Jisoo oversaw the setup—tents arrived, chairs were arranged, an elegant ice sculpture was placed at the reception area, and dozens of butterflies, a symbolic touch he knew Celeste would love, were being prepared for release.

Everywhere he looked, Celeste's favorite flowers were being arranged, filling the space with vibrant colors and soft, delicate fragrances. The menu was set, the cake was ordered, and everything was falling into place.

All that was left was for Celeste to find her dress and say, "I do."

Celeste's wedding dress was nothing short of breathtaking. She had chosen a timeless yet modern gown that embodied elegance and grace. The dress featured an off-the-shoulder sweetheart neckline with delicate lace appliqués cascading down the fitted bodice. The fabric was a blend of soft satin and chiffon, allowing it to flow effortlessly with every step she took. The back had an intricate illusion lace design with tiny pearl buttons trailing down the spine, adding a touch of vintage charm. A long, flowing train, embroidered with floral patterns, trailed behind her, creating a regal yet ethereal effect. She wore a simple yet elegant veil that fell just past her waist, and her hair was styled in soft curls, pinned on one side with a delicate pearl-and-crystal hairpiece.

As they prepared to see each other fully dressed for the first time that day, a hush seemed to settle over the room. Celeste adjusted the hem of her gown, catching her reflection and taking a deep breath, while Jisoo's eyes lit up as he admired her. For a brief moment, the world outside faded away—there was only the two of them, each a perfect complement to the other, radiating love, excitement, and the quiet anticipation of the vows they were about to share.

Jisoo stood tall and proud in a classic black tuxedo, perfectly tailored to his frame. He chose a modern slim-fit style, with a crisp white dress shirt and a black satin bow tie. The jacket featured subtle satin lapels, giving it a refined, polished look. A single white orchid boutonniere was pinned to his lapel, matching the ones in Celeste's bouquet. His hair was styled effortlessly, with a clean yet slightly tousled look that gave him an air of natural charm and sophistication.

The mothers of the bride and groom both looked stunning in their elegant gowns. Jiyeon Jisoo's mother, wore a traditional hanbok in soft lavender with gold embroidery, symbolizing warmth and prosperity. The delicate silk fabric draped beautifully, and her look was completed with pearl earrings and an elegant updo. Diane, Celeste's mother, opted for a floor-length navy-blue gown with intricate beading along the neckline and sleeves. The dress featured a flowing A-line silhouette, which she paired with a subtle diamond bracelet and earrings, keeping her look classic and refined.

Clara, Celeste's assistant and dear friend, was the Maid of Honor. She wore a soft blush-pink gown with a fitted bodice and a flowing chiffon skirt, exuding simplicity and beauty. The dress featured delicate lace cap sleeves, adding a touch of romance to her look.

Jisoo's Best Man, Mr. Park , looked dignified in a charcoal gray tuxedo, paired with a deep burgundy tie that complemented the wedding's color theme. His presence as Best Man symbolized not just friendship but the deep bond and support Jisoo had found within the Little Hanseong community.

As they all stood together, dressed in their finest, it was clear that this wedding was not just a celebration of love but also of unity, family, and the blending of two beautiful cultures.

After the wedding, Jisoo and Celeste spent the evening enjoying their family and guests. They sipped champagne, nibbled on delicious food, and basked in the warmth of love surrounding them. Laughter echoed through the night as friends from Little Hanseong and New Beginnings mingled, sharing stories and well-wishes for the newlyweds.

As the evening wore on, Jisoo gently took Celeste's hand and whispered, "Let's slip away for a moment."

They quietly stole away from the celebration, finding refuge under the soft glow of lanterns near the ocean's edge. The sound of the waves rolling against the shore created a melody just for them.

Jisoo pulled Celeste into his arms, holding her close as he gazed into her eyes. "I can't believe this has happened," he murmured, his voice filled with emotion. "Celeste Monroe, I love you, and this is the happiest moment of my life. Thank you for being my wife."

Celeste smiled up at him, her fingers tracing the lapels of his tuxedo. "You are everything I didn't know I needed, Min Jisoo. Today, you've made me the happiest woman alive." She cupped his face tenderly. "I love you. We get to spend the rest of our lives together."

Jisoo leaned down, capturing her lips in a long, passionate kiss, pouring every ounce of love and devotion into that moment. When they finally pulled apart, he rested his forehead against hers.

"Just a few more moments, love," he whispered. "I want to savor this."

Celeste chuckled, resting her hands on his chest. "I still can't believe this is real. This day has been more beautiful than I ever imagined."

Jisoo brushed a loose curl away from her face. "It's real, Celeste. You are my wife now. And I will spend every day making sure you never regret this decision."

Tears welled in Celeste's eyes, but they were tears of joy. "I could never regret loving you, Jisoo. You are my heart, my home. No matter what comes, we'll face it together."

Jisoo smiled, pressing another lingering kiss to her lips before sighing. "You're right, we should get back before they come looking for us."

Celeste laughed softly, taking his hand in hers. "Yes, let's go celebrate with our family and friends—our new beginning."

Hand in hand, they walked back toward the reception, where laughter, music, and the warm glow of lanterns awaited them. Their journey as husband and wife had only just begun, and in that moment, with love surrounding them, they knew they were exactly where they were meant to be.

Chapter 24

In-law Bonding

The following morning, Celeste's parents, Ronald and Diane, took Jisoo's parents, Si-woo and Jiyeon, out for breakfast and a morning of shopping. Laughter and conversation flowed easily between them as they explored boutiques and shared stories about their children. Later, they made their way to the country club for a relaxed afternoon of golf, deepening their bond as in-laws.

Meanwhile, at home, Celeste and Jisoo enjoyed their first day as husband and wife. The house was tranquil, a stark contrast to the lively festivities of the previous night. Jisoo pulled Celeste into his arms as they stood by the floor-to-ceiling windows, gazing out at the ocean.

"I still can't believe we're married," he murmured, pressing a kiss to her temple.

Celeste leaned into him, smiling. "Believe it, Mr. Min Jisoo, because you're stuck with me now."

Jisoo chuckled, tightening his embrace. "Stuck? More like blessed." He turned her to face him, his expression turning serious. "I want to talk about going to Korea together. We can plan when we'll go, and also, where would you like to go for our honeymoon?"

Celeste exhaled softly, resting her hands on his chest. "Jisoo, you know I have a job, and Micah has school. We can't just pack up and leave."

Jisoo sighed, cupping her face gently. "I know, but we'll figure it out. I want us to start this journey together, no matter where we are."

She smiled, standing on her toes to kiss him. "We will. But let's talk about it later today. Right now, let's enjoy being husband and wife."

Jisoo grinned, taking her hand and leading her toward the sunlit patio. "Agreed. No plans, no worries—just us."

With that, they spent the rest of the morning wrapped in each other's presence, soaking in the joy of their new life together.

Later that afternoon, as the warm sun filtered through the tall windows of the country club lounge, Si-woo and Jiyeon sat across from Ronald and Diane on a quiet terrace. The clinking of silverware and distant laughter from the golf course filled the silence between them until Jiyeon, her hands nervously clasped together, finally spoke.

As the soft afternoon breeze carried the faint sounds of golfers in the distance, Si-woo and Jiyeon exchanged a quiet glance, both feeling the weight of the conversation they were about to have. The casual clinking of cutlery and muted laughter around them seemed to fade, leaving only a shared understanding: some matters required honesty, even when difficult. Jiyeon took a steadying breath, gathering her thoughts before speaking, while Mr. Min's hand rested lightly on hers, a silent gesture of support and reassurance.

"Ronald… Diane," she began gently, her voice edged with both sincerity and hesitation. "There is something we feel we must ask. It is not easy for us to bring this up, but as Jisoo's parents, and now Celeste's as well… we feel it's necessary."

Ronald and Diane exchanged a glance; their expressions calm and open.

Si-woo cleared his throat, his voice low and measured. "You see, in our country, when someone like Jisoo—an actor, a public figure—marries, the entire family becomes part of that story. The media does not distinguish between one's private life and their loved ones. What affects him affects us all. And there has already been… attention."

Jiyeon nodded. "Some of it is harsh. Speculative. People are curious about Celeste's past. About her marriage. And as her family, we need to be prepared. We need to know how to defend her. To defend our son. Because we intend to stand with them, fully, but in Korea, family means standing as one, especially when the world is watching."

There was a beat of silence before Diane leaned forward, her gaze steady, her voice unwavering.

"We understand," she said gently. "This world our children live in—it doesn't always leave room for grace, does it?" She reached across the table, placing her hand over Jiyeon's. "Celeste has always carried herself with strength and dignity. But yes, she was married once, to a man who also lived under the weight of the spotlight."

Ronald's jaw tightened slightly as he added, "Marcus was a rising star—handsome, talented, and driven. But when he lost his parents and suffered that career-ending injury, everything changed. He spiraled. Fame can be a cruel master, and he lost sight of the things that truly matter… like family.”

Diane's voice softened. “He was a good man who became lost in grief and pride. And when he couldn't find his way back, Celeste had to choose herself… and her son.”

Ronald nodded. “She gave her all to that marriage. She fought for it. But in the end, she chose peace and chose to build a new life. And we supported her every step of the way.”

A moment passed before Si-woo said, quietly but firmly, “Thank you for telling us. That helps… more than you know.”

Jiyeon offered a small smile, one that carried the weight of understanding. “Celeste is our daughter now. We are proud of her. We want to protect her, just as we would Jisoo.”

Diane squeezed Jiyeon's hand. “Then we will protect them together.”

The four of them sat there for a long moment, the silence between them no longer heavy, but filled with shared understanding, and the bond of two families now joined by love—and by purpose.

That evening, as the sun dipped low and painted the sky in hues of lavender and gold, the house stirred with the gentle hum of returning life. Ronald and Diane returned with Jiyeon and Si-woo after a long but joyful day of breakfast, shopping, and a friendly round of golf. Their laughter echoed down the hallway as they kicked off shoes and shrugged off jackets, clearly refreshed from their outing.

As the parents returned home, the joyful energy from their outing mingled with the calm serenity that had settled over the house. The contrast between the lively adventures of the day and the quiet intimacy inside made the home feel even warmer—a place where laughter and love coexisted effortlessly.

It was a reminder that while the families were reconnecting and bonding, Celeste and Jisoo were carving out their own peaceful world together, savoring the simple moments of their new life as husband and wife. Inside, the house was warm with the scent of fresh tea and the cozy quiet that only newlyweds know.

Celeste and Jisoo had spent the entire day lounging around, curled up on the couch, exchanging quiet conversation, slow kisses, and contented silence. It was their first full day as husband and wife, and they'd basked in it with full hearts and slow smiles.

Micah returned not long after, bookbag slung over one shoulder, damp hair from swim practice sticking to his forehead. He greeted everyone with a polite but tired grin, and just as he was about to retreat to his room, Si-woo spoke.

"Micah," he said, with a gentle warmth, "can we talk for a moment?"

Micah paused, a bit startled. "Uh… sure, Grandfather."

The family gathered casually in the living room, the soft lighting casting a golden glow over everyone's faces. Si-woo sat across from Micah, his posture kind and relaxed.

"I was wondering," he said, "what classes are you taking at school? And what do you enjoy doing? I want to get to know you better."

Micah blinked, suddenly aware of everyone's attention on him. He scratched the back of his neck, a bashful smile tugging at his lips.

"Well… I'm in mostly AP classes. That means Advanced Placement. They're like college-level classes, but in high school. You get college credit if you pass the exam," he explained, clearly trying to sound casual despite the growing pink in his cheeks. "I'm taking AP English Language and Composition, AP World History, Honors Chemistry, Precalculus, and… Mandarin."

There was a quiet beat as everyone digested his words. Si-woo's eyebrows lifted, clearly impressed. Jiyeon placed a hand over her heart, her eyes lighting with pride.

"Mandarin too?" Ronald said with a low whistle. "That's not an easy load, son."

Micah gave a modest shrug, eyes dropping. "I mean… yeah. It's hard sometimes, but I like it. Helps keep me focused. I'm also on the swim and track teams. Swimming especially helps me relax after long days."

"And your grades?" Jiyeon asked gently, smiling at him with a mother's warmth.

"I'm expected to keep at least a 3.0," Micah said with a sheepish grin, "but Mom and Jisoo expect a 4.0."

He paused for dramatic effect, then added with a half-smirk, "And I have a 4.0."

Laughter bubbled through the room—soft and proud. Celeste leaned over, pressing a kiss to Micah's temple, beaming with pride. Jisoo rested his hand on Micah's shoulder, giving it a light, affirming squeeze.

The adults looked at one another, their expressions filled with admiration and a touch of wonder. This young man, once a stranger to them, had clearly become someone very special—not just to Celeste and Jisoo, but now to them as well.

Micah, meanwhile, did his best to disappear into the couch cushions, rolling his eyes with the embarrassed flush of a teenager who'd just received too much praise.

Still, he couldn't hide the small smile tugging at the corner of his mouth.

It was one of those rare moments—quiet and unspoken—when everyone in the room knew: they weren't just blending families. They were becoming one.

Chapter 25

Parents' Departure

The following day unfolded quietly, the house humming with the gentle rhythm of everyday life settling back in.

Celeste returned to work, her presence missed but her purpose understood. Micah left for school, his backpack slung over one shoulder, his goodbye quick but loving. Jisoo spent the morning tucked away in his office, catching up on emails, scripts, and quiet reflection. The silence of the house was peaceful, grounding.

The quiet of the morning lingered for a while, giving Jisoo a moment to breathe and reflect on the calm after the whirlwind of recent days. Yet, even in this stillness, the house carried a subtle energy, a gentle hum of life that hinted something comforting and familiar awaited him just beyond the office door.

When he finally stepped out of his office around midday, he was greeted by a warm, nostalgic aroma that immediately made him smile. It was the unmistakable scent of home—garlic, sesame oil, soy, and the savory depth of something slowly simmering on the stove.

In the kitchen, his mother stood at the stove, apron tied neatly around her waist, moving with grace and familiarity. She turned with a warm smile when she saw her son.

"I'm making a feast," she said. "Lunch and dinner. Ronald and Diane will be leaving tomorrow morning, and this is my last chance to cook for them here. And..."—her voice softened—"your father and I will be leaving the day after. I wanted to make sure you and Celeste have plenty of your favorites before we go."

Jisoo smiled, heart tugging at the thought. He moved to the breakfast bar and sat down, watching his mother work, a mix of love and quiet gratitude in his eyes.

She placed a steaming bowl of bibimbap in front of him with a small bottle of soju. "Eat," she said gently. "You've been working all morning."

Jisoo ate slowly, savoring each bite—not just the flavors, but the love behind them. When he finished, full and content, he kissed his mother on the cheek and told her, "Thank you, Mother."

"Go rest," she said with a soft chuckle, "You're no good to Celeste if you're tired all the time."

He took her advice and drifted off into a peaceful nap, the kind that only comes when your heart is whole.

While he slept, Jiyeon continued cooking, her movements purposeful but calm. Diane entered the kitchen not long after, still glowing from the sun, her arms full of fresh vegetables.

"Need a sous chef?" she asked warmly.

Jiyeon smiled. "Only if you're ready for a proper Korean kitchen."

The two women fell into an easy rhythm, prepping, chopping, laughing. The kitchen filled not just with food, but with the comfort of shared womanhood, of mothers bonding across culture and experience.

Outside, Ronald and Si-woo lounged by the pool, their conversation drifting from family stories to their careers. Ronald spoke of his years in medicine, the families he'd helped, the lives he'd seen change. Si-woo listened thoughtfully, then shared his own journey through architecture—the legacy he hoped to pass on, the pride he took in building not just structures, but spaces for memories.

It was a simple afternoon, yet profoundly meaningful. The kind of day that stitches people together, thread by invisible thread.

Celeste arrived home just as the sky began to soften with the approach of evening. She walked through the front door to find the house humming with delicious smells and soft voices. She peeked into the bedroom and found her husband still curled up, deeply asleep. A smile spread across her face as she slipped into something casual and gently climbed beside him.

She kissed him sweetly. "Wake up, honey."

Jisoo stirred, blinking groggily, and then smiled as her face came into focus. "I slept the whole afternoon?"

She laughed softly, "You must've needed it."

Downstairs, Micah returned from school and swim practice, kicking off his shoes before heading straight to the kitchen. He greeted his grandparents with warm hugs and set the table with practiced ease, the familiar clatter of plates and silverware echoing through the house.

By the time dinner was ready, the table was full of people, of food, of warmth. Everyone gathered, plates overflowing, conversation lively.

Before anyone could take the first bite, Micah cleared his throat.

"I just wanted to say goodbye to Grandpa Ronald and Grandma Diane before they leave tomorrow," he said, a little shy but sincere. "I won't see you in the morning before school. Thank you for coming. I love you."

Ronald and Diane pulled him into a hug, clearly touched.

As Micah's words hung in the air, a warm hush settled over the room, each family member taking a moment to savor the closeness around the table.

Plates of food glistened under the soft glow of the lights, but more than the meal, it was the shared laughter, gentle smiles, and unspoken affection that filled the space. Stories were exchanged, small jokes prompted chuckles, and hands occasionally reached across the table in quiet gestures of connection.

It was an evening that didn't need grand declarations—its beauty lay in the simple presence of one another, a prelude to the bittersweet farewells that would come with the morning.

"We love you too, Micah," Diane whispered. "Take care of your mom and Jisoo for us."

Dinner continued with laughter and heartfelt toasts, the kind of evening that would live in everyone's memory—tucked away in the quiet corners of their hearts.

Tomorrow, the goodbyes would come. But tonight was about togetherness, about family, about love—spoken and unspoken.

The following morning began quietly and early. Micah had swim practice before school and was out of the house before anyone else stirred. A note scribbled on the kitchen counter read: "Have a great trip back. I'll miss you! Love, Micah."

Ronald and Diane were next, as their morning flight required them to return the rental car by 8 a.m. The house stirred with warm embraces and heartfelt goodbyes. Hugs lingered a little longer, and eyes were just a little misty. There had been laughter, love, and new bonds formed—now it was time to part, for now.

Celeste left for work with a soft kiss to Jisoo's cheek and a warm goodbye to his parents. "I'll see you this evening," she said, "we'll go to Little Hanseong together."

With the house a little quieter, Jisoo spent the day with his parents, showing them more of the home he and Celeste had built together. As they sat outside with coffee in hand, he turned to them and said, "Father, Mother, Celeste, and I made a promise to the community in Little Hanseong. Before you go back to Korea, we want to take you there to say goodbye properly."

Jiyeon smiled warmly. "That's very thoughtful of you. We'd love to go."

Still, the long days had taken their toll. "But first," Si-woo said, stretching, "your mother and I need a little nap. This trip has been wonderful, but we're not as young as we used to be."

Later that afternoon, Celeste returned home from work, slipping off her shoes and letting the hum of her home wash over her. Jisoo met her at the door with a soft kiss. "Ready?" he asked.

Together with Si-woo and Jiyeon, they made their way to Little Hanseong.

The familiar faces of their cherished community awaited them—Park Dae-jung, the kind-hearted restaurant owner; his spirited granddaughter Hana Park; Moon Ji-won, the wise and gentle bookstore owner; and Mrs. Kim, ever elegant and warm, the tea shop's proud proprietor. They had all gathered to honor the parents of the man they now considered one of their own.

A table was laid with love, a meal that could rival royalty—grilled fish, vibrant vegetables, delicate rice cakes, and hot pots brimming with flavor. Stories were shared, laughter echoed, and the gentle clinking of glasses punctuated heartfelt goodbyes.

At the end of the meal, each elder presented Jiyeon and Si-woo with parting gifts—hand-sewn scarves, rare teas, and a framed calligraphy piece reading "Gratitude in every step." Their eyes glistened with emotion as they accepted the tokens.

Jisoo stood and bowed respectfully. "Thank you all for the kindness you've shown to me, Celeste, and now to our family. We are grateful beyond words. We need to get home so my parents can finish packing for their flight tomorrow, but tonight is a memory I will always cherish."

Back at home, the evening was quiet. Si-woo and Jiyeon retreated to their room to pack the last of their belongings. As she folded one final blouse, Jiyeon handed her son a small stack of carefully wrapped gifts. "Can you ship these to us once we get back to Seoul?" she asked gently.

"Of course, Mother," Jisoo replied with a nod. "I'll take care of it."

Everyone began to settle in for the night. As the lights dimmed and the house hushed, a soft knock came at Si-woo and Jiyeon 's door.

It was Micah, pajama-clad and slightly sleepy. "I just wanted to say goodbye before I go to bed. I won't see you in the morning before school."

Both grandparents wrapped him in a tight embrace. Jiyeon. smoothed his hair affectionately. "We are so proud of you, Micah. Take care of your mom and Jisoo, okay?"

"I will," he said with a small smile. "Promise."

And with that, the house settled into silence, full hearts carrying the warmth of family, love, and beginnings that had only just taken root.

The following morning began with the soft stillness of goodbye. Micah had already left for school, but not before leaving a handwritten note on the kitchen counter: "Have a safe flight. I'll miss you! Love, Micah."

Jisoo drove Celeste to work, stealing a few quiet minutes alone together before the busyness of the day began. He kissed her gently and promised to see her later, then returned home to find his parents finishing up their morning tea.

They spent their last meal together—just the three of them— talking and laughing, savoring the closeness of family. Mrs. Park lovingly packed the last of their gifts, and Jisoo loaded the car with their luggage, careful not to forget anything.

Just before they left, the phone rang. It was Ronald and Diane, calling to say one final goodbye to Si-woo and Jiyeon. Warm words were exchanged, promises to visit again were made, and gratitude for the unforgettable time they shared flowed freely between them.

On the way to the airport, Jisoo made a quick stop at a shipping center to ship the thoughtfully wrapped gifts his mother had entrusted to him. Once everything was taken care of, he picked up Celeste from work so they could drop his parents off together.

The goodbye at the airport was heartfelt—tearful smiles, long hugs, and soft words of love and blessing. Jiyeon held her son tightly, whispering, "Take care of your wife. You've made us proud." Si-woo clasped his shoulder, firm and reassuring. "This is a good life you're building, son. Don't lose sight of that."

With final waves, they disappeared through the departure gate.

Jisoo and Celeste drove home in thoughtful silence; fingers interlaced on the center console. That evening, they shared dinner with Micah—a simple, comforting meal full of quiet joy in just being together.

After dinner, Jisoo made a few business calls to Korea to check in on his upcoming projects. The house slowly settled, and the night wrapped around them like a soft blanket.

Later, in their bedroom, Jisoo climbed into bed beside Celeste. She was already fast asleep, her face peaceful in the moonlight spilling through the window. He lay beside her, watching her for a long moment, his heart full. *This is home,* he thought.

With a deep sigh of contentment, he let his eyes close and drifted off to sleep beside the woman he loved.

Saturday morning arrived with the soft hush of a house finally at rest. Everyone slept in, wrapped in the quiet comfort that followed a whirlwind of family, love, and farewells. Sunlight spilled lazily through the windows as the day began to warm.

Jisoo was the first to stir. He stretched, smiled at the sleeping figure next to him, then slipped out of bed and knocked gently on Micah's door. "Hey, you want to join me in the gym?"

Micah blinked awake, yawned, and nodded. "Give me five."

Soon, the two were side by side in the gym, music playing softly as they moved through their workout—grunts, encouragement, and the occasional joke filling the space between sets. It was a quiet, but meaningful time—father and son bonding in the rhythm of shared effort.

Meanwhile, Celeste tied her robe around her waist and padded into the kitchen. She hummed as she prepared breakfast—fluffy scrambled eggs, fruit, bacon, and toast. The scent wafted through the house, greeting the men as they emerged from the gym, sweaty but smiling.

After breakfast, the three headed outside for a refreshing swim under the soft morning sun, laughter echoing over the water.

Later, Micah's phone buzzed. A grin spread across his face as he read a message. "Can I go hang out with some friends for a couple of hours?"

Immediately, the parental litany began: "No smoking, no drugs, no girls—"

Micah rolled his eyes, grinning. "—no alcohol, no rides with strangers, etcetera, etcetera, etcetera. I know the rules. I always obey the rules, guys."

Jisoo and Celeste exchanged amused looks and chuckled. "Alright, have a good time," Jisoo said, tousling Micah's hair as he headed out.

Once the door closed behind him, Jisoo turned to Celeste, eyes playful. "My wife," he murmured, amusement warming his voice. "Come here." She barely had time to protest before he scooped her up and headed for the bedroom. Celeste giggled. The afternoon melted into soft laughter, whispered words, and tender moments shared between two people in love.

They woke around 2 p.m., tangled in each other's arms. After a warm shower, they headed back outside for another swim, basking in the sunlight and the joy of simply being together. Later, they shared a snack in the kitchen, the ease between them as natural as breathing.

Around 6 p.m., Micah returned home. He greeted them, then disappeared into his room to unwind with video games and finish up some studying.

Jisoo looked across the table at Celeste, admiration in his voice. "You should be proud of the job you did raising Micah on your own all these years."

Celeste's smile softened, pride shining in her eyes. "I think he used to worry about me when we first left and came here. He worked extra hard, I think… to make sure he didn't add any stress to my life."

She paused, emotionally veiling her voice.

"We took care of each other."

Jisoo reached across the table and took her hand, giving it a gentle squeeze. "And now… we all have each other."

Chapter 26

Ring of Reckoning

"Hello? Jisoo-ya!" "Sang-ho—it's great to hear your voice," Jisoo said, smiling as he leaned back in his chair.

"How are you, my friend? Ready to do that article?"

"Yes, that's actually why I'm calling. How's two weeks from now?"

"That sounds good," Jisoo replied, glancing toward the kitchen. "But I need to check with my wife first."

There was a brief pause on the line before Sang-ho's voice returned, full of surprise and excitement.

"Your wife, Jisoo-ya? You got married? That news hasn't reached the media here yet."

Jisoo chuckled softly. "Let's try to keep it that way—at least until you get your exclusive."

"Man… what about your parents?"

"They were here. They came for the wedding."

"Wow, man. So, they're okay with this whole thing?"

"They love her," Jisoo said with pride. "It means everything to me."

"Well, let me know for sure about the dates so I can book my flight. You think a week will be long enough for the interview and photos?"

"More than enough. Just get here."

As he ended the call, the door opened. Celeste walked in, tired but smiling, her presence instantly brightening the room.

"You're home," he said, crossing the room to greet her with a kiss.

"I am. Long day."

"I just got off the phone with Sang-ho. He wants to come in two weeks for the article. I told him I'd check with you first."

Celeste nodded, setting her bag down. "That should be fine. Just remind me of the exact days."

"Thanks, babe." He hesitated for a second before bringing up what had been on his mind. "While we're talking… we should really decide about Korea. I need to know if you're coming with me."

Celeste sighed, her shoulders tensing. "Jisoo, I just don't know if I can take three months off work. There's so much happening at New Beginnings."

Jisoo's frustration began to rise. "Celeste, I can't go to Korea and concentrate on filming knowing you're back here. You remember what happened last time."

"I do, but we haven't heard from Marcus in months," she said gently. "And the last time… he seemed sorry. He was trying to get his life together."

Jisoo stepped closer, his voice low and full of emotion. "Celeste, I felt completely helpless last time. I cannot, I will not accept that again. You're my wife. I refuse to leave you behind, unprotected."

She looked up at him, her eyes wide and uncertain. The tremble in her lips said what she didn't.

"Baby," he said, softening his tone, reaching for her hands, "I'm not trying to control you. I need you to understand. I only make one film a year. Just one. And—" Her phone rang.

They both looked at it.

Celeste froze. The name flashing on the screen sent a chill through the room.

Marcus. The expression on her face said it all.

She answered quietly. "Hello… Marcus?"

Jisoo stood silently, watching her, his heart pounding.

And everything changed.

"Hello, Celeste. How are you?"

Celeste's voice was calm but guarded. "What do you want, Marcus?"

"I need your address. You moved, and I want to see my son. I also want to give you some money for him."

"We don't need your money, Marcus," Celeste replied, her tone sharp but steady. "And I need to talk to Micah first—if he even wants to see you."

"He's my son, Celeste. A boy needs his father."

Celeste sighed. "Micah is no longer a boy. He's a young man now—one who's perfectly capable of making his own decisions."

There was a pause on the other end. Then Marcus's voice dropped.

"Have you been bad-mouthing me to him?"

"Of course not, Marcus. We don't talk about you at all."

The silence that followed was heavy. Then Marcus asked, "Are you still with the same man I saw you with?"

Celeste didn't answer right away.

"Is he the reason you won't let me see my son?" Marcus continued. "Damn it, Celeste… Micah is all I have left."

Celeste's voice softened just slightly but remained firm. "I'll talk with Micah when he gets home. Call me back on Tuesday."

She didn't wait for a response.

"Goodbye, Marcus."

And with that, she ended the call, her hand trembling slightly as she lowered the phone.

"What was that all about, Celeste?" Jisoo asked, his voice low but tense. "He doesn't sound as peaceful as before."

Celeste didn't respond right away, but Jisoo's eyes didn't leave her.

"And you want me to leave my family here unprotected?" he continued, stepping closer. "Celeste, a man doesn't do that. You and Micah cannot stay here without me. Do you understand now?"

Celeste looked into his eyes, the gravity of his words settling in. She nodded slowly.

"You either come with me," he said softly but firmly, "or I buy my way out of this contract and quit acting."

Just then, Micah walked through the door. He paused immediately, sensing the tension that hung heavily in the air.

"Is everything okay?" he asked, looking between the two of them.

Jisoo glanced at Celeste, who took a breath and nodded.

"Please sit down, Micah. We need to talk."

He took a seat cautiously. Celeste met his eyes.

"Your father called," she began gently. "He wants to see you."

Micah blinked but didn't speak.

"I told him I would talk to you first. I don't want him knowing where we live, and if you decide to see him, it'll have to be in a public place, somewhere safe, and only if you agree." Micah was quiet for a long moment, then said softly, "Mom… I understand. I remember what he did to you."

Celeste looked at him, surprised.

"I always knew why we left," Micah continued, his voice steady. "And honestly… I'm not sure I want to see him."

"He'll call on Tuesday," Celeste said gently. "You don't have to decide right now, but he'll want an answer."

Micah gave a slight nod. "I'll let you know."

As Micah walked away toward his room, Jisoo turned to Celeste, his brow furrowed with concern.

"I'm not comfortable with Marcus being alone with Micah," he said quietly.

"We don't know what state he's in, or what he's really after. Something about this doesn't feel right."

Celeste exhaled slowly. "Marcus would never hurt Micah, Jisoo. He always directed his anger at me… never at our son. Micah is his child, and as much as it pains me to admit it, I'd like him to get to know his father—on his own terms."

Jisoo took a deep breath, his hands resting lightly on her shoulders as he looked into her eyes. "I understand, Celeste. I really do. I just… I can't help worrying. After everything, I need to know he's safe. I want to respect your choices, but I also have to protect our family." His voice softened, losing the edge of tension. "It's not about control. It's about care. We'll take it slow, step by step, and make sure Micah feels comfortable." I agree," Jisoo said, his voice softer now. "I just think… the first couple of visits should be supervised. That's all I'm saying."

"We don't even know what Micah is going to decide," Celeste replied, her tone growing tired. "So maybe we don't need to have this conversation yet."

Jisoo didn't respond. He turned and walked out of the room, the silence between them lingering longer than Celeste liked.

She sat still, the emotional weight of the day pressing heavily against her shoulders. Her mind drifted back to something Jisoo had said earlier—about quitting acting if she refused to go with him to Korea. The thought made her chest ache.

She knew how much acting meant to him. It wasn't just his career—it was his art, his passion. Just as poetry fed his soul, performing gave him a sense of life. Celeste never wanted to be the reason he gave that up. She understood his fears, his frustration, and his need to protect her. But it was all just too much tonight.

Too tired to think anymore, she leaned back on the sofa and closed her eyes, exhaustion from work and stress overtaking her.

Later, Jisoo came out of the gym. He stopped in the doorway when he saw her curled up on the sofa, fast asleep. His expression softened. Quietly, he walked over, gently scooped her into his arms, and carried her to their bedroom. He laid her down carefully, brushing a few strands of hair from her face before pulling the blanket over her.

He stood for a moment, just watching her. Then, without a word, he turned off the light and quietly left the room.

Celeste woke with a start, blinking against the dim light in the bedroom. She glanced at the clock—it was late. Stretching, she sat up, ran a hand through her hair, and quietly got out of bed. After slipping off her clothes, she stepped into a warm shower, letting the water wash away the stress of the day.

The day's tension lingered in her muscles, a subtle weight that even the warm shower hadn't fully washed away. Her mind wandered over the conversation with Jisoo, the heavy words about Marcus and Micah, and the careful balance of protecting her son while allowing him to form his own relationship with his father. She felt a mix of exhaustion and quiet relief—the relief of having voiced her thoughts, and the exhaustion of carrying the responsibility of decisions that affected more than just herself.

Once she was clean and relaxed, she put on her nightclothes and robe, then padded down the hallway toward the kitchen. As she entered, she was greeted by the smell of pizza and chicken wings. On the breakfast bar sat an open box and a still-warm platter. She looked around—no one in sight.

With a small smile, she grabbed a cold beer from the fridge, took a slice of pizza and a wing, and made her way to the living room. She turned on the TV, curling into the corner of the couch just as Jisoo rounded the corner.

"See, you found the food," he said with a gentle smile, walking over to her. "I went to wake you, but you weren't there." He leaned down and kissed her forehead.

Celeste smiled up at him. "Thanks, baby. This hits the spot." She took a bite, chewed, and then sighed. "There was a crisis at the center today."

Jisoo's expression shifted, concerned. "What happened?"

"A man attacked his wife in the parking lot," she said, her voice steady but tired. "Security got to him before it got too bad. She has some scrapes and bruises, but nothing more serious, thank God."

Jisoo sat beside her, listening intently.

"My assistant—you remember Clara?" she asked.

Jisoo nodded.

"She was incredible today. Handled everything like a pro. She interviewed the client, took her to the hospital, and handled all the paperwork. I didn't have to lift a finger. She even gave the police all the information they needed."

Jisoo reached over and gently squeezed her hand. "Sounds like you've got an amazing team."

"I do," Celeste said softly, a glimmer of pride in her eyes. "It was awful, but... I was proud of how everyone came together. It reminded me why I do this work."

Jisoo smiled and pulled her closer. "You're changing lives, Celeste. Even when you think you're too tired to move, you still show up. I love that about you."

Celeste leaned into him, resting her head on his shoulder. For a moment, they said nothing—just shared the quiet, the food, and the comfort of being together.

For the next few days, life settled into a comfortable rhythm. Celeste went to work each morning, Micah kept up with school and practice, and Jisoo spent his days studying his new script and writing poetry. The calm was a welcome change, a soft lull after the recent whirlwind of events.

By Tuesday, Jisoo suggested taking Celeste to lunch—a simple break in the middle of their day together. They agreed he would drop her off at work in the morning and return to pick her up for lunch. Afterwards, they'd meet with the metalworks company installing the customized wall art they had ordered—the letter "M," in both English and Korean, to hang above their fireplace.

Late that morning, Jisoo called to say he was on his way. Celeste, already getting ready to leave her office, smiled when her receptionist buzzed her line.

"Tell Jisoo I'm on my way down," Celeste said, assuming it was him.

There was a pause. "Actually, Ms. Monroe… there's a Mr. Marcus Hollaway here to see you."

Celeste froze. The name hit her like a wave, crashing into her carefully constructed calm.

"Ms. Monroe? Are you still there?"

"Yes," she said quickly, trying to steady her voice. "Ask him to have a seat. I'll be right down."

Her stomach twisted as she stepped into the elevator, her heart pounding in her chest. But the second the doors opened, her eyes met Jisoo's. He was walking through the building's entrance, smiling—until he saw her face. His smile faded instantly, his stride quickening.

He reached her just as she stepped forward, his arm instinctively moving to her back. And then he saw Marcus.

The moment stretched long and tense. Marcus faltered slightly when he recognized Jisoo, realizing they were still together. Jisoo didn't flinch. With calm precision, he gently guided Celeste so that he stood between her and Marcus.

"Hello, Marcus," he said smoothly. "Celeste and I were just about to head to lunch—would you like to join us?"

His voice was friendly, but firm. The way he moved, the tone he used—it was so composed that anyone watching would've thought nothing was amiss. Celeste, still rattled, focused on Jisoo, letting his steadiness ground her.

Outside, the fresh air helped Celeste begin to shake off her shock.

Marcus declined the invitation. "I came to talk to you about our son," he said, emphasizing the word our while glancing at Jisoo.

Jisoo's face remained unreadable, calm as ever.

Celeste took a breath. "Marcus, I gave Micah your message. He said he'd let me know, but he hasn't decided yet and you were supposed to call tonight."

Marcus tried to speak again, but she held up her hand.

"You need to call this evening, and I'll give you Micah's answer. But right now, I have to go."

Without another word, Jisoo took her hand and guided her toward the car. They walked in silence for a few paces before Jisoo let out a small chuckle.

"Now I can't even let you go to work without me," he said, shaking his head.

Celeste laughed, the sound soft but real. "I know, right?"

She gave his hand a gentle squeeze, grateful for him—for his strength, his calm, and the way he always seemed to know just what she needed.

Chapter 27

Micah meets Marcus

They arrived at the restaurant and settled into a quiet booth. Celeste glanced over the menu briefly and said, "I'll have a salad, dressing on the side, and a cup of tea, please."

Jisoo raised an eyebrow at her. "Fried chicken and a salad for me," he told the waiter, then turned to Celeste. "Baby, what's the problem? You barely ordered anything."

Celeste gave a small sigh. "My clothes are getting a little tight," she admitted.

Jisoo smiled, reaching across the table. "Then join me in the gym, honey, if that's what you're worried about. You look great to me, just the way you are."

Celeste gave him a soft smile, but then grew thoughtful. "Can we talk about what just happened? Marcus showing up like that… once again, he crossed a line."

Jisoo nodded, his tone calm but serious. "I told you something didn't feel right."

The tension between them lingered for a moment, unspoken but understood. Both knew the weight of the situation—Marcus's unpredictable presence, the history they carried, and the fragile balance of their family's peace. Yet beneath it all, a quiet understanding settled between them, a shared commitment to trust each other and protect Micah's right to choose. The moment passed, replaced by a softer energy, one that allowed them to shift their focus back to the simple joys of the afternoon: a meal together and the excitement of returning home.

Celeste nodded in agreement. "I know. But I still want Micah to have the chance to get to know his dad, to make that decision for himself."

Jisoo reached over and squeezed her hand. "Okay. I trust you."

She smiled, then added, "Let's eat up. I'm excited to get home and see the artwork."

After lunch, they returned home just as the metalworks company arrived. The workers carefully unboxed the custom letters and mounted them over the fireplace. The large "M" in English sat beside the square Hangul symbol for "M," a simple yet striking contrast against the wall.

One of the workers stepped back and asked, "If you don't mind me asking—what's the story behind the letters and the square?"

Jisoo beamed, glancing at Celeste. "Actually, that square *is* the letter 'M' in Korean. We chose them because we're a Korean American family. The letter M represents each person in the house—my wife's last name is Monroe, our son's name is Micah, and my last name is Min. It was actually my wife's idea."

The workers smiled, clearly impressed. Once they finished cleaning up, they said their goodbyes and left.

Celeste stood in front of the fireplace, admiring the final result. "It's perfect," she whispered.

Jisoo watched her, smiling to himself. "If you're happy, I'm happy."

Just then, Micah walked through the door. He dropped his bag by the stairs, then headed toward them.

"Hey," Celeste greeted him, "Marcus came by my office today to talk about seeing you."

Micah furrowed his brow. "I thought he was going to call tonight?"

"He was," Celeste said. "I don't know why he showed up."

Micah shook his head. "Okay. When he calls, let me know."

He went upstairs, dropped his book bag, then returned to the kitchen, opening the fridge.

Celeste's phone rang.

"Hello? Yes, Marcus… hold on, Micah wants to talk to you."

She handed the phone to Micah.

"Hello? Yeah, I know who you are. Sure, we can meet up. Let me check first." He looked over at Jisoo, who glanced up from the book he was reading.

"*Appa*, are you available Saturday?" he asked.

Jisoo nodded. "Yes."

Micah spoke back into the phone. "Okay, Saturday is fine. 1 o'clock?" He looked at Jisoo again, who nodded. "1 o'clock is good. How about we meet at Sal's Pizza Place? Okay, see you then."

He handed the phone back to Celeste and then returned to the fridge.

"I'm starving. Coach really gave us a workout today, and I have way too much homework to do. Is it okay if I eat in my room? I promise I won't make a mess."

"Sure, honey," Celeste replied. "But first, give your mom a big kiss."

Micah smirked. "How about a hug, Mom?"

She laughed. "Fine. I'll take what I can get."

He hugged her and headed to his room with a plate full of snacks.

Jisoo leaned in close to Celeste and whispered, wonder soft in his voice.

"He called me Appa, Celeste. Did you hear?"

Celeste laughed softly, the warmth in her eyes matching the joy in his.

Micah texts Kai

Micah:
You busy?

Kai:
Nah, just chillin', what's up?

Micah:
Gotta tell u something kinda big.

Kai:
uh oh 😬 what'd u do this time lol.

Micah:
Nothing like that.
I'm meeting my father… my real father . Marcus.

Kai:
Wait fr?? When??

Micah:
Saturday. 1pm. Sal's Pizza.

Kai:
Dang… that's huge, man. How u feelin?

Micah:
idk… weird. Nervous, I guess.
Feels like I'm meeting a stranger who's supposed to be family.

Kai:
Yeah, that's heavy. u sure u wanna do it?

Micah:
Yeah. I just… need to see for myself, you know?
but can I ask u a favor?

Kai:
Always. What u need?

Micah:

Can u get there early, grab a table outside on the patio where u,& Jisoo can see everything inside?
Wanna know someone's there in case it gets awkward or… whatever.

Kai:

Say less. I got u, bro. I'll blend in, pretend I'm just there for the pizza 😄

Micah:

Lol thanks. just don't make it obvious.

Kai:

I'll be in stealth mode. Silent pepperoni watcher. 🍕

Micah:

Haha, appreciate it, man. Means a lot.

Kai:

you got this. Seriously. No matter how it goes, I'm right there if you need me.

Micah:

thanks, Kai. fr. 🙏

The heat of the afternoon pressed down as Jisoo guided the car into the lot at Sal's Pizza Place. The patio was dotted with red umbrellas, their fabric faded by too many summers. Cicadas droned in the distance, and the smell of garlic and cheese drifted out through the open doors.

The tension in the car was thick but measured, a quiet anticipation settling over them. Jisoo rested a reassuring hand on Micah's shoulder, his presence calm and steady, while

Micah's gaze flicked between the familiar faces and the patio ahead. Every detail—the red umbrellas, the hum of cicadas, the scent of pizza—seemed amplified, marking the moment as something significant. With a slow, grounding breath, Micah nodded, drawing courage from the support surrounding him, and prepared to take the first step toward a meeting that could change everything.

Micah shifted in his seat as they pulled into the parking lot. "He's here," Jisoo said, spotting the broad frame of Marcus already seated at a patio table near the far railing.

Kai had chosen his spot wisely. He sat on the opposite side of the patio, a Coke sweating on the table in front of him, phone idle in his hand. From where he sat, Jisoo would have a clear view of all the seats inside the pizza place without being obvious. When Micah and Jisoo stepped out of the car, Kai gave a slight nod of acknowledgement, steady and reassuring.

Jisoo touched Micah's shoulder lightly. "We'll be right here," he said, his voice calm. "Go at your own pace."

Micah nodded, then drew a breath and crossed the patio toward his father.

Marcus stood when he saw him. His face carried a tight smile that didn't quite reach his eyes. "Micah," he said, voice low, almost careful. He glanced over Micah's shoulder toward Jisoo and Kai, then back at his son. "Why don't we get a table inside? A little quieter. Just you and me."

Micah hesitated, shifting his weight, his gaze flicking back toward Jisoo on the patio. Jisoo's calm presence and Kai's steady watch both anchored him.

Still, the decision would be his to make.

After finishing their pizza, Micah and Jisoo dropped Kai off at his house. On the drive home, silence settled over the car again, but it wasn't the uncomfortable kind. It was thoughtful. Heavy with everything that hadn't yet been said.

Back at the house, Jisoo pulled into the driveway and cut the engine. Micah stayed still, staring ahead.

"I think I'm ready to talk to Mom," he said quietly.

Jisoo nodded. "I'll be right there with you."

Inside, Celeste was sitting on the couch with a cup of tea. She looked up as they entered, her expression softening when she saw Micah.

"You okay?" she asked gently.

Micah nodded and took a seat across from her. Jisoo sat beside him, giving him a reassuring look.

"Mom… I need to know what happened. With you and Marcus. I need to understand."

Celeste hesitated. She looked at Jisoo, who nodded slightly, then turned back to her son. She sat forward, hands clasped in her lap.

"All right," she said. "It's time you knew."

She took a breath. "Marcus and I met in college. He was this rising star—big personality, full of dreams. When he got drafted, we thought we had it all. You were born during his second season in the NFL, and things were good for a while. Your grandparents, Taylor and Sarah Hollaway, adored you. They couldn't wait to come visit."

Micah watched her closely. He'd never heard her speak of Marcus's parents before.

"It was during the offseason," she continued, her voice growing quiet. "They were on their way to visit us. They were excited—Taylor had just retired, and Sarah had planned a weekend full of things to do with you. But on the way, a drunk driver ran a red light on the highway. Hit them full speed. They were gone before the paramedics even got there."

Micah's breath caught. "I didn't know…"

"You were still so young," Celeste said gently. "We didn't want you to carry that pain. But for Marcus… it broke something in him."

She paused. "Not long after that, he took a bad hit—shattered his knee. It was the kind of injury you don't come back from. He tried rehab, but the doctors were honest: he'd never play professionally again."

Micah's face was unreadable, but his eyes glistened.

Celeste's voice was softer now. "The man who had been defined by his strength, by football, by that dream… suddenly had nothing. He started spiraling. The night I knew something had changed was when I found him alone, watching his teammates on TV. His knee was swollen, pain meds on the counter… and this look on his face like he was hollow inside."

"That's when the anger started," Jisoo said quietly.

Celeste nodded. "He never hurt you. He wouldn't. But he wasn't kind to me. His grief turned into rage, and I tried to hold it together—for you—but I couldn't live like that. I didn't want you to grow up thinking that kind of anger was normal. So, I left. We left."

Micah leaned forward, elbows on his knees. "And you never told me because…?"

"Because I thought I was protecting you," she whispered. "And maybe I was. But you deserve the truth now."

Micah sat back, the pieces slowly falling into place. He thought about how tired Marcus looked earlier, how the years seemed to weigh on his shoulders.

"He apologized today," Micah said. "He said he wanted to build a connection. But I told him I remember how he treated you. I told him not to call you again. If he wants to talk, he has to call me directly."

Celeste blinked back tears but nodded with quiet strength.

"I'm proud of you," Jisoo said.

Micah looked at him, then at Celeste. "Thanks, Appa. Thanks, Mom. I just… needed to know everything. I don't know what I'm going to do yet, but I'll figure it out."

Celeste stood and wrapped her arms around him. "Whatever you decide, we're with you. Always."

Jisoo joined the hug, holding them both. The past may have shaped them, but it didn't have to define them. They had each other—and that was enough to carry them forward.

Later that night, Jisoo got a call from his old military comrade, Sang-ho, the familiar voice on the other end bringing a strange comfort.

"Two days, Jisoo," Sang-ho said. "I'll be in Solmere. We'll talk, film, and clear the air. No more letting strangers tell your story."

Jisoo glanced out the window, the moonlight catching the edge of the ocean. "Thanks. ... keep it real, okay? No dramatics."

"I wouldn't dare," Sang-ho said with a chuckle. "But don't try to pretty it up either. The truth has its own beauty."

The call ended with a promise of honesty. Jisoo leaned back, heart steady but braced. The interview wasn't just for him—it was for Celeste, for Micah, for their new life.

The next morning, the rhythm of routine resumed. Celeste left for work, her satchel slung over one shoulder and a kiss pressed to Jisoo's lips. Micah grabbed his backpack, earbuds in, eyes half-lidded with sleep but still offering Jisoo a casual, "Later, Appa."

School was its usual blur. But during lunch, Micah checked his phone—and froze.

Dad (Marcus):
Hey, son. I know you probably don't want to hear from me. I've been thinking a lot since we saw each other. That pizza place—seeing you walk in—it shook something loose in me I didn't even know was still there. You've grown up into someone strong and steady. I'm proud of you. I know I don't have the right to ask for anything, but I want to be honest with you.
That first meeting meant more to me than you'll ever know. I didn't expect forgiveness. I still don't. But I'm hoping for a chance—a chance to show you who I'm trying to become. Not to erase the past, but to build something new.

If you're open to it, maybe we can meet again sometime. No pressure. Just two people figuring out what this could look like.
I know I missed out on a lot. But I'm here now, and I'm not running from the hard parts anymore.
Dad

Micah stared at the message, his stomach tightening. Around him, the cafeteria buzzed, but it all faded to a low hum. He reread the text. Once. Twice.

He didn't respond. Not yet.

Instead, he tucked the phone away and tried to breathe.

Chapter 28

Perfect Score

When Micah got home from school, the familiar smell of garlic and ginger hit him as he stepped into the house. He dropped his backpack and shoes by the door and followed the sounds of laughter and chopping into the kitchen.

Jisoo and Celeste stood side by side at the stove, a gentle rhythm between them. Celeste stirred something in a pan while Jisoo diced green onions with practiced ease. The soft hum of jazz played in the background.

Micah leaned against the counter. "Hey."

Celeste looked up and smiled. "Hey, baby. How was school?"

"It was fine," he said, hesitating a little. "I got a text. From Marcus."

That made both Jisoo and Celeste pause. Jisoo set down the knife. Celeste wiped her hands on a towel and walked over, her face full of softness. She wrapped her arms around Micah and held him for a long moment.

"You, okay?" she asked gently.

He nodded into her shoulder. "I haven't answered yet."

Celeste pulled back, brushing his hair from his face. "We're here for you. Whatever you decide. There's no pressure, okay?"

"Okay," he said, his voice low.

He turned and headed up to his room. Sitting on his bed, he stared at the message for a while, then finally typed back:

Micah:

I'm not sure what to say. It was… a lot seeing you again. I'm not making any promises, but I'll think about it and just remember—you contact me directly—no contact with my mom.

He hit send before he could second-guess it.

Back in the kitchen, Jisoo was plating food, and Celeste was setting the table. Micah slid back onto a stool and exhaled.

"I answered him," he said quietly.

Jisoo nodded, handing him a spoonful of rice. "Good. Just do what feels right, not what anyone expects."

"Thanks," Micah said. Then, looking between them, he added, "Also, don't forget—Sang-ho's coming in two days."

Jisoo smiled. "Right. The great Solmere interview. We should probably clean the guest room."

Celeste chuckled. "And stock up on snacks. Journalists run on caffeine and sugar."

Micah gave a small laugh, and for a moment, the tension lifted. There was still a lot to figure out—but here, in this kitchen, with the people who had his back, he felt a little more ready.

The next morning, sunlight filtered through the kitchen windows as Celeste poured herself a cup of coffee, still dressed in her robe. Jisoo stood by the counter, scrolling through his phone and sipping his tea.

"Hey," Celeste said, glancing toward the small pile of mail on the counter. "Have you seen anything from the College Board? Micah's PSAT scores were supposed to come this week."

Jisoo shook his head. "Nothing yet. They should've arrived by now. Maybe we need to follow up."

Celeste nodded thoughtfully, then glanced at the time. "I'd better get going, or I'll be late for the hospice team meeting." She kissed his cheek, grabbed her bag, and headed out the door.

Jisoo cleaned up the breakfast dishes and wandered to his office, where he settled in to write. The day crept by—just the rustling of wind outside, the tapping of his keyboard, the occasional creak of the house.

As the afternoon drifted slowly into evening, the soft golden light of the setting sun began to filter through the curtains, casting warm patterns across the floor. Jisoo glanced up from his screen, stretching his shoulders, while the house settled into a quiet rhythm—the distant hum of the fridge, the occasional creak of the floorboards, and the faint rustle of leaves outside.

Somewhere in the back of his mind, he felt the familiar pull of routine and comfort, knowing soon the kitchen would come alive again with chatter, clinking dishes, and the smells that always made this house feel like home. By evening, the three of them were gathered around the dinner table, plates full of roasted chicken, rice, and stir-fried vegetables. The table was cozy, conversation easy.

Celeste passed the salad bowl to Micah. "How was school?"

"Fine," he said, reaching for more rice.

Jisoo looked up from his plate. "Any news from your teachers or clubs?"

Micah shrugged. "Not really."

Celeste sipped her water, then tilted her head. "What about your PSAT scores? Still nothing in the mail?"

Micah blinked. "Oh—they came. I forgot to show them to you."

Jisoo nearly dropped his fork. "You what? Where are they? How did you do?"

Celeste's eyes widened. "Micah! We'd like to see them. That's a big deal."

Micah looked sheepish. "I did okay."

Celeste raised an eyebrow. "Go get them. How could you forget something so important?"

With a dramatic sigh, Micah stood and trudged to his room. A minute later, he returned with a sealed envelope and handed it to Jisoo.

Jisoo opened it, his eyes scanning the score report. Celeste leaned in, and suddenly they both gasped and shouted in unison:

"Micah!"

Micah winced. "What?"

"You got a perfect score!" Celeste exclaimed, practically glowing. "Oh, my Lord—a perfect score!"

Jisoo grinned widely, holding the paper like it was a golden ticket. "You crushed it, kid."

Micah shrugged. "It's not a big deal. Kai got a perfect score, too."

Celeste stood up and pulled him into a hug. "I am *so* proud of you."

"Thanks, Mom," Micah mumbled. "Can I go now? And please don't call everyone. It's embarrassing."

Celeste laughed, still beaming. "No promises."

Jisoo gave Micah a playful pat on the back as he passed by. "You earned it. Even if you're too cool to celebrate."

As Micah disappeared upstairs, Celeste and Jisoo exchanged a look, their hearts full. Their boy was growing up— intelligent, humble, and still their greatest joy.

After dinner, dishes were done, and the kitchen lights cast a soft golden hue over the countertops. Celeste leaned against the counter, her arms folded as she watched Jisoo pour them both a glass of ginger tea.

The warmth of the kitchen lingered around them, the soft clink of the glasses and the faint aroma of ginger tea creating a quiet comfort. Celeste's eyes wandered to Micah's empty chair at the table, and a small smile tugged at her lips. Thoughts of how quickly he was growing up—and how much he deserved to feel celebrated—bubbled up inside her, sparking an idea that made her heart race with a mix of mischief and affection.

"We have to do something huge for Micah," she said suddenly, her eyes twinkling with excitement. "Maybe we could throw him a surprise party—invite his friends, decorate the house, get a cake shaped like a Scantron sheet or something fun."

Jisoo chuckled, setting his tea down gently. "Umm... maybe we should ask him what he'd like first. I'm not sure he's a party kid. You know how he is—cool on the outside, all nerves on the inside."

Celeste sighed with a smile, nodding. "Maybe you're right. Once Sang-ho leaves, we can plan something lowkey but special. I want him to feel seen, celebrated, you know?"

Jisoo stepped closer and brushed a curl from her cheek. "He already does. Because of you."

Celeste softened, her smile turning playful. "Well, tonight, my darling husband, I believe you said you had something romantic in mind?"

Jisoo grinned. "Is that right, my beautiful wife?"

She took a teasing step toward him, eyes glinting. "Yes, how would you like me to play the role of your leading lady and help you rehearse your lines?"

Jisoo placed a hand over his heart dramatically. "Would I ever. Though... do you think your Korean has gotten that good?"

Celeste raised a brow, smirking. "I'll have you know I've been practicing. And according to a very reliable source—my son—I'm almost reading and speaking as well as he does."

Jisoo laughed, then reached for her hand. "Then come on, my muse. Let's run lines under moonlight. And maybe, if the mood is right, we'll improvise a scene or two."

She took his hand, laughing as he pulled her toward the living room, where the script and a candlelit mood awaited.

"Lead the way, director," she whispered.

"Only if you promise to steal every scene," he replied.

And just like that, their evening faded into something soft and full of love—lines blurring between real and pretend, between everyday life and something out of a film.

The morning began like any other.

Micah headed off to school, backpack slung over one shoulder, earbuds in, offering a quick "See you later" before disappearing out the front door. Celeste kissed Jisoo on the cheek, adjusted the collar of his shirt, and headed to work, her heels clicking softly against the hardwood as she left.

Chapter 29
Sang-ho Exclusive

Jisoo stood for a moment in the quiet, sipping his coffee, then glanced at the time. He had a guest to pick up.

By noon, he was waiting at the arrivals terminal of Solmere Regional Airport, shifting his weight from one foot to the other until he spotted a familiar figure coming through the gates—Sang-ho, his old friend and military comrade. The two embraced with an easy, brotherly warmth, clapping each other on the back.

"You haven't aged a day," Sang-ho joked, rolling his suitcase.

Jisoo laughed. "Liar. But I missed you."

They loaded up the car, catching up in bits and pieces as the city slipped past the windows. "Thought we might stop in Little Hanseong for lunch," Jisoo suggested. "Or head back to the house. Up to you."

"Lunch sounds good. I want to meet this community I've been reading about."

So, they went.

The moment they stepped into Seojin's Kitchen, the familiar scents of gochujang, sesame oil, and fresh garlic greeted them like an old song. Mr. Park, the owner, recognized Jisoo instantly and came bustling over with a wide grin.

"Jisoo-ya!" he exclaimed. "And you must be the famous journalist. Welcome, welcome."

As they moved deeper into the restaurant, chairs scraped softly against the floor and the low hum of conversation wrapped around them. Plates clinked, steam curled through the air, and the warmth of the space settled in—not just from the food, but from the familiarity of the place itself. It felt less like a restaurant and more like a living room that had learned to cook for dozens, a space ready to welcome them fully.

Within moments, the lunch crowd was buzzing. Familiar faces from Little Hanseong came by to greet them—Mrs. Moon from Haneul Pages, Hana with her shy smile, and even a few elders who nodded solemnly in approval.

The food came in waves—kimchi pancakes, spicy tofu stew, bulgogi sizzling on a hot plate. Over bites of mandu, Sang-ho listened as Mr. Park spoke with unexpected fire.

"All this outrage in the Korean media," Mr. Park said, shaking his head. "It's nothing new. Age-old racism, nationalism, classism, sexism, envy—name it. Brutal everywhere, but back home?" He tapped his chest. "Sometimes even worse."

He looked directly at Sang-ho. "Koreans should support Koreans. They shouldn't tear them down because of who they love, where they live, or how they speak their truth. Jisoo hasn't forgotten his heritage. He's honored it—in every poem, every action. And this community stands behind him."

Sang-ho nodded slowly, clearly moved. "I can see that."

After lunch, Jisoo drove Sang-ho back to the house, letting the silence between them hold the weight of everything they'd just heard.

"I figured you'd want to rest and freshen up," Jisoo said as they pulled into the driveway. "And then… we talk."

Sang-ho gave him a look part gratitude, part determination. "We talk."

And as they stepped into the quiet of Jisoo and Celeste's home, something shifted. The interview wasn't just a story anymore. It was a responsibility.

Sunlight streamed through the tall windows of the coastal home, casting golden rays across the sleek hardwood floor. A gentle breeze from the ocean lifted the sheer curtains as Jisoo poured tea for Sang-ho, who sat on the sofa with a small digital recorder in hand and a leather-bound notebook resting on his lap.

The presence of home softened the edges of the moment. With Celeste nearby—quietly supportive, thoughtful in her gestures—the space felt less like a formal interview setting and more like a conversation unfolding in trust. Once she stepped away, leaving the two men alone with their thoughts, the air shifted subtly, settling into a focused stillness.

Celeste brought over a plate of honey cookies and placed them on the coffee table. "Let me know if you need anything else," she said warmly, then smiled at Jisoo before heading to her office to give them space.

Sang-ho adjusted the recorder's settings and looked up. "You ready?"

Jisoo gave a nod, a calm but steady presence. "Let's do it."

Sang-ho clicked the red button. "This is Lee Sang-ho, interviewing Min Jisoo, actor, poet, and recently revealed to the world as Eun Sol. Thank you for letting me be the one to tell your story."

Jisoo offered a small smile. "I trust you. That's rare, these days."

"Let's start with the obvious" Sang-ho said. "Your fans know you as a celebrated actor, but many were surprised to learn you're also the poet Eun Sol. Why did you keep that part of yourself private for so long?"

"As I said when it was revealed that I was Eun Sol—'I wrote in shadows, afraid that my voice would not be enough," Jisoo replied. "But if my words have brought even one person comfort, then they were never just mine to keep."

"What does poetry give you that acting doesn't?"

"When I act, I'm living someone else's vision—a character that another writer created. But my poetry? That's mine. It's my personal expression of my thoughts, my feelings, my joys, and pain. No camera, no costume. Just truth."

"How did your time in the military shape your identity and your work both as an artist and as a man?"

"I returned to civilian life with a new sense of discipline, purpose, and mental strength. I learned perseverance and gained a deeper understanding of the true meaning of responsibility. My poetry became deeper, more profound, infused with the understanding that suffering and growth are two sides of the same coin. When facing personal and public scrutiny for my choices—my decision to move to America, to love Celeste despite societal backlash—I leaned on that inner strength forged in the military."

"The Korean media had mixed reactions to your life in America. What would you like to say to those who feel you've abandoned your roots?"

With a quiet breath, he said, "I missed the food, the people, the culture so much that my lovely wife found us a Korean community here in Solmere. And as you saw today, they embraced us. We're not isolated. We're part of something. I didn't forget where I came from."

"You're married to Celeste Monroe, an older African American woman. That's challenged many cultural expectations. How do you navigate that personally and publicly?"

"I've always dated older women. It's not something I planned it just happened. Celeste is only two years older than me, which isn't significant. In the past, I dated women who were four or five years older than me. What matters isn't the number it's the connection, the love, the respect. I don't see her age. I see her heart. Love doesn't follow rules, especially not the ones society tries to impose."

"What does 'home' mean to you now?"

Looking toward the hallway where Celeste had disappeared, "Home is a place shared with the people you love—in comfort and peace. That's what we've built here. That's home."

"And the Korean American community here in Solmere, how have they helped you feel grounded?"

"It's a small version of Korea. They've welcomed me, Celeste, and Micah like family. We get a newsletter, celebrate holidays together, share meals… They came to our wedding. They're part of our everyday life now. And now, they're part of my parents' lives too."

Sang-ho paused the recorder and leaned back. "This… this is the story the world needs to hear. Not the gossip, not the backlash. Just the truth."

Jisoo smiled quietly. "Then tell it."

After wrapping up the initial interview with Jisoo, Sang-ho paused the recorder and glanced toward the kitchen.

"Do you think Celeste might be open to talking for a few minutes?" he asked, his tone respectful.

Jisoo nodded. "She'd want to. Let me get her."

A moment later, Celeste entered, now in a soft cardigan and jeans, her hair pulled back in a loose ponytail. She gave Sang-ho a warm but curious smile as she took a seat across from him.

"I hear you want to interview me now?" she said lightly.

"If you're willing," Sang-ho replied, sitting forward slightly. "I think your voice is just as important in this story. You and Jisoo… you're building something rare. And people need to hear from both of you."

Celeste folded her hands in her lap. "All right. But I'm not as poetic as my husband."

Sang-ho smiled. "That's okay. I'm here for the truth, not the polish."

He switched on the recorder again.

"Celeste, thank you for speaking with me. I know your life has undergone significant changes over the past few years. If I may ask… how did you and Jisoo first connect?"

Celeste smiled. "Through poetry. We met on a literature forum, initially anonymously. I knew him only as 'Eun Sol,' and he knew me only by my initials. We exchanged verses, slowly building trust with our words. By the time I learned who he really was, we had already shared something deeper than names. We had found a mirror in each other."

"What was it like for you—falling in love with someone from such a different world?" Sang-ho asked.

"It wasn't easy" Celeste said. "There were cultural gaps, language barriers, and, of course, public scrutiny. But love real love —teaches you to listen. To be humble. To hold space for difference. We've both had to learn and unlearn things. But we never gave up on each other."

"Can I ask—when did you realize this wasn't just a relationship, but something that would change your whole life?"

Celeste's expression softened. "Probably the moment Jisoo showed up in Solmere and looked at me like I wasn't a secret worth hiding. Like I was home. I'd been surviving for so long… I didn't know I could still choose joy. He reminded me that I could."

"There's been a lot of public commentary—about your age, your background, your past. How have you managed to stay grounded?"

Celeste said quietly, "By remembering who I am. "I'm a mother. I'm a woman who survived an abusive marriage and started over. I work in crisis support. I sit with people in their darkest moments. That gives you perspective. The gossip fades. What matters is the life I've built—with Jisoo, with Micah, with the community that welcomed us."

Sang-ho nodded slowly, visibly moved. "There's been backlash—harsh criticism. You've seen what the Korean media has said. How do you deal with it?"

Celeste took a breath. "I don't take it personally anymore. What people don't understand, they try to destroy. But this love—it's built on truth, not approval. Jisoo and I... we've weathered worse."

"What's been the hardest part of this journey?"

Celeste paused, watching Jisoo carry the burden of trying to protect everyone. He's an artist, but he's also a son, a public figure, a husband, a father. Sometimes I see the weight on his shoulders, and I wish I could take some of it from him. But I support him by standing beside him—not in front, not behind."

"What does Jisoo mean to you?"

Celeste's voice softened, "He is... my second chance. My anchor. My sunrise. With him, I feel seen—not just for what I've endured, but for what I've become."

"And your son, Micah? How has he handled all of this?"

Celeste smiled, pride glowing in her eyes. "Micah is extraordinary. He's kind, thoughtful, and strong. He accepted Jisoo into our lives not because he had to—but because he saw who Jisoo really was. And now, they're closer than I ever imagined possible."

Sang-ho checked the time, then set down his pen. "I was hoping to speak with him, too."

Celeste nodded. "He won't be back until late—he's got swim practice and then a study session at Kai's. But he'll be home tomorrow. I'm sure he'd be willing to talk then."

"Good," Sang-ho said, rising from his chair. "This isn't just an article anymore. It's a portrait of your life. I want to do it justice."

Celeste stood too, offering her hand. "Then you already are."

They shook hands, a quiet understanding passing between them.

The evening settled into a warm hush, the last hints of twilight stretching across the sky like watercolors bleeding into dusk. Out by the pool, a soft breeze carried the scent of jasmine and sea salt, mingling with the gentle clink of glasses and laughter.

The soft twilight and the gentle rustle of the evening set a serene backdrop as the meal was laid out. The scents of the food mingled with the ocean breeze, promising comfort and ease. It was a quiet, unhurried moment—a pause where conversation could linger, laughter could rise softly, and the simple act of sharing a meal became a small celebration of presence and togetherness.

Dinner was light—grilled vegetables, seasoned chicken skewers, a small tray of kimchi and pickled radish, and bowls of rice. On the side table, a half-full bottle of soju glistened beside three small shot glasses.

Jisoo poured with practiced ease, offering the first glass to Sang-ho, then one to Celeste. Sang-ho reached for the bottle, a familiar smile passing between them, and filled Jisoo's glass in return.

"To old friends," he said, raising his glass.

"To new beginnings," Celeste added with a soft smile.

They clinked glasses and drank, the soju burning just enough to warm them, but not overwhelm.

The pool lights shimmered beneath the surface, casting soft ripples of gold and blue across the patio. Music played low from a speaker nearby—classic jazz, something Celeste always gravitated toward in the evenings.

After a few more rounds of drinks and shared memories, Celeste leaned back in her chair, letting the warmth of the moment settle into her bones.

"Well," she said, stretching a little, "this has been lovely, but I think I'm going to turn in early. Long day."

She rose, placing a gentle hand on Jisoo's shoulder. "Don't stay up too late," she teased, then turned to Sang-ho. "It's good having you here. Rest well and thank you—for telling our story with care."

Sang-ho stood politely, bowing his head slightly. "Thank you for trusting me with it."

Celeste gave Jisoo one last smile before heading inside, leaving the two men in comfortable silence as crickets chirped softly in the background.

Jisoo leaned back, exhaling deeply. "It's strange," he said. "Some nights I forget who I used to be before all of this."

Sang-ho topped off Jisoo's glass. Jisoo took the bottle and returned the favor. That's not a bad thing, Jisoo. It means you've grown. But don't forget him completely. He's the one who survived the storms."

Jisoo raised his glass again, this time without words, and Sang-ho mirrored the gesture.

"Can I ask…" Sang-ho said what did your parents think of all this? Of Celeste? Of your life here?"

Jisoo smiled faintly, eyes on the horizon. "At first… it was hard for them. Not just because of who Celeste is, but because of everything she represented—freedom, change, America. But they came here. They met her. They saw the life we're building." He paused.

"They gave us their blessing. Maybe not all at once… but they gave it."

Sang-ho nodded, visibly moved. "That says a lot."

Chapter 30

Sang-ho's Departure

The morning air was crisp and golden, sunlight spilling through the trees as Jisoo steered his car down the quiet suburban street. He pulled up in front of Kai's house and texted Micah.

A few seconds later, the front door opened. Micah stepped out with Kai beside him, both boys laughing about something. Kai gave Jisoo a polite wave before heading back inside.

The morning moved with a gentle, unhurried rhythm. The quiet streets stretched out before them, bathed in soft sunlight, while the air carried the faint scent of dew and fresh coffee from nearby houses. Jisoo stole a glance at Micah, noting the easy camaraderie he shared with Kai, and felt a small swell of gratitude. It was one of those rare, calm mornings when the world seemed to pause just long enough for connection, and he hoped this moment would help set the tone for the conversation ahead.

Micah climbed into the passenger seat, tossing his bag in the back.

"Morning, Appa," he said casually, buckling in.

Jisoo smiled. "Morning. Did you sleep okay?"

Micah shrugged. "Yeah. Kai's mom made breakfast and everything."

As they drove, the town slowly began to wake up—dog walkers, joggers, early coffee runs. Jisoo glanced at his son from the corner of his eye.

"You remember Sang-ho? My friend from the military?"

Micah nodded. "Yeah. He's the reporter, right?"

"He's staying with us for a few days," Jisoo said. "He wants to talk to you today, if you're up for it. Just a short conversation, about what life's been like, how you're feeling, maybe even how you see all of this… with your mom and me."

Micah didn't answer right away. He stared out the window, thoughtful. "Do I have to?"

"No," Jisoo said gently. "But I think he'd really value your perspective. You don't have to say anything you don't want to. He's not looking to push you. Just… listen. Talk if you feel like it."

Micah gave a slow nod. "Okay. I guess it wouldn't hurt."

Jisoo reached over at the next red light and squeezed his shoulder. "That's all I ask."

They pulled into the driveway a few minutes later. The house stood quiet, peaceful under the soft light of morning.

Inside, the kettle was already whistling. Sang-ho stood in the kitchen with a mug in hand, wearing a comfortable t-shirt and jeans. He looked up and smiled as they walked in.

"Micah," he said warmly. "Good to see you."

Micah gave a small smile in return. "Hey."

Jisoo clapped a hand on his back. "Why don't you two sit out back? I'll bring out some juice and tea."

Sang-ho nodded. "That sounds perfect."

As Micah led the way to the back patio, Jisoo lingered for a moment, watching his son's posture, cautious but open. And that was enough.

The morning sunbathed the patio in soft light as Micah settled into a chair across from Sang-ho. A light breeze rustled the leaves, and the distant sound of waves gave the space an almost meditative calm.

Sang-ho took a sip of his tea and smiled gently. "Thanks for sitting down with me, Micah. I know this isn't the usual way you'd want to spend your morning."

Micah shrugged, leaning back. "It's okay. Jisoo said you were a friend. From the military."

Sang-ho nodded. "He said you were the reason he could face the backlash. The rumors. The pressure. He told me you grounded him."

Micah looked down at his hands, then out at the ocean. "It's been… a lot, all of it. I mean, I love Jisoo. And I'm glad he's here. But everything changed fast, you know?"

Sang-ho nodded slowly. "That makes sense. You were already going through a lot before all of this. And now the spotlight's bigger than ever."

There was a beat of silence before Sang-ho continued. "I don't want to pressure you. I'm not here to pull soundbites or twist your story. I'm trying to tell the truth. And your voice… it matters in that truth."

"What's it been like" Sang-ho asked, "having someone like Jisoo become your stepdad?"

Micah looked down at his hands for a long moment. "At first… weird. I didn't know what to think. He was famous. My mom was… healing. I was scared for her. But Jisoo, he never pushed. He just showed up. Again, and again. And eventually, I realized… he wasn't trying to replace anyone. He was trying to be someone I could count on."

"Now?" Micah said, "He's Appa."

Sang-ho smiled. "That's a strong word. It means a lot."

"Yeah." Micah said quietly. "He does."

They sat quietly for a moment, the ocean breeze swirling between them.

"Thanks for telling me that," Sang-ho said softly. "I know you didn't have to."

Micah nodded. "Just… don't make it sound like it was easy. It wasn't. But we got here. Together."

Sang-ho reached into his notebook and scribbled something down. Then he closed it, looking up with a smile. "That's exactly the kind of story I want to tell."

The late afternoon sun filtered through the windows of the guest room as Sang-ho sat at the small desk overlooking the sea. His notebook lay open, pages already filled with scribbled impressions and quotes, but this page remained blank for now.

For a moment, Sang-ho simply let himself absorb the room—the soft lapping of the waves, the golden light spilling across the desk, the quiet rhythm of a house that had already lived through so much. It was a pause that felt deliberate, as if the world itself was giving him permission to settle, focus, and prepare. Then, pen in hand, he allowed the story before him to finally take shape.

He took a slow breath, letting the ocean air steady his thoughts. Then, in neat, careful writing, he began:

Journal Entry — Solmere

I came here to write a story about a famous man who caused a stir in Korea by falling in love with someone unexpected.

What I found instead… was a family. A real one. Imperfect, but whole.

Jisoo isn't just an actor or a poet. He's a son who asked for his parents' blessing. A man who left everything he knew to protect the woman he loves, a father by choice, not biology.

Celeste is strength wrapped in grace. She carries the scars of her past with quiet dignity, and yet she laughs with a freedom that tells you she's survived it all.

And Micah, he's the bridge between them. Intelligent, observant, a little guarded… but deeply good.

They don't fit into the easy molds. They've carved out their own shape, their own rhythm, their own home.

Tomorrow, I'll start writing.

Tonight, I'm just grateful to have witnessed it.

"Sometimes the most extraordinary stories are not found in the spotlight, but in the quiet spaces between heartbeats, in the steady gaze of a teenage boy who has weathered more than most adults, or the quiet grace of a woman who chose peace over pride. And in a man once revered only for his image, now known for the truth behind his words."

The room seemed to hold its breath as Sang-ho reflected, the quiet hum of the ocean outside blending with the soft scratch of his pen. Each memory, each observation, settled onto the page like careful brushstrokes, shaping not just a story, but a portrait of a life lived with courage, resilience, and quiet love. It was a moment suspended between thought and action, where insight transformed into narrative.

Sang-ho paused, tapping his pen gently against the paper. He thought of Micah's eyes, transparent, guarded, but honest. Of Celeste's warmth and steel. Of Jisoo's quiet strength and the way he seemed to have grown into the fullness of who he was meant to be, not on stage, but in this house, among these people.

"Min Jisoo, or Eun Sol, is not simply a star—he is a survivor of silence, a poet of resilience. He has not abandoned his heritage; he has redefined it, carrying it with him into a new land, a new language, a new kind of family."

He set the pen down for a moment, looking out at the water.

He reflected on Korea, how harsh it could be to those who veered from expectations. He considered how Jisoo's story might still cause controversy. But he also understood: the truth held power. And this truth… was worth sharing.

"In a world quick to judge and slow to understand, this story is not about scandal, it's about survival. It's about choosing love, again and again, even when the world tells you not to."

Satisfied, Sang-ho closed his notebook. The real work was only beginning, but the heart of the story had revealed itself.

And it beat here, in this house by the sea.

First Draft – Sang-ho's Article

Title: *Between Two Worlds: The Quiet Courage of Min Jisoo*

By Lee Sang-ho

For Seoul Chronicle, International Arts & Culture Feature

In a quiet coastal town thousands of miles from Seoul, the man once known only as an idol, a leading man, and a heartthrob walks barefoot across his garden, carrying a mug of tea and a book of poetry, his own.

Min Jisoo, actor. Eun Sol, poet.

It's a truth that stunned the Korean public: that one of our most celebrated screen icons had, all along, been pouring his soul into verse under a pseudonym. That the man adored for his roles in dramas and films had also been living a second life, one shaped by introspection, quiet rebellion, and eventually, love.

What began as whispers, a fan analyzing the handwriting in a rare autograph, ended in a single post from his long, dormant private social media account:

"Yes. I am Eun Sol."

Now, in an exclusive conversation, Min Jisoo breaks his silence about poetry, service, scandal, and the love that took him across an ocean.

"I wrote in shadows, afraid that my voice would not be enough," he tells me one night over soju by the pool. "But if my words brought even one person comfort, then they were never just mine to keep."

Min Jisoo's journey through military service, enduring bitter winters and blistering drills, transformed not just his body but his soul.

"When I returned," he says, "I was different. No longer just a dreamer. My poetry deepened. I understood that suffering and growth were two sides of the same coin."

That resilience was tested again when his relationship with Celeste Monroe, a community activist, hospice minister, and older American woman, went public.

The backlash in Korea was immediate. The hate was loud. But so was the support.

Here in Solmere, Min Jisoo and Celeste are not tabloid fodder. They are neighbors. Family. They share Sunday dinners in Little Hanseong, a vibrant Korean American enclave where the fish market smells like Noryangjin and Mrs. Moon's bookstore stocks both Emily Dickinson and Han Kang.

Their home, a sanctuary by the sea, is filled with floor-to-ceiling windows, music, books, laughter… and a teenage boy named Micah.

"He calls me Appa now," Jisoo says quietly. "Not because I asked him to. Because he wanted to."

Micah, Celeste's son, is bright, thoughtful, and already well on his way to building a future as extraordinary as his present. When asked what he thinks of his stepfather, he answers:

"He didn't try to replace anyone. He just showed up."

Jisoo has not abandoned his heritage. He's expanded it. He speaks of Solmere and Seoul in the same breath. Of loyalty and love. It takes courage to choose happiness in a world that punishes deviation.

"Home," he tells me, "Is wherever we're allowed to love in peace."

The morning light spilled gently through the windows of the Solmere home. In the kitchen, Celeste stood barefoot, flipping pancakes while humming softly to herself. The smell of sizzling bacon and fresh coffee lingered in the air.

Jisoo was setting the table; his hair still damp from the shower. Micah dragged himself down the stairs, still in his sleep shirt, yawning.

"Something smells good. Is this for Sang-ho's last breakfast?"

"Yes, Micah, so be nice and stay awake long enough to say goodbye."

Sang-ho entered the room with his bag slung over one shoulder. He paused in the doorway, absorbing the scene of the family moving with the effortless rhythm of love and familiarity.

"Did I step into a commercial for peace and pancakes?" Sang-ho teased.

Jisoo laughed "You wish."

Everyone sat down together. The table was full, pancakes, bacon, eggs, fruit, juice, and coffee.

Celeste raised her mug, "To friends who become family."

Micah mutters, "Even if they take the last slice of bacon."

Laughter followed.

After the meal, Sang-ho extended his hand to Micah. "You're a good kid, Micah. Stay true to yourself."

"Thanks," Micah replied. "Safe travels."

Sang-ho turned to Celeste and Jisoo. "You didn't just give me a story. You gave me something real. Something I won't forget."

As they finished packing up the last of Sang-ho's things after breakfast, Jisoo walked him out to the car waiting in the driveway. The morning sun was warm on their backs, and the sea breeze carried the scent of salt and pine.

Sang-ho glanced at Jisoo, his duffel slung over one shoulder. "It's hard to leave. This place… it feels good. Real."

Jisoo smiled, sliding his hands into his pockets. "It is real. Took a while to get here, but we're building something solid."

Sang-ho nodded, then raised an eyebrow. "And when do you head back to Korea?"

Jisoo's expression softened. "June. I'll be there all summer, filming from June through August."

"Ah, so the mystery man returns," Sang-ho teased. "And Celeste and Micah?"

"They're coming with me," Jisoo said. "We'll stay in my apartment in Seoul. Still got it. Figured it's time to bring my family home… at least for a little while."

Sang-ho looked genuinely moved. "That's going to make a hell of a follow-up article."

Jisoo chuckled. "Let's see how this first one goes."

Celeste hugged him. "We're glad you came. Tell the truth, and take care of our Jisoo's reputation while you're at it."

"He'll tell the story right. He always does." Jisoo replied.

Jisoo and Sang-ho shared one final embrace, the kind that carried the weight of shared pasts and evolving futures. As Sang-ho climbed into the car, he leaned out the window.

"Don't forget, Jisoo—truth speaks louder than the noise. And your story? It's worth hearing."

Jisoo nodded, watching as the car pulled away, knowing the next chapter was already beginning.

As the car pulled away, Celeste rested her head on Jisoo's shoulder and sighed. "Do you think they'll understand back home?"

"Some will. Some won't. But what matters is that we do." Jisoo responded .

Chapter 31

Seoul Chronicle

Over the next few weeks, Marcus kept his promise by regularly reaching out to Micah. Sometimes it was just a short text checking in:

Marcus:

Hey son. Just thinking about you. Hope school's going well. Let me know if you need anything.

Other times, it was a call, always respectful, never demanding. He kept the conversations light, talking about sports scores, new music, and upcoming movies. He didn't push. He just tried to stay present.

One Friday evening, after Micah got home from swim practice, he found a new message waiting:

Marcus:
Hey Micah. I was wondering if you'd want to catch a movie this weekend, or we could hit the outlet mall if you need new sneakers. Your call. Whatever you feel up for. Just let me know.

Micah stared at the screen for a long moment, then set his phone down on his desk without answering right away. He didn't know how he felt yet, not really. But he'd noticed something different in Marcus lately. No pressure. Just... consistency.

At dinner that night, the topic came up as they sat around the table.

"Marcus texted me," Micah said, glancing at both Jisoo and Celeste. "He wants to hang out. Movie, shopping… he said I can choose."

Celeste was quiet for a moment, her fork resting on the edge of her plate. "How do you feel about that?"

Micah shrugged, chewing his food slowly. "I don't know. He's been reaching out every week. Nothing intense, just checking in. It's weird… but not bad."

Jisoo nodded thoughtfully. "You don't have to decide right now. But if you ever do want to go… I can take you and stay nearby. Just in case."

Micah gave a small smile. "Thanks, Appa. I'll think about it." And he meant it.

It was late Saturday afternoon when Micah and Kai sat on the rocky overlook above Solmere's coast, their bikes propped behind them and the ocean stretching endlessly below. The sky was streaked with soft golds and pinks, and the salty breeze tangled gently through their hair.

Micah picked up a smooth pebble and tossed it, watching it skip once before sinking. He had been quiet for a while, too calm for Kai.

Micah sat quietly for a moment, letting the sound of the waves fill the space between them. His thoughts drifted over the past few weeks—the texts from Marcus, the awkward yet steady attempts to reconnect, and the whirlwind of Jisoo's life now laid bare for the world to see. It all pressed against him at once, a mix of pride, uncertainty, and the strange weight of being caught between so many expectations.

"What's going on in that genius brain of yours?" Kai asked, nudging his shoulder.

Micah exhaled slowly. "It's been a lot lately."

Kai gave him a knowing look. "Start from the top."

Micah leaned back on his elbows; eyes focused on the horizon. "There was the interview with Sang-ho about Jisoo… and my mom. I listened to parts of it while they were recording. It was real. Honest. I didn't expect it to hit me that hard."

"You mean the whole world finally seeing who you guys are?" Kai asked.

"Yeah," Micah nodded. "And then Marcus—my father, he's been calling, texting. He wants to meet up again. A movie, shopping, just… stuff." He paused. "He's not pushing, but it still feels like… pressure."

Kai was silent, letting him talk.

"And then there's Korea," Micah continued. "We're all going in June. I've never been. Jisoo has his apartment there. I'll be living there all summer, and I don't know the language or the culture that well... I just… I feel like I'm floating between two worlds."

Kai nodded slowly. "You are. But you're not alone. Jisoo will be there. Your mom will be there. And you've got me, even if I'm stuck here sending dumb memes across time zones."

Micah chuckled, but his smile faded fast.

"I guess I'm scared," he admitted. "Scared that I won't fit in anywhere, not with Marcus, not in Korea. I'm proud of my family, proud of what we've built… but what if the world still sees me as a kid stuck in between?"

Kai picked up a pebble and tossed it. "Micah, you're one of the most grounded people I know. You've already done what a lot of adults can't—facing the truth, setting boundaries, staying open even when it hurts. You're not in between. You're building something new."

Micah looked over at him, eyes glinting with quiet gratitude.

"You really believe that?"

"I do," Kai said with a grin. "But if you start spouting poetry, I'm biking home alone."

Micah laughed, the sound light and true. "Deal."

As the sun dipped lower and the sky blushed deeper, the boys sat in silence, the kind that only true friends could share. And for the first time in weeks, Micah felt something like peace.

The sky over Solmere was a soft gray, with low but not heavy clouds. The coastal breeze carried a quiet stillness, as if the air itself were holding its breath.

Jisoo stood in the doorway of his home office, coffee in one hand, phone in the other. Celeste leaned against the wall across from him, a towel wrapped around her head, fresh from the shower. Micah padded barefoot into the kitchen, searching for cereal.

"Has it posted yet?" Celeste asked, her voice low with anticipation.

Jisoo checked the time. "It's 9:00 in Seoul."

His phone buzzed.

[1 New Notification: Feature article by Lee Sang-ho is now live on Korea Insight.]

He opened the link and exhaled.

"Between Two Worlds: The Life of Actor Min Jisoo"

By Lee Sang-ho – Seoul Chronicle, International Arts & Culture Feature

"Some truths are best whispered into the dark until we are strong enough to sing them aloud."– Eun Sol

For over a decade, the world has known Min Jisoo as a beloved actor, charming, talented, often cloaked in mystery. But few knew that, behind the screen, behind the curated interviews and award show smiles, he was also the elusive poet Eun Sol. Fewer still understood the quiet life he had chosen to build in America, with a woman, a son, and a community far from Seoul's spotlight.

Living quietly in Solmere, Min Jisoo steps away from the constant glare of cameras and expectations to explore the parts of himself that have long remained hidden. Between morning walks along the coast, visits to the local bookstore, and Sunday dinners with Celeste and Micah, he has discovered a rhythm of life that balances creativity, love, and reflection—one that would prepare him to finally share his story with the world.

In this exclusive feature, Jisoo opens up for the first time about his decision to reveal his identity as Eun Sol, the controversy surrounding his relationship with American community activist and hospice minister Celeste Monroe, and the new life he's built in the town of Solmere.

"Why did I keep it private?" Jisoo reflects. "Because I wrote in shadows, afraid my voice would not be enough. But if my words brought even one person comfort, then they were never just mine to keep."

The revelation shook fans across Korea, inspiring many and leaving others skeptical. But what emerges clearly in my time with Min Jisoo is a man rooted in conviction, shaped by hardship, and unwilling to apologize for the form his joy takes.

His time in the Korean military, where we once served together, taught him endurance and self-discipline, qualities he would need later when public opinion turned sharply after his relationship with Celeste became known.

"When I am acting, I become someone else. When I write, I become myself."

In Solmere, Jisoo walks freely down the streets, stopping at a bookstore in Little Hanseong or sharing meals at a local Korean restaurant. Here, he is not the celebrity, but a neighbor, a husband, a father.

And the community has welcomed him wholeheartedly.

"Koreans should support Koreans," said Park Dae-jung, owner of Seojin's Kitchen.

"Jisoo has not abandoned his roots. He has carried them with him."

Jisoo's wife, Celeste Monroe, is a hospice chaplain and poet in her own right. Their love story, unconventional in age and culture, is quiet but deeply authentic. He speaks of her with reverence, and of her son, Micah, as his own.

"They didn't just give me love. They gave me a new life."

His parents, who recently visited the United States, were hesitant at first, but after spending time in Solmere, they offered full support. "What affects him affects us," his father told me. "But now we understand this is his truth."

Min Jisoo plans to return to Korea this summer to resume filming. He will bring his family with him.

"Home is no longer just Seoul or a city by the ocean. It's the space we create, the people we carry."

Conclusion:

Min Jisoo's story is not one of abandonment; it is one of transformation. In a world quick to judge and slower to understand, he offers a different way: a man unafraid to love deeply, write honestly, and live freely.

And in that way, perhaps, he is not living between two worlds but building one of his own.

When Jisoo finished reading, he didn't speak.

Celeste crossed the room and wrapped her arms around him from behind. "It's beautiful," she whispered.

Micah appeared beside them, spoon still in his mouth, having read it over their shoulders. "Dang," he said. "Sang-ho can write."

Jisoo laughed. "Yes, he can."

Celeste looked up at him. "Are you ready for what comes next?"

Jisoo set his coffee down and turned to her. "I am. Because I'm not walking into it alone."

The article hit newsstands and online platforms overnight, and by morning, it had ignited a digital firestorm.

Jisoo's name was trending in both Korea and the U.S., not for a drama premiere or an award, but for living his truth. The feature written by Sang-ho was deeply personal, layered with poetic reflections, candid conversations, and honest glimpses into Jisoo's life in Solmere with Celeste and Micah.

The reactions came fast. And they were intense.

Some praised him for his courage:

"Jisoo didn't abandon Korea; he's living abroad, but his heart is still Korean. You can't erase that."

"He served. He sacrificed. He writes like a true son of the peninsula. Stop acting like he turned his back on us."

Others were… less kind:

"Why not a Korean wife? Really?"

"I feel sorry for his poor parents. Can you imagine the shame?"

"She is still a Black American divorced woman with a child. That's a no. Period."

"What is this, Joseon? Why are we still policing who people love?"

"You can't say he abandoned Korea when he still has his apartment here. He's not running away; he's expanding his life."

The online world became a mirror reflecting admiration, confusion, curiosity, and prejudice in equal measure.

Jisoo didn't respond. He logged off entirely. Celeste, seeing the comments, felt a slow ache in her chest, not for herself, but for him. And for Micah.

But inside their home, it was quiet. Safe.

A sanctuary.

"I think we were naïve to think it would all be positive," Jisoo admitted to Celeste that evening, sitting on the porch with the ocean at their feet. "But I don't regret it."

She reached for his hand. "You told the truth. And the people who matter? They see you."

Jisoo nodded. "And soon… we go home, to Korea, and we face everything together."

The morning after the article's whirlwind release, Jisoo's phone buzzed with a familiar number. His heart skipped. He answered quickly.

"Mother?"

"Jisoo-ya," his mother's voice came through warm and steady. "We read the article."

Jisoo held his breath.

"It was beautiful," she said. "Honest. Thoughtful. We can see Lee Sang-ho told it well."

His father's voice followed. "It sparked more support than I expected. Maybe this… was the right time. You've given people something real to reflect on."

Jisoo swallowed hard, the emotion catching him off guard. "Thank you. That means a lot."

"And how are Celeste and Micah?" Mrs. Park asked gently. "Looking forward to coming to Korea?"

Jisoo glanced toward the living room, where Celeste was helping Micah look through his old passport photos. Laughter echoed faintly down the hall.

"They're excited. Nervous. But ready."

His mother paused. "We're looking forward to welcoming them. Truly."

Meanwhile, across town in Little Hanseong, Hana Park posted a comment beneath the article's official digital release:

"A well written piece. Deeply moving. I've always admired Eun Sol's poetry, but now I admire the man behind it even more. Solmere is lucky to have him, and so is Korea."

Mrs. Moon left her own quiet endorsement on the community board:

"It's rare to see a public figure speak with such softness and strength. May this be the beginning of more open hearts."

Back in Seoul, Sang-ho's editor at *The Seoul Chronicle* wrote a private message to him:

"You delivered something powerful. Not just a profile, this was a portrait of transformation. Of love, exile, and reclamation. We've already received a dozen reader letters. This one will stay with people, Sang-ho."

Sang-ho read the message, then looked out over the Han River from his window. A quiet smile tugged at the corner of his lips.

He'd told the truth.

And the truth had found its home.

Chapter 32

Family Flight to Korea

Back in Solmere, Celeste wrapped an arm around Jisoo's waist as they stood on the deck, looking out at the sea.

"Two more weeks," she said softly. "Then we're in Seoul."

"Are you ready?" he asked.

She leaned into him. "With you and Micah by my side? I think I'm more than ready."

Inside, Micah held his freshly printed passport in one hand and texted Kai in the other.

"Guess who's officially travel-ready?"

The reply came almost instantly.

"LET'S GOOOOO. Bring me back something Korean and cool."

Micah grinned.

For the first time in a long while, everything felt like it was coming together.

And, they'd walk into Korea not just as visitors but as a family.

On Friday afternoon, as Micah sat on the edge of his bed scrolling through his phone, a familiar ping lit up his screen. It was Marcus.

Marcus (Text):
Hey, son. Just checking in. How about we meet up this Sunday? I was thinking Sal's Pizza—1:00 if you're free.

Micah stared at the message for a moment, thumb hovering over the screen. After a few seconds, he typed back.

Micah (Text):
Okay. I'll be there.

Later that evening, Micah walked into the kitchen where Jisoo and Celeste were prepping dinner. Jisoo glanced up from the cutting board and gave him a nod.

"Hey, what's up?"

Micah rubbed the back of his neck. "I'm meeting Marcus at Sal's on Sunday at one. Can you give me a ride?"

Jisoo nodded, keeping his tone casual. "Of course. Just let me know when you're ready to go."

Micah gave him a quick thanks and disappeared back into his room. He sat back down on his bed, pulling up the conversation thread with Marcus.

Micah (Text):
Just so you know, I'll be in Korea for the summer. We leave in June, back in August.

The reply came within minutes, but it wasn't a text. It was a call.

When Marcus arrived at Sal's Pizza that Sunday, he spotted Micah already at a booth near the window, sipping a soda. Marcus approached with a hopeful smile, but when Micah casually mentioned the upcoming trip to Korea, Marcus's expression faltered for a split second—tightening around the eyes, jaw clenched just slightly.

Marcus paused for a moment, running a hand through his hair as he tried to mask the mix of surprise and concern bubbling beneath his calm exterior. He studied Micah across the table, noticing the casual way he sipped his soda, the ease that belied the weight of the news. The mention of Korea lingered in the air between them, unspoken questions hanging just below the surface—how long he'd be gone, what it would mean for their time together, and whether the distance might widen the gap they were still learning to close.

"Korea, huh?" he said, trying to keep his tone light. "That's… a long time."

Micah shrugged. "Jisoo has a project there, and we're spending the summer with his family.

Marcus nodded slowly, clearly trying to process the information. "Okay, okay… well, maybe when you get back, we can figure something out. Go catch a game or something."

Micah gave him a small smile. Let's talk about it when I get back.

Marcus chuckled, though there was a trace of hurt behind the laugh. "Fair enough."

Micah leaned back, more relaxed now. "We can keep texting while I'm away. That's cool with me."

"Yeah," Marcus said, his voice softer now. "I'd like that."

And for the rest of the lunch, they stuck to safer subjects: food, school, and small talk. It wasn't perfect. But it was something.

The SUV was packed with suitcases neatly stacked in the trunk, carry-ons at their feet, and the quiet hum of anticipation hanging in the air. Celeste sat in the passenger seat, double-checking their passports and itinerary, while Jisoo drove with one hand on the wheel and the other resting on her knee. Micah sat in the back, earbuds in, staring out the window, the early morning light casting shadows across his face.

"Everyone has their documents?" Celeste asked, not for the first time.

Jisoo gave her a look. "Yes, darling. You've asked us three times."

She smiled sheepishly. "Just making sure."

Micah pulled out one earbud. "I've got mine. And my charger. And my snacks. We're good, Mom."

The drive to the airport wasn't long, but it felt heavy with unspoken thoughts. There was excitement, of course, but also nervousness. A new chapter awaited them on the other side of the world.

Jisoo glanced at Micah in the rearview mirror. "You doing okay back there?"

Micah gave a small nod. "Yeah. Just thinking."

Jisoo didn't press. He knew how much was going on in Micah's head: Marcus, the article, leaving the country, and being in Korea for three months. It was a lot.

Inside the bustling terminal, they made their way through check-in and security, each step drawing them closer to departure. The air was vibrant, with travelers rushing past, announcements echoing, and the distant scent of coffee and jet fuel mingling.

Once they reached their gate, there was a lull, a moment to just… breathe.

Jisoo wrapped his arms around Celeste from behind as they watched Micah peer through the large window at the planes on the tarmac.

"You okay?" he asked softly.

She nodded. "I'm ready."

Jisoo turned his attention to Micah and walked over. "First time flying international, huh?"

Micah smirked. "Yeah. Pretty cool."

"You'll love Seoul. I promise."

They boarded shortly after, each of them settling into their seats. Jisoo and Celeste sat side by side, while Micah had the window seat behind them. As the plane taxied down the runway, Celeste reached for Jisoo's hand and squeezed it.

"Here we go," she whispered.

He turned to her with a soft smile. "Together."

As the plane lifted off, Micah stared out at the shrinking city below. He felt the weight of everything he was leaving behind—and the possibilities of what lay ahead. He pulled out his phone and sent one last text before switching to airplane mode:

Micah (Text to Marcus):
On our way to Korea. Talk to you soon.

He didn't expect a reply, and none came.

He leaned back in his seat and closed his eyes, letting the gentle hum of the engines and the steady rhythm of the air around him lull him into sleep.

He was ready to begin again.

Ten hours into the flight, the cabin was dimmed for rest. The occasional beep of a flight attendant's call button and the gentle rustling of blankets were the only sounds in the cool, quiet cabin.

Micah scrolled through the entertainment menu for the fifth time, his eyes dry and unfocused. He had already watched a movie, eaten both meals, and played two rounds of trivia against Jisoo, who beat him once and then let him win the second.

In the row in front of him, Jisoo was fast asleep, his head tilted slightly toward Celeste, who was quietly mouthing Korean phrases from a language learning app, earbuds in and a small notebook in her lap.

Micah leaned forward and tapped her shoulder.

She pulled out one earbud. "What's up, baby?"

He shrugged. "Can't sleep. And I already ate everything."

She smiled. "Want some gum? Or tea?"

"Gum," he said, and she passed a piece back to him.

After a moment, he added, "You nervous?"

Celeste thought for a second. "Maybe. But it's more like… anticipation. I'm excited to see your Appa in his element. And I'm excited for you. It's your first time there, your first time really connecting with that side of our life."

Micah nodded, chewing slowly. "It's weird. I feel… I don't know, caught between stuff. Like home and not-home."

"That's okay," Celeste said softly. "It just means you're growing."

Micah sat back again, processing. Then he smiled slightly. "Can I get some of that tea now?"

Celeste chuckled and signaled the flight attendant.

By the time they landed in Seoul, the airport was alive with motion, clean, efficient, quietly bustling despite the late hour. Their layover before the final connecting flight to Jeju Island gave them just enough time to stretch their legs, grab a meal, and refresh.

Jisoo led the way through the sleek, glass-and-steel terminal with the ease of someone who'd passed through dozens of times before. Celeste, wide-eyed and slightly jet-lagged, kept pace while Micah took photos of everything, the architecture, the robot information assistant, even the ceiling.

"Yo, this place is futuristic," Micah muttered. "They have a freakin' spa and gardens in here."

"They also have jjajangmyeon," Jisoo added, "and I know just the place."

They found a small, clean food court tucked beside one of the terminal gardens, where Jisoo ordered steaming bowls of black bean noodles, kimchi, and fried dumplings for all of them.

Micah hesitated at first, then slurped a bite and froze. "Okay… this slaps."

Jisoo grinned proudly. "Welcome to the motherland."

They ate quietly, the warm food grounding them in a moment that felt like both an end and a beginning.

Later, while Celeste freshened up in the lounge bathroom, Jisoo and Micah sat beside a giant window, watching planes roll by on the tarmac. The glow of the city lights pulsed beyond the runway, and the quiet buzz of Korean and English filled the space around them.

Micah glanced at his phone. A text from Kai blinked on screen:

"Safe flight, bro. Can't wait to hear all about it."

Micah smiled and texted back:

"Already ate better noodles than we ever had. Wish you were here."

Jisoo nudged him. "Ready for the last leg?"

Micah nodded. "Yeah. Ready as I'll ever be."

As they waited at the gate for their connecting flight to Jeju, Jisoo tried to keep a low profile, hood up, glasses on, posture casual. But there were always eyes, especially in Korea.

He kept his head down, scrolling through his phone as Celeste leaned into his shoulder, half-dozing, and Micah munched on a pack of shrimp chips nearby.

That's when it happened.

A girl in her early twenties paused mid-step, phone in hand, eyes wide as recognition struck. She didn't scream. She didn't run. She took a picture, quietly, carefully, and then walked away as if nothing had happened.

Jisoo didn't notice.

But the internet did.

By the time they boarded, the photo had already circulated through several fan accounts:

MIN JISOO SPOTTED AT INCHEON HEADING TO JEJU. He's not alone. 👀 👀 👀" #Min Jisoo #Jeju Arrival #Spotted

Comments exploded:
- "Wait… is that Celeste with him?"
- "They're really together. Wow."
- "I thought they were in America. Why Jeju? A honeymoon?"
- "Omg Micah is with them. His son???"
- "Leave them alone! Let them breathe."
- "This is going to be a media circus."

When they landed in Jeju, the airport was already buzzing with the ripple effects.

As Jisoo, Celeste, and Micah made their way toward baggage claim, they were met with a subtle but unmistakable shift in the air, people glancing up from their phones, whispering, discreetly taking photos. It wasn't a mob… but it wasn't peace either.

A young man wearing a face mask bowed respectfully to Jisoo. Two older women giggled as Celeste passed by, then turned to whisper furiously to each other. Someone behind them muttered, "That's the poet. The actor. That's his foreign wife."

Jisoo sighed quietly, his arm wrapping protectively around Celeste's back. "I think we've been found."

Celeste gave him a look, equal parts amused and resigned. "You think?"

Micah rolled his eyes. "This is gonna be weird, huh?"

Jisoo gave a short nod. "Probably. But we stick together."

At the exit, Jisoo's cousin, Min Jiho, stood waiting, grinning broadly—blissfully unaware of the social media wildfire erupting in real time.

"Jisoo!" Jiho called, waving them over. "Welcome home!"

Jisoo returned the smile and guided his family forward. "Jiho," he said warmly, then turned slightly, his hand settling at the small of Celeste's back. "This is my wife, Celeste. And this is Micah."

Min Jiho's expression softened at once. He gave Celeste a respectful nod before dipping slightly toward Micah. "Welcome to Jeju," he said. "You've traveled a long way. Our family is honored."

"Thank you," Celeste replied, returning the nod, her tone calm and gracious. Micah followed her lead, straightening instinctively.

Jisoo returned the smile and led his family forward, murmuring, "Let's make the best of it."

Outside, the island breeze was fresh and clean. But behind them, the quiet hum of gossip and flashing cameras made one thing clear:

This summer in Korea would not be quiet.

Chapter 33

Jeju Island

The humid Jeju air greeted them as they stepped out of the small regional airport. The scent of salt and citrus clung to the breeze, and above them, a brilliant blue sky stretched endlessly across the island. A sleek black van pulled up to the curb just as Jisoo adjusted his cap and sunglasses. The driver greeted them in polite Jeju dialect before helping load their luggage.

As the van pulled away from the airport, Jisoo settled into the back seat beside Celeste while Micah leaned against the window, eyes tracing the coastline.

"This is Jeju Island," Jisoo said softly, placing a hand on Micah's shoulder. "Not just a tourist spot. It's where Jiho lives. We used to visit his family every summer when I was your age."

Micah glanced back at him. "So… this is like a family reunion?"

Jisoo nodded. "Sort of. But it's also about something more."

Celeste looked over, curious. Jisoo met Micah's eyes in the rearview mirror.

"I wanted you to see this part of Korea," Jisoo said. "The slower side. The peaceful side. Min Jiho and I… we were like brothers growing up. And now that we're here as a family, I wanted you to meet his family. I wanted them to meet you."

Micah leaned his head back against the seat. "Are they nice?"

"They're the kindest people you'll ever meet," Jisoo said with a soft smile. "They've been watching everything from afar. The article, the interviews. They're proud."

The van wound through narrow roads bordered by stone fences and endless rows of tangerine trees. Jeju's unique charm revealed itself in quiet villages, colorful rooftops, and the mountains rising in the distance.

"Jeju has always been a place to breathe," Jisoo said, glancing out the window. "And after everything this past year… I thought we could all use a deep breath."

Celeste reached over and squeezed his hand.

Micah nodded slowly, taking in the scenery. "Okay," he said quietly. "Let's breathe then."

The house was nestled among the gentle slopes of Jeju's countryside, framed by wind-kissed stone walls and the soft rustle of tangerine trees swaying in the breeze. Inside, the air smelled faintly of sea salt and simmering doenjang jjigae. Jiho's home was modest but warm, filled with family photos, children's laughter, and the kind of peace that came from living close to the earth.

The warmth of the afternoon sun spilled through the wide windows, bathing the room in a soft glow that seemed to hold time still for a moment. The gentle hum of the countryside—rustling leaves, distant birdsong, and the faint lapping of water somewhere beyond the property—blended with the quiet chatter of the family inside. Micah let out a small sigh, feeling the tension of travel and anticipation melt just slightly, as the scent of fresh tea and sweet pastries promised a rare kind of comfort he hadn't realized he'd been craving. Jisoo, Celeste, and Micah sat on the floor of the sunlit sitting room, sipping barley tea as Jiho's wife, Kim Soo-ah, brought out a tray of homemade Yakgwa. The children, two boys with their father's quick eyes and their mother's easy smile, played quietly nearby with wooden blocks and a small puppy that had taken a liking to Micah.

"It's been too long," Jiho said, raising his cup in a small toast. "Seeing you with your family like this... it feels like a dream."

Jisoo smiled. "It feels good to be here. Safe. Real."

Celeste leaned against Jisoo, her fingers laced with his. "It's so beautiful," she said softly. "I see why you love it here."

Jiho nodded. "This place... it heals you if you let it."

There was a long, comfortable, quiet pause. Outside, a wind chime rang lazily in the breeze. Soo-ah sat down beside them, offering more tea.

"I saw the article," she said gently, her eyes meeting Jisoo's. "We're proud of you, Jisoo. Not just for what you've accomplished, but for the life you're building."

Jisoo bowed his head slightly. "Thank you. That means everything."

Micah, curled up with the puppy in his lap, looked up. "Do you guys live here all year?"

Jiho chuckled. "All year. The island life suits us. Slower, but good."

Micah smiled, then nodded. "I like it."

The quiet moment stretched, unspoken understanding, shared tea, and the feeling of family that needed no bloodline to make it real.

The late afternoon sun bathed the orchard in a golden hue, casting long shadows between the rows of tangerine trees. The soft rustle of leaves and the faint chirping of birds made the air feel alive, but peaceful. Soo-ah walked beside Celeste, her wide, brimmed sunhat tilted just slightly as she reached up and plucked a ripe fruit from a low-hanging branch.

Celeste followed Soo-ah's steps, the sunlight catching on the soft green of the leaves and the golden hue of the ripe fruit. She reached up to touch a tangerine herself, marveling at how peaceful it all felt—the quiet hum of life in the orchard, the gentle sway of the branches, and the distant laughter of children playing nearby. For a moment, it was easy to forget the world outside this little sanctuary, the headlines, the fans, the pressures waiting beyond the grove.

"You're lucky," Soo-ah said, her voice warm and unhurried. "This is the best time of year. Everything is sweet right now, ripe and full."

Celeste smiled, taking in the scent of citrus that seemed to hang in the breeze. "It's beautiful here. Quiet in a way I didn't know I needed."

Soo-ah handed her the tangerine and motioned for her to peel it. "Jisoo used to run through these rows when he was little. Always chasing butterflies and never listening when we told him not to ruin his shoes." She chuckled fondly. "But even back then, he was different. Thoughtful. Dreamy."

Celeste peeled the fruit slowly, the zest spritzing her fingers. "He still is."

Soo-ah paused, her expression turning more serious. "He loves you. That much is obvious. I've never seen him look at anyone the way he looks at you."

Celeste looked down, her cheeks warming. "He's… everything I never expected. And everything I needed."

They stopped beneath an ancient tree; its limbs gnarled with age but heavy with fruit. Soo-ah placed a gentle hand on Celeste's arm.

"I wanted to tell you something," she said. "I know it hasn't been easy. The world sees you, judges you, for your age, for being different, for simply loving him. But here, in this place, you are family. And I wish you a long and happy marriage. From the deepest part of my heart."

Celeste's eyes shimmered. "Thank you. That means more than I can say."

Soo-ah smiled, picking two more tangerines and placing them in Celeste's hands. "These are from our oldest tree. A small gift. May your marriage be like this tree, weathered, but generous. Rooted, but still reaching for the sun."

They walked on, the orchard stretching quietly around them, the sunlight painting the trees in gold.

Back at the house, the late afternoon breeze fluttered the sheer curtains as laughter echoed from the backyard. Micah had kicked off his shoes and was now chasing two of Jiho's kids across the grass, their squeals ringing out as they darted between the trees and around the garden beds. One of the twins, a tiny girl named Yuna, had claimed Micah as her favorite and clung to his back like a little koala as he galloped playfully across the yard.

"Cousin, faster!" she cried.

"Cousin Micah, catch me!" the older brother, Hyun-woo, shouted, zigzagging wildly.

Micah laughed, breathless but happy, his heart lighter than it had felt in weeks.

From the shaded porch, Jisoo and Jiho sat with two chilled drinks between them. The sunlight filtered through the woven awning above, casting patterned shadows over the table.

"You've got a good one," Jiho said, nodding toward the yard. "Micah's got such a kind way about him. My kids adore him already."

Jisoo watched with a soft smile. "He's a good kid. Smart, thoughtful. He's been through more than most boys his age, but he carries it with so much grace."

"And you," Jiho said, giving him a sideways glance. "You look… settled. Happy."

Jisoo chuckled, rubbing the back of his neck. "I am. It's a strange thing, how peace can come after chaos. Celeste, Micah… they gave me something real."

Jiho leaned back in his chair, eyes thoughtful. "I remember when we were in university, and you used to talk about disappearing—writing under a fake name, living quietly by the sea, far from the press, far from your parents' expectations."

Jisoo laughed. "And now I live in a coastal town, married to a poet in disguise, raising a brilliant teenager who calls me Appa." He paused, then added, "Funny how some dreams look different when they come true."

Jiho lifted his glass. "To dreams realized—no matter how they take shape."

Jisoo clinked his glass against his cousin's. "To family," he said softly. "And finding your way home."

They drank, the moment stretching into comfortable silence. The children's laughter floated through the air, blending with the rustle of leaves and the faint song of cicadas.

It was the kind of day that asked nothing—only offered peace.

As the sun dipped lower, painting the sky in soft oranges and pinks, the family lingered in the orchard a little longer, savoring the warmth of the late afternoon. Micah chased the puppy one last time, the children's laughter ringing through the trees, while Jisoo and Jiho exchanged quiet smiles, letting the calm settle around them.

The scents of tangerines and fresh earth mingled in the air, a subtle reminder of the simple joys of being together. Slowly, the group began making their way back inside, carrying the lingering serenity of the orchard with them into the welcoming warmth of the house.

That evening, the house was filled with the gentle clatter of dishes, soft conversation, and the savory aroma of grilled mackerel and doenjang jjigae. Jiho's wife, Soo-ah, had laid out a simple but delicious spread across the low dining table:

seasoned vegetables, perfectly steamed rice, fresh fruit, and her homemade kimchi, which she proudly served with a wink.

They all sat cross-legged on the floor, the children chattering excitedly as they recounted their afternoon playing with Micah. Celeste sat beside Soo-ah, her posture respectful and her Korean careful but steady as she offered thanks.

"The food is really delicious," Celeste said with a smile. "Thank you so much for preparing this."

Soo-ah replied. "Your Korean is really good. Truly. You speak with such heart."

Jiho nodded in agreement. "And Micah too—when he spoke to Hyun-woo earlier, I was surprised. His accent is almost perfect."

Micah ducked his head a little, chewing a bite of galbi, clearly pleased but trying not to show it. "Jisoo's been helping," he said casually. "We've been practicing at home."

Jisoo grinned proudly. "They both work hard. I think they're going to surprise a few people when we get to Seoul."

Jiho raised a brow. "Speaking of Seoul… you saw what happened after the fan spotted you at the airport."

Jisoo sighed, his shoulders tensing slightly. "Yeah. I hoped we could stay under the radar a bit longer, but it's already circulating online."

Celeste reached for his hand under the table and squeezed it gently.

"I'm going to contact my management company tomorrow," Jisoo said, glancing between them. "We may need to arrange security and possibly a driver to take us to Seoul. It's better if we avoid more unexpected encounters."

Jiho gave a knowing nod. "Smart. Things can escalate quickly once word spreads."

Soo-ah leaned over to refill everyone's cups with barley tea. "You're always welcome to stay as long as you need," she said warmly. "This house is quiet and safe."

"Thank you," Celeste said sincerely. "It means so much, especially with everything going on."

Jisoo looked around the table, his heart full at the sight of Celeste chatting comfortably with Soo-ah, Micah laughing with the children, and Jiho watching over it all like a proud older brother.

"I think this is exactly what we needed," he said softly.

The rest of the evening passed gently, soft conversation, laughter, and warm company the kind of dinner where everything felt whole.

Later that night, the house was wrapped in stillness. The children had long gone to bed, and Jiho and Soo-ah had retired to their room. Celeste and Jisoo stepped onto the back porch, wrapped in the soft hush of the Jeju night. The stars above shimmered clearly, and the distant waves whispered against the coast beyond the orchard.

Celeste leaned against the wooden railing, sipping from a small mug of ginger tea. Jisoo stood beside her, close enough for their shoulders to touch.

"It's beautiful here," she murmured.

"It always feels like time slows down in Jeju," Jisoo replied, his voice low and thoughtful. "Like the noise of the world fades."

Celeste smiled gently. "You needed this. We all did."

Jisoo nodded, then turned slightly to face her. "I saw your face at dinner—when Soo-ah praised your Korean."

Celeste chuckled. "I think I blushed down to my toes."

"Well," Jisoo teased, brushing a strand of hair behind her ear, "you should be proud. You've worked so hard to learn. For me… for us."

Celeste set her cup down and reached for his hand. "I'd do it again a hundred times. I'm not trying to be Korean. I want your world to feel like mine, too."

Jisoo's thumb brushed across her knuckles. "It already does."

There was a pause before he continued. "When we get to Seoul… it might be overwhelming. With the media, the fans. But no matter what happens, I want you to remember this—right here. This peace. This love."

Celeste leaned her head against his shoulder, the moment held like a sacred hush between them.

"I'll remember," she whispered.

The next morning, Jisoo woke early. The sun had just begun to rise, casting gold across the quiet Jeju landscape. After showering and dressing, he stepped into the sitting room, took his phone, and called his management company.

When the call connected, he greeted his assistant. "Hello, Seung. It's Jisoo."

"Jisoo! I saw the news last night. You're in Jeju?"

"Yeah. A fan spotted us at the airport. I need help keeping the next steps quiet. We'll be heading to Seoul tomorrow—can you arrange a car and light security?"

"Already on it," Seung replied. "We'll have a driver meet you at the ferry port. No flashy vehicles. Just subtle coverage."

"Thanks, I appreciate it."

Jisoo ended the call and sat for a moment, thinking, then dialed his parents.

His mother answered first. "Jisoo-ya! Are you still in Jeju?"

"Yes, Mother. We're staying with Jiho and Soo-ah. It's been peaceful."

"I'm glad," she said warmly. "When will we see you?"

"We're heading to Seoul tomorrow. I'll take Celeste and Micah to my apartment first, settle in, then come to the family home later that evening or the next morning. I wanted to let you know ahead of time."

"That sounds wise," his father's voice came through now. "Better to ease into it."

"We're looking forward to seeing you," his mother added. "And tell Celeste and Micah we said hello."

"I will," Jisoo smiled. "See you soon."

As he hung up, Celeste stepped into the room.

"Good morning," she said sleepily. "Who were you talking to?"

"Management and my parents," Jisoo replied. "Everything's set for tomorrow. One more quiet day before Seoul."

Celeste smiled. "Then let's make the most of it."

Chapter 34

Tranquility

The sky was still blushing with the first soft strokes of dawn when Jisoo gently nudged Celeste awake. The air was calm and quiet, the kind of stillness that only came just before a day began in earnest.

"Time to go, honey," he whispered, brushing a kiss across her forehead.

Within the hour, the family was ready—luggage packed, jackets zipped, and sleepy smiles exchanged with Jiho's family as they stood outside the front door. Soo-ah handed Celeste a small bag of fresh fruit from the orchard, and the children hugged Micah goodbye, still barefoot from their early play in the garden.

Jisoo double-checked the straps on the luggage as he glanced at Celeste and Micah. "Everyone got everything?" he asked, though he knew the answer already. Celeste nodded, adjusting the bag of fruit, and Micah gave a sleepy thumbs-up. The morning air was crisp, carrying the faint scent of the orchard behind them, and for a moment, Jisoo allowed himself to savor the calm—the quiet before the controlled chaos of the city awaited.

"Come back soon," Jiho said, clapping Jisoo on the shoulder. "You'll always have a place here."

Jisoo smiled, his voice low. "Thank you.. You've given us a peaceful start."

A sleek black van pulled into the long gravel drive—unmarked and tinted. It was sent by Jisoo's management company and driven by someone discreet, someone trusted. No logos. No attention.

The driver stepped out, bowed respectfully, and quickly loaded their luggage. Jisoo guided Celeste and Micah inside, pulling the door closed behind them. As the van pulled away, Jiho and his family waved from the gate, the morning sun cresting over the orchard behind them.

Inside the van, Micah leaned against the window, watching Jeju's coastline slip by as they made their way to the airport.

"Are you nervous?" Celeste asked Jisoo, her voice hushed.

He glanced over at her. "Not nervous. Just… cautious. Seoul is louder. Busier. And more eyes are watching." He gave her hand a gentle squeeze. "But we'll be okay."

At Jeju International Airport, they were ushered through a side entrance used by VIPs and public figures—a courtesy extended by the airline and arranged by Jisoo's team. No one stopped them. No fans. No flashing cameras. Just security, check-in, and a quiet waiting lounge.

Onboard the short flight to Gimpo, Jisoo sat between Celeste and Micah. Celeste closed her eyes and leaned her head on his shoulder while Micah tucked his hoodie over his head and started a movie on the in-flight screen.

Jisoo glanced out the window as the plane ascended. The island grew smaller, the ocean swallowing the land in blue. He inhaled deeply, as if preparing himself for what awaited them in Seoul.

Touching down at Gimpo Airport, they were met at a secured private terminal exit by the same driver who had previously handled Jisoo's press-sensitive moves. He gave another respectful bow and opened the doors of a black sedan, roomy and tinted for discretion.

The car moved smoothly through the city traffic, taking a quiet route toward Jisoo's apartment in Gangnam. Celeste looked out the window, taking in the rising skyline of Seoul— so different from Solmere and Jeju, yet beautiful in its own way.

Micah stirred from a nap as they neared the complex.

Jisoo looked back at him. "We'll rest a little at the apartment. Then tonight, we'll go see my parents, okay?"

Micah nodded, rubbing his eyes. "Sounds good."

As the driver pulled into the private parking beneath Jisoo's building, the family exhaled as one.

So far, so good.

No crowds.

No flashing lights.

Just a soft, quiet return to the city that once defined Jisoo's life—now ready to meet the family who had reshaped it.

Micah strolled back into the living room, barefoot, a banana in hand, his face lit up with a mix of curiosity and amusement.

"Okay, so this place is insane," he said, flopping onto the couch. "You press a button, and the blinds close. Another button? Mood lighting. I found the bidet remote in the bathroom and I'm just saying it's an experience."

Jisoo chuckled from the kitchen. "Korea takes its technology seriously."

"No kidding," Micah said, biting into the banana. "The mirror in the hallway talks, by the way. I think it wished me good morning. I wasn't ready for that level of friendliness from furniture."

Celeste laughed as she returned with a short list of essentials. "Did you figure out how to turn on the shower? Or do we need to send a tech support team in there?"

Micah grinned. "I figured it out—eventually. It's like a spaceship. I almost called NASA for help."

Jisoo leaned against the counter, arms crossed, watching his son with quiet pride. "And the trip so far? Still glad you came?"

Micah's expression turned more thoughtful. He glanced out at the hazy Seoul skyline. "Yeah," he said after a beat. "It's different here. Busier, louder—but also… kind of exciting. I don't feel out of place, even when I am the only one who looks like me. People stare, but it doesn't mean anything. Just curious."

Celeste walked over and gently brushed her fingers over his curls. "You're handling it well."

Micah smiled. "It helps having you both here. And Appa— thanks for letting me pick my room. I picked the one with the smart mirror, obviously."

Jisoo laughed. "Of course you did."

Micah stood and stretched. "I'm gonna go take a shower before I break something else trying to figure out the washer."

Jisoo shook his head, amused. "He's adjusting faster than I did."

"Teenagers adapt," Celeste replied, smiling as she took Jisoo's hand. "And he feels safe. That's what matters most."

Micah sends a text message to Kai, "Yo, you're not gonna believe this trip

First off, the second we landed in Jeju, a fan recognized Jisoo and posted it online. By the time we left the airport, it was like the entire island knew he was here. We had to switch up our plans and dodge cameras like we were in a spy movie.

His cousin's place is dope though—peaceful, has an orchard. I've been playing with the little kids, and Jisoo's catching up with his fam. Mom and Soo-ah (his cousin's wife) went for a walk through the trees like it was a scene from a K-drama lol.

Now we're in Seoul. His apartment is insane—super high-tech, automatic everything. I swear the toilet speaks Korean better than I do. I picked a room, and now we're just settling in. It's wild, but kinda cool too.

Please remind me to tell you about all this in person when we get back. Miss you, bro."

Later that evening, the city lights of Seoul shimmered through the tall apartment windows. Celeste, now in comfortable clothes, sat curled on the sofa with a cup of barley tea. Jisoo was checking the kitchen pantry, making mental notes of what was missing. Micah had disappeared into his new room, already syncing his playlist to the Bluetooth speakers and marveling at the automatic blinds and voice-controlled lighting.

Micah wandered back into the living room and flopped down beside Celeste, still buzzing from the flight. "This place is… wow. Everything's so sleek, and quiet in a weird way for being in the middle of Seoul." He glanced around, eyes wide at the gleaming surfaces and hidden gadgets. "I think I need a manual just to figure out how to turn on the lights." Celeste laughed softly, reaching for his hand while Jisoo shook his head with a fond smile, watching Micah explore his new surroundings with a mix of awe and mischief.

A moment later, Jisoo leaned against the doorway , rubbing the back of his neck. "Okay, so… we've got instant ramyeon, some fruit, and half a carton of eggs. Not bad, but we definitely need to shop."

Celeste smiled, stretching her legs out. "I'll make a list tomorrow. You said you moved most of your stuff to Solmere, right?"

"Yeah," he said with a sheepish grin. "Didn't think I'd be back so soon, or with my whole family."

Just then, Micah's phone buzzed. He glanced down and laughed., "Kai says this whole thing sounds like a K-pop spy drama," he laughed. "He wants pictures."

Celeste chuckled. "Tell him no photos until we're out of the 'witness protection program.'"

Jisoo looked at Micah with a smirk. "You good with your room?"

Micah nodded. "Yeah. The toilet's terrifying but awesome."

"That's Korea," Jisoo grinned.

There was a soft buzz on Jisoo's phone. He glanced at it. "It's my management team. They've confirmed a driver for tomorrow. He'll pick us up around ten. Quiet vehicle, tinted windows, VIP route—should keep us under the radar getting to my parents' house."

Celeste exhaled. "Good. I just want things to go smoothly."

"They will," Jisoo said, gently taking her hand. "We're together. That's the only part that really matters."

From his spot by the window, Micah glanced out at the city. "Seoul's a lot. Loud, fast, different... but kinda cool." He paused. "You think we'll ever really fit in here?"

Jisoo turned to him. "We don't have to fit in. We have to be true to who we are. That's enough."

Micah nodded slowly, taking that in.

Later that night, with the lights dimmed and the city humming below them, the three of them stood on the balcony. The air was warm, carrying the faint scent of street food and the warmth of summer. Celeste leaned into Jisoo's side, and Micah leaned on the railing beside them.

"Tomorrow's a big day," Celeste said quietly.

"Yeah," Jisoo agreed. "It's the beginning of something new."

Micah didn't say anything—he just looked out at the glowing skyline and let the moment settle in.

The morning sun streamed gently into the apartment as Celeste fastened the final button on her light blouse. Her nerves were quiet but present, humming under her calm exterior. Jisoo emerged from the bedroom in a crisp short-sleeved shirt, his hair still damp from the shower. He smiled when he saw her.

"You look perfect," he said, offering his arm. "They're going to be happy to see you."

Celeste smiled softly. "Let's just hope no one's waiting outside."

At exactly 10:00 a.m., a sleek black van with tinted windows pulled into the private lot below. The driver, dressed in a discreet black suit, gave a respectful bow as Jisoo, Celeste, and Micah stepped into the vehicle. The ride was smooth, quiet, luxurious, without drawing attention.

Micah stared out the window at the bustling city. "This is wild," he muttered, eyes following the blur of people, scooters, and street vendors.

Jisoo nodded. "It's home in a different way. Fast, sharp, beautiful chaos."

It took less than thirty minutes to reach the Jisoo family residence. It was a traditional hanok-inspired house tucked in a quiet neighborhood of northern Seoul. The wooden gate opened slowly as the van approached, revealing a courtyard shaded by gingko trees and lined with stones.

As they stepped out of the car, his mother, , was already waiting at the entrance in a soft mint hanbok. Her smile bloomed the moment she saw her son. Beside her, his father stood dignified in a tailored gray suit, his expression unreadable but not unkind.

"Mother, Father," Jisoo said, bowing low. "We're here."

His mother stepped forward and took Celeste's hands warmly. "Celeste, welcome. It is so good to see you again."

Celeste returned the bow, her Korean steady. "Thank you for welcoming us. It is good to be here."

Jisoo's father gave a respectful nod to Celeste, then turned to Micah. "You've grown since the last time we saw you."

Micah bowed politely. "Thank you, sir."

Jisoo placed a reassuring hand on Micah's back. "Let's go in."

The interior of the Min house was serene: cool marble floors, paper doors open to the gardens, and the gentle scent of incense drifting through the air. Jiyeon led them into the sitting room, where a low table was already prepared with tea and light refreshments.

"You must be tired from the trip," she said. "Please, sit."

They all gathered around the table, sipping tea. The conversation began lightly—updates on the flight, reflections on Jeju, laughter about how Micah had eluded fan mobs. Jiyeon was especially pleased to hear that they'd visited Min Jiho's family.

"He said Soo-ah adores Celeste," Jiyeon added with a teasing smile. "And the children think Micah is some sort of movie star."

Micah blushed and quickly sipped his tea. "They were really cool," he said.

Eventually, Jisoo's father set his cup down and addressed them all. "You've returned to Korea at an important time. The media is still talking about you, Jisoo, and now that the article is out, there's a lot of conversation. Some of it... difficult."

Jisoo nodded solemnly. "I expected that."

"But," his mother said, interrupting gently, "there is also growing support. People are beginning to see more clearly."

She turned to Celeste and Micah. "You are family now. And what people say, they will learn. In time."

Celeste bowed her head slightly. "We're grateful to be here. Truly."

Jiyeon stood. "Then let's eat something more than tea. You've traveled far, and I've prepared a meal."

They moved to the formal dining area, where a quiet lunch awaited: grilled fish, banchan, japchae, and bowls of hot soup. Celeste was careful to use both hands when pouring tea for Jiyeon and accepted food graciously. Micah remembered to turn his head politely when drinking water, a gesture that made Jiyeon smile proudly.

As the meal wound down, Jiyeon looked across the table. "Micah," she said gently, "you've improved your Korean."

Micah smiled. "Thank you. I've been practicing."

"We're impressed," Mr. Min added. "Both of you."

Jisoo glanced at Celeste with a quiet smile, knowing how much effort she'd put into learning the customs and the language. This was more than just acceptance—it was the beginning of true belonging.

When the meal ended, Jiyeon stood. "Rest now. You are welcome here for as long as you need. Tomorrow, we can plan the rest of your visit."

As they stepped into the guest rooms prepared for them, the peaceful hum of wind through the garden leaves wrapped around them like a quiet blessing.

Chapter 35

Nesting

The house had quieted after dinner. The moonlight spilled gently through the paper doors, casting soft silver patterns across the wooden floors. Celeste and Micah had already turned in for the night, their voices faint behind the sliding doors of the guest quarters.

Jisoo stood alone in the garden for a while, gazing up at the dark sky. The scent of pine and old stone comforted him—familiar and grounding. Eventually, he made his way toward the study where the warm glow of a lamp beckoned from inside.

His father was seated at the low table, glasses perched on the bridge of his nose, reviewing architectural sketches in a leather-bound portfolio. His mother sat nearby, knitting a fine piece of embroidery in quiet concentration. When Jisoo entered, both looked up.

"You're still awake," his mother said, setting her embroidery aside.

"I couldn't sleep," Jisoo replied, taking a seat across from them. "There's something about being here... it always stirs things up."

His father closed the portfolio, folding his hands. "Sit. Speak freely."

Jisoo inhaled deeply. "I wanted to thank you both. For everything. For coming to Solmere. For being open to Celeste. For treating Micah with warmth and dignity."

"You are our son," his mother said softly. "And they are your family. That makes them ours too."

Jisoo hesitated. "Were you… ever ashamed? When the news first broke?"

There was a pause. His father leaned back, eyes steady on his son.

"We were… confused," his father admitted. "Not ashamed. But we were afraid. Afraid that the life you were building might collapse under pressure, that people's words would become knives."

His mother nodded. "And we didn't know her yet. Only what the media chose to show us."

Jisoo's voice softened. "She saved me, Mother. After the military, after the pressures of this life, I felt lost. Writing helped, yes. But Celeste… she gave me something more. A place to be myself. Fully."

His father considered this for a long moment. Then he said, "She carries herself with grace. She did not flinch once when we met. Not even when I asked difficult questions, that tells me she is strong—and sincere."

Jisoo smiled faintly. "She's the strongest person I know."

His mother's voice was quiet. "And Micah… is remarkable. So respectful. So smart. He speaks with the weight of someone twice his age."

Jisoo chuckled softly. "He's always been that way. An old soul in a teenage body."

The garden seemed to hold its breath for a moment, the soft rustle of leaves echoing the unspoken feelings between them. Jisoo let himself linger in the quiet, letting the warmth of his parents' words settle deep in his chest. He realized that this—this connection, this understanding—was as much a part of him as any achievement or dream. The weight of gratitude, pride, and love blended into a gentle resolve, and he felt ready to embrace whatever came next, carrying both his family's legacy and his own heart forward.

There was silence again, filled only by the sound of the garden breeze.

Then his father looked directly at his son. "Are you happy, Jisoo?"

Jisoo didn't hesitate. "Yes, Father. I am. More than I've ever been."

His father nodded slowly. "Then we've done our job. And now it is time for you to continue your own legacy."

His mother reached out and touched her son's hand. "Just promise us one thing."

"Anything."

"Protect them. Fiercely. Love them without apology."

Jisoo's eyes misted. "Always."

His father rose first. "Then go. Rest. Tomorrow will come fast—and so will the world's expectations. But for tonight, just be a son in your parents' home."

Jisoo stood, bowed slightly, and smiled.

"Good night, Mother. Father."

"Good night, Jisoo."

The aroma of sizzling eggs, warm rice, and freshly brewed barley tea filled the kitchen as the morning sun poured through the large window. Jisoo stood at the stove, flipping kimchi pancakes while his mother sliced fruit with the same ease she'd had since his childhood. Celeste helped set the table, her Korean improving just enough for the casual banter Jiyeon now teased her with. Si-woo sat with the morning newspaper folded neatly beside his tea, nodding occasionally at the quiet conversation around him.

The soft warmth of the morning seemed to linger in the kitchen, wrapping everyone in a quiet sense of togetherness. Jisoo paused for a moment, watching his mother's practiced movements and Celeste's careful gestures, and felt a simple contentment settle over him. The clinking of dishes, the gentle hum of conversation, and the golden sunlight spilling across the table made the house feel alive in a gentle, comforting rhythm—a small, perfect pause before the day truly began.

Micah wandered in, still in his pajama bottoms and a T-shirt, hair slightly tousled. "Morning," he mumbled, rubbing his eyes.

"Good morning, champ," Jisoo said, placing a platter on the table. "You're just in time."

Everyone took their seats, filling their plates and bowls with familiar comfort. The conversation flowed easily until Jisoo, glancing at Celeste, gave Micah a sly grin.

"So… I was thinking about your PSAT scores," Jisoo said casually, reaching for his tea.

Micah narrowed his eyes, suspicious. "Okay…?"

Jisoo grinned. "You said not to call everyone. You didn't say anything about telling anyone."

Micah groaned, setting down his chopsticks. "You told them?"

Jisoo leaned back smugly. "Of course I did. You got a perfect score. That's not something you keep to yourself, son."

Jiyeon's eyes sparkled with pride as she looked over at Micah. "A perfect score? That's amazing."

Celeste chimed in, beaming. "Both he and his best friend Kai got perfect scores. We're so proud of them."

Si-woo nodded approvingly. "Then it seems intelligence runs strong in this household."

Micah gave a bashful smile and blushed. "Thanks. But please, no surprise parties or anything."

"No promises," Jisoo teased, earning a playful nudge from Celeste.

After a few more bites, Jisoo glanced at his phone. "I need to start prepping for work tomorrow. And we still need to restock the apartment. A lot is missing since I moved most things to Solmere.”

His mother wiped her hands gently and looked at Celeste. “Why don’t you and I go shopping together today? I can show you where to find everything.”

Celeste smiled warmly. “I’d love that. It’ll be nice to explore with you.”

Jiyeon turned to her husband. “And Micah, you can spend the day with your grandfather. If that’s alright with you.”

Si-woo looked over at Micah with a mild shrug. “I was going to visit the design institute and walk through the cultural district. You’re welcome to join me.”

Micah nodded. “Sure. That sounds cool.”

Jisoo looked around the table and smiled. “Perfect. Everyone’s got a plan.”

Celeste reached over and squeezed his hand. “And tonight, we’ll all meet back at the apartment for dinner?”

Jisoo nodded. “Exactly. One last quiet evening before the real chaos begins.”

They all shared a moment of quiet joy simple, easy, and full of a sense of family that had grown from choice and love.

The streets of Seoul bustled with weekend energy, but inside the quiet boutique, time seemed to slow. Celeste walked beside her mother-in-law through neatly arranged aisles, the soft hum of instrumental music playing in the background. The store featured a refined blend of modern and traditional Korean housewares ceramic dishes with delicate floral patterns, wooden trays, silk table runners, and minimalist teapots that gleamed under warm lighting.

Celeste picked up a set of white porcelain bowls, each etched with a subtle wave pattern along the edge. "These are beautiful," she said quietly.

Jiyeon examined one with a nod of approval. "They're from a ceramicist in Gangjin. Excellent quality. They'll last forever if you care for them."

Celeste smiled, touched by the gentle pride in Jiyeon's voice. "We want the apartment to feel like home while we're here, even if it's temporary."

Jiyeon paused, glancing at her. "You're already making it one."

Celeste felt the warmth of those words settle in her chest. As they moved toward a small display of traditional linens, she asked, "Is there anything you think we're forgetting? Something essential?"

Jiyeon tilted her head in thought. "Every Korean kitchen should have a proper set of chopsticks and soup spoons. And tea Jisoo likes barley tea, doesn't he?"

Celeste grinned. "He does. And so does Micah now. I'll make sure we grab enough for the summer."

They made their way through the shop slowly, choosing practical items and a few decorative touches: soft cushions for the window seats, a woven table mat, and small, framed calligraphy art for the kitchen nook. Jiyeon seemed to enjoy explaining each item's origin, and Celeste listened intently, grateful for the guidance.

After checking out, their arms filled with shopping bags, they stepped into a nearby café. Over warm citron tea and sweet red bean buns, Jiyeon spoke softly, watching Celeste across the table.

"I want you to know, you've made a deep impression on me, Celeste. And not just because of how happy my son looks." Her eyes glinted with affection and sincerity. "You're strong. Thoughtful. Patient in ways I wasn't sure I'd see from someone not raised in our ways. You care enough to learn, and that means something."

Celeste blinked, taken aback for a moment, then smiled. "Thank you, Mother," Celeste said softly. "That means more than I can say."

They sat in companionable silence for a while, sipping tea and watching people pass outside the window.

For the first time since landing in Korea, Celeste felt not only accepted—but fully seen.

While Celeste and Jiyeon browsed kitchenware and teacups across Seoul, Micah found himself in a very different world: the peaceful garden courtyard of Jisoo's parents' traditional hanok-style home.

Si-woo, dignified yet relaxed in a light linen shirt, led Micah around the property with quiet pride. "The architecture here," he said, gesturing toward the curved tiled roof and wooden beams, "has not changed in hundreds of years. It's designed for harmony—with the seasons, with nature, and with the family that lives inside."

Micah looked around, impressed. "It's really peaceful here."

His grandfather smiled slightly. "It keeps the mind still. Come, let's go inside. I have something to show you."

Inside, the air was cool and clean. Si-woo led Micah into a back room, where a large desk stood beneath a wall of shelves lined with books, scrolls, and framed architectural sketches.

"This was my study," he explained. "Where I drafted designs for many years. I've since passed the firm to my juniors, but the work… still lives in me."

Micah's eyes widened as he took in the drawings. "You did all of these?"

"Yes," his grandfather said. "Each one began with a pencil, not a computer. You must understand a building with your hands before you build it with machines."

Micah walked slowly along the shelves, taking it all in. "You ever think about designing something in Solmere?"

His grandfather gave him a curious look. "Why do you ask?"

Micah shrugged. "Just thinking… I like the way you talk about this stuff. It's like it means something bigger."

There was a long pause, and then his grandfather chuckled softly. "You're more perceptive than I thought."

They moved to the sitting area, where Jiyeon had earlier set out a tray with fruit, rice cakes, and barley tea. Mr. Min poured Micah a cup, then one for himself, settling across from him.

"I know this trip is a lot," he said after a moment. "New culture, new pace, new expectations. And meeting your father… again."

Micah looked down at his cup, swirling the tea a little before taking a sip.

"I'm okay," he said. "I mean, not all the way. But I know who's here for me. And that helps."

His grandfather studied him for a moment, nodding with approval. "It's good to question things. Even the people we come from. Just be sure you don't forget who you are along the way."

Micah met his gaze. "That's something Jisoo says too."

"As he should." his tone warmed slightly. "He is my son, after all."

The afternoon passed easily, with talk about music, sports, architecture, and Korean history. He even showed Micah how to use an old ink brush to write simple Hangul characters—one of which Micah proudly signed with his own name by the end of the session.

By the time Celeste and Jiyeon returned, the two were deep in a discussion about traditional Korean hanok versus modern steel-and-glass homes.

Jiyeon leaned into Celeste and whispered, amused, "They're already debating."

Celeste smiled. " He is in good hands."

And he was.

Chapter 36

Break A Leg Appa

Micah sat under the curved eaves of the hanok's tiled roof, legs stretched out on the cool wooden floor of the daecheong maru. A light breeze swept through the open courtyard, rustling the leaves of the persimmon tree in the center. He took a bite of the pear Jiyeon had sliced earlier, then pulled out his phone and opened a chat with Kai.

Micah:
yo. today's been wild.

Kai:
👀 what happened? Have you met any K-pop idols yet lol

Micah:
nah. no celebrities. just spent the whole day with Jisoo's dad
place is straight out of a movie. it's this traditional hanok house—wooden floors, rice paper windows, the whole vibe.

Kai:
okay that actually sounds kinda dope

Micah:
It is. peaceful. like... ancient but not old.
Grandfather is cool tho. quiet, super observant. but he talks to me like I'm already a grown man.

Kai:
that's gotta feel different

Micah:

yeah. he asked me what I want to do with my life. I said I'm figuring it out. he just nodded and said, "There is wisdom in not rushing." 😐 bro hit me with a proverb like he's in a drama.

Kai:

lololol he *is* in a drama. you're living one 😄

Micah:

fr. he took me to this little stream behind the house and told me he used to go there as a kid when his thoughts were too loud. said he was glad I came.

Kai:

Yo that's actually really sweet

Micah:

it was. idk, man. It's quiet here in a way that makes you think differently but I miss spicy chips. and you. and real sarcasm.

Kai:

lmao aww miss you too bro. don't forget you gotta bring me back something cool. no tourist junk

Micah:

noted oh and I almost got chased by a rooster in the courtyard earlier do not ask.

Kai:

Okay now you're officially in a Korean drama

Micah smiled as he looked out across the yard, where his grandfather was tending to a small garden in the corner. It wasn't flashy, and it wasn't fast—but there was something about this day, about this man, that felt solid.

For the first time in a long while, Micah wasn't thinking about Marcus, or the noise of the outside world.

Micah lingered a moment longer in the quiet of the hanok, letting the calm seep into him. The air was gentle, carrying the faint scent of earth and blossoms, and for once, the world beyond this courtyard felt distant, almost paused. Somewhere else in the city, life was waking with its usual rhythm—sunlight spilling across floors, kitchens coming alive, and the subtle hum of morning routines beginning anew. It was a bridge between two worlds: one of serene reflection, and one of bustling, familiar life waiting just beyond the door.

Just the soft creak of wood, the rustle of leaves, and the steady presence of someone who expected nothing of him— except to simply be.

The morning sun filtered through the tall windows of the Seoul apartment, casting long streaks of light across the floor. Celeste was up early, tying her robe as she padded softly through the kitchen, brewing coffee and setting out toast and fruit.

Jisoo emerged from the bedroom looking sharp and focused casual black slacks, a crisp gray T-shirt, and a light jacket. His hair was styled but not overly done. He looked like himself just polished enough for the cameras.

"First day," Celeste said, sliding a mug into his hand.

Jisoo took it with a small smile. "Feels strange. I haven't worked here since before everything changed."

Celeste stepped closer, smoothing the front of his jacket. "You're going to be brilliant. You always are."

Micah came out rubbing his eyes, yawning. "You look famous already," he teased.

Jisoo laughed. "Only look famous?"

Micah grinned and sat down to eat. "Break a leg, Appa."

Jisoo's heart caught slightly at the word, but he recovered quickly and gave Micah a wink. "Thanks, kiddo."

Soon after breakfast, the apartment buzzed with quiet activity. A black SUV arrived with a discreet security team, and a driver provided by Jisoo's management company. As promised, they were keeping everything low-key to avoid drawing attention from fans.

The quiet hum of the apartment lingered in Jisoo's chest as he stepped into the waiting SUV. Even amidst the gentle chaos of the morning—bags, breakfast dishes, and soft chatter—there was a thread of calm that followed him. With Celeste's words echoing in his mind, he felt grounded, ready to step into another world for the day, carrying the warmth of home with him as the city blurred past the windows.

Before heading out, Jisoo kissed Celeste on the forehead. "Text me if you need anything."

She nodded. "Go do your thing, actor man."

The ride to the set was smooth. The production had rented a historic hanok village on the edge of the city—a popular filming location for period dramas. As they arrived, crew members bowed respectfully, actors gathered in costume, and the director approached Jisoo with visible excitement.

"Jisoo-ssi, we're honored to have you back."

Jisoo bowed politely. "I'm honored to be here."

He changed into his hanbok, a rugged scholar-warrior from the Joseon era, draped in deep indigo robes with hand-stitched detailing. The wardrobe director helped with final touches, and soon Jisoo stood on set, his presence commanding even without dialogue.

The cameras rolled.

In the first scene, he stood at a cliff's edge, overlooking the sea, eyes haunted by betrayal. As the camera zoomed in, Jisoo's expression shifted—just a breath of anguish, a flicker of rage, then stillness.

"Cut!" the director called. "Perfect. That's the take."

Jisoo nodded, stepping off the rock and back into himself.

During lunch break, a young actor approached nervously. "Jisoo-ssi I grew up watching your work. It's surreal to be here with you."

Jisoo smiled kindly. "Thank you. You'll be great. Just stay true to the character and breathe."

The young man bowed deeply, clearly moved.

Later, while waiting for lighting adjustments, Jisoo stepped aside and texted Celeste: "First scene done. Everything feels right again. Miss you."

Her reply came almost instantly: "So proud of you. Bring that character to life. We'll be waiting when you get home."

Jisoo exhaled slowly, the tension easing from his shoulders. He was back in Korea, standing in the spotlight again. But this time, he wasn't standing alone.

After lunch, the crew resumed filming with a more intense scene. Jisoo stood in the courtyard of the reconstructed hanok, facing off with a fellow actor playing his on-screen rival. The dialogue was heavy with tension—betrayal, loyalty, and the weight of honor.

Jisoo's delivery was sharp, his movements measured but full of restrained emotion. The camera followed him as he stalked forward, his voice low and simmering with anger.

The director leaned toward the monitor, murmuring, "He's still got it. That's real conviction."

After the scene, Jisoo walked off set, a towel around his neck, sipping water. One of the assistant directors caught up to him, clipboard in hand, with an apologetic expression.

"Jisoo-ssi, sorry to bother you. We've had a minor script change. The writer requested a new flashback scene. It's scheduled for late afternoon—just wanted you to be aware."

Jisoo took the update in stride. "No problem. I'll review the pages."

As he stepped into the shade and sat down to read, the wardrobe designer, a cheerful woman named Eun-ji, approached with a grin. "Your robe's starting to fray from that fight scene. That means you're really acting."

He chuckled. "Tell the wardrobe team they're miracle workers."

A few feet away, two younger actors whispered excitedly about the scene they'd just witnessed.

"Did you see the way he shifted tone mid-line? That's master-level stuff."

"I know. It was like watching a drama class in real time."

Jisoo caught their words but said nothing, only offering a subtle smile as he flipped the script pages.

Then the producer, a man in his late forties with a professional but friendly demeanor, approached with his assistant. "Jisoo-ssi , we've been following your article—the one Sang-ho wrote. Beautifully done. Honest. Brave."

Jisoo bowed slightly. "Thank you."

"We just want you to know we support your decision to live openly. Bringing your family here, being transparent… it means something."

Jisoo nodded, quietly moved. "I appreciate that more than I can say."

The rest of the afternoon flew by in a blur of choreography, dialogue, and camera work. By the time the sun began to set, painting the sky in streaks of gold and lavender, the day's final scene was wrapping up.

"Cut!" the director called again, and applause broke out on set—not for the scene alone, but for Jisoo himself.

The crew gathered briefly for a group photo to mark the first day of filming. Jisoo stood in the center, robe slightly wind-tousled, surrounded by co-stars, production staff, and the quiet magic of a new story taking root.

As they all began to pack up, the young actor from earlier approached again.

"Jisoo-ssi… do you ever get nervous?"

Jisoo smiled, placing a hand on the young man's shoulder. "Of course. I just don't let it stop me."

And with that, he changed out of his stage clothes, texted Celeste that he was on his way home, and climbed into the waiting SUV with the driver who would carry him back through the busy streets of Seoul to his family, his second home—and the quiet arms of love waiting on the other side of the door.

As the sun began to dip lower in the sky, casting golden hues across the skyline of Seoul, Celeste and Jiyeon returned to the apartment, arms full of shopping bags and quiet laughter trailing behind them.

They stepped through the front door, the soft clatter of their shoes echoing off the polished floor. Celeste kicked hers off first, sighing with relief.

"I haven't walked this much in a day since Micah's sixth-grade field trip to the botanical gardens," she said with a chuckle, stretching her shoulders.

Jiyeon smiled, setting her bags down neatly. "You kept up beautifully. And your taste… Celeste, you've got an eye. That navy hanbok you picked out—it'll look stunning for the family portrait."

Celeste blushed lightly, waving off the compliment. "You're too kind. I just took your lead and tried not to embarrass myself too much."

"Nonsense," Jiyeon said. "You're graceful, Celeste. And you're learning. That matters."

They moved into the kitchen, instinctively beginning to unpack their finds, the counters quickly filled with groceries, herbal teas, Korean side dishes from a local shop, a box of fresh tangerines, and a few beautifully wrapped gift boxes—souvenirs and housewarming offerings for upcoming visits.

Celeste held up a small, delicate ceramic dish with a soft blue floral pattern. "This reminded me of something my grandmother used to keep earrings in."

Jiyeon paused for a moment, her expression thoughtful. "It's beautiful. And it suits you. There's something comforting about surrounding yourself with things that hold quiet memories."

Celeste nodded, taking a deep breath. "I think that's what this whole trip is about, for all of us."

Jiyeon turned, her hand resting gently on Celeste's shoulder. "Thank you for today," she said, sincere and warm. "I know this isn't always easy—blending cultures, learning new rhythms—but you are doing it with so much heart."

Celeste met her gaze, surprised by the sudden well of emotion in her chest. "That means more than I can say."

The door swung open with a burst of energy as, Jisoo, his father, and Micah stepped inside, their laughter already announcing them.

Celeste smiled, glancing toward the entryway. "I guess we beat the boys."

Jiyeon laughed. "Let's see how their day compares to ours."

They exchanged one more glance—this one lighter, filled with the unspoken understanding of two women who, in their own ways, were both figuring out what it meant to share a family.

"We didn't break anything, Mother!" Jisoo called out playfully, helping Micah shrug off his jacket.

Jiyeon appeared from the kitchen with a raised brow. "That's a very specific thing to say. What almost broke?"

Micah grinned, brushing past her with his usual casual charm. "Let's just say I got a little too confident trying to use a traditional ink brush at the hanok. But Appa here saved the day."

Jisoo held up his hand, modestly triumphant. "One reflex left from my action movie days."

Celeste stepped forward, smiling as she tucked a curl behind her ear. "And here I thought you were just filming love scenes."

Jisoo shot her a wink. "That too."

Micah dropped onto the couch, stretching like a cat. "Grandfather knows everything about old houses. He showed me how the ondol floors work, the secret to keeping the doors from sticking in the summer, and told me a story about dad's grandmother chasing chickens with a fan."

"I didn't even know that one," Jisoo said, shaking his head fondly. "Father only shares the really good stories with people he likes."

"Guess I passed the test then," Micah said with a smirk.

Jiyeon approached with a glass of water and offered it to Micah. "You always pass, dear."

Jisoo walked over to Celeste and gently kissed her temple. "How was your day?"

"We shopped Seoul clean," Celeste said, stepping back to admire him. "But it was lovely. I think your mom and I are figuring each other out."

Jisoo smiled, clearly touched. "I knew you would."

They all gathered around the open kitchen island as the sun dipped fully below the skyline, warm amber light softening the edges of the evening. Grocery bags were unpacked, stories were traded, and there was a quiet ease between them—each of them slowly claiming this new rhythm as their own.

Jisoo looked around at the faces he loved most and exhaled contentedly. "Feels like home, doesn't it?"

Celeste nodded, looping her arm through his. "It really does."

The scent of simmering stew and roasted vegetables filled the apartment, mingling with the soft strains of jazz playing low in the background. Dinner was a warm, unhurried affair.

Chapter 37

Curtain Call

Jiyeon returned from her brief visit to a nearby friend just in time to join them, slipping off her shoes at the door and greeting everyone with a smile that spoke of both tiredness and contentment.

Celeste plated the last of the dishes—braised short ribs and lotus root, glazed carrots, and a big bowl of sesame spinach—and Jisoo set the table with practiced ease. Jiyeon reached over to ruffle Micah's hair as she passed by, and Si-woo clapped Jisoo on the back when he stepped into the room.

Everyone gathered at the table, and for a while, it was just the comforting hum of conversation, the occasional laughter, and the shared language of family. Even in a space that still felt new, there was a growing familiarity that stitched them all together, meal by meal, day by day.

When the dishes were finally cleared and the leftovers tucked away, Jiyeon and Si-woo said their goodnights, promising to return the next day. Micah retreated to his room with a book and his earbuds, waving sleepily as he disappeared down the hallway.

Later, in the quiet of their bedroom, Celeste stepped out of the ensuite bathroom in her robe, her hair wrapped up in a silk scarf. She climbed into bed beside Jisoo, who had been lounging g with a script open on his chest but not reading it.

She looked over at him, smile soft. "Today was good."

Jisoo nodded, turning toward her. "Yeah, it was. I loved seeing Micah with my father today. He looked… peaceful."

Celeste leaned her head on his shoulder. "Your parents have been wonderful."

"They love you," he murmured. "I think my dad's just trying to show it in his quiet, brooding, architect way."

Celeste chuckled. "He doesn't need to say anything. I feel it." She paused for a moment, then added, "Your mom and I bought so many things today. Linens, organizers, lamps, rugs—beautiful things. She has such a good eye."

Jisoo wrapped an arm around her waist and pulled her close. "I'm glad you had that time with her."

"She said they're coming over tomorrow to help put it all away and create a beautiful space together."

"I like the sound of that," Jisoo said, kissing her hair.

Celeste tilted her head to meet his gaze. "So do I. This is starting to feel like a real home."

He smiled, brushing a hand down her arm. "It is. Because you're here."

They fell into a comfortable silence, the kind reserved for those who have nothing to prove, only love to share. The soft hush of the city outside their window was the only sound as they drifted toward sleep—two souls, anchored in one another.

The internet was ablaze.

Social media, fan forums, and gossip sites were teeming with speculation. Photos of Jisoo had surfaced—blurry shots taken from afar as he walked through Seoul or stepped out of a car—but none included the woman he'd married. None featured the teenage boy who had become part of his life.

"Is he ashamed of her?"

"Is she ugly?"

"Why is he hiding her?"

"Is she too proud to show her face?"

"He used to care about his fans—what happened?"

The rumors swirled like wildfire, and even those who supported Jisoo began to ask questions. His management team, watching the rising chatter and feeling the temperature rise in the press, called an emergency meeting.

"We need to address this," one of the managers said bluntly. "Jisoo, the speculation is out of control."

Jisoo took a slow breath, letting the weight of the situation settle in. The room felt smaller somehow, the buzz of speculation pressing against the calm he tried to hold. He looked around at the team he trusted, each face a reminder that this wasn't about appeasing the crowd—it was about protecting the people he loved. His mind raced through possibilities, weighing respect, safety, and dignity, until a plan began to form—one that would allow the world a glimpse without compromising the peace they had fought so hard to create.

"I know," Jisoo replied, his voice calm but firm. "I never meant to hide my family. I just wanted to give them peace."

Another team member leaned in. "Then let's give the fans what they need. Not a press conference. Just something light. You come out, talk about the new movie, and sign a few autographs. Then we bring Celeste and Micah out. You introduce them. They greet the fans, bow, say thank you in Korean, and leave the stage."

Jisoo thought for a moment, then gave a small nod. "Alright. But no questions. No microphones in Celeste or Micah's face."

"Of course," the manager agreed. "Simple. Elegant. Let them see the truth with their own eyes."

Jisoo, glancing around the table, then added, "Before that night, I want them to come here. To the set. I want to introduce them to the team, let them see how things work. That way, when they stand beside me, they won't feel like strangers in my world."

The room went quiet for a moment, the weight of his words settling in. This wasn't about publicity—it was about protection, about making sure the two people he loved most were steady before the lights and cameras ever found them.

The apartment was quiet when Jisoo returned, the scent of garlic and herbs drifting from the kitchen. Celeste had set the table, a simple dinner—roast chicken, rice, and vegetables steaming in their bowls. Micah was already seated, drumming his fingers on the edge of his plate until Celeste gave him a look that made him stop.

Jisoo slipped off his coat and came to the table, his face softened by fatigue but lit by quiet determination. He sat, reached for Celeste's hand briefly, and then folded his napkin across his lap.

"Smells wonderful," he said.

Celeste smiled, pouring him a glass of water. "You look tired. Long day?"

He nodded, then glanced at Micah. "Busy. But important. That's why I wanted us to sit together tonight. I have something to tell you both."

Micah leaned in, curious. Celeste waited, calmly watching Jisoo.

"There's going to be an event in a few days," Jisoo began. "Something for my most faithful fans. Not a press conference— more of a gathering. I'll talk about the new movie, sign a few autographs, nothing heavy."

Micah's fork clinked against his plate. "And we're going too?"

"Yes," Jisoo said, his tone careful but firm. "But I don't want you thrown into it without knowing what to expect. Tomorrow, I want you both to come to the studio. Meet the staff, see the set, understand how things work. That way, when the event comes, it won't feel so strange."

Celeste studied him, her expression unreadable for a moment. "You're sure about this? Putting us out there like that?"

Jisoo's gaze met hers, unwavering. "I'm sure. I want people to see you—not as strangers, but as part of my life. But I'll control how it happens. No microphones. No questions. Just introductions."

Micah grinned, excitement bubbling in his voice. "So… I'll actually get to go behind the scenes. See how they make the movie?"

Jisoo chuckled, his shoulders easing. "Yes, you will. And tomorrow, you'll meet everyone. They'll take care of you. By the time the event happens, you'll already know the faces in the room."

Celeste exhaled slowly, her fingers tracing the rim of her glass. There was risk in this, she knew, but also a strange relief— Jisoo wasn't hiding her anymore. He was folding her and Micah into his world with deliberate care.

Celeste felt a flutter of anticipation mix with her relief, the weight of the decision settling like a gentle tide. She watched Jisoo carefully, the steadiness in his eyes grounding her, and glanced at Micah, who was already buzzing with excitement. In that quiet moment, the three of them felt a subtle shift—what had been uncertainty and hesitation now began to stretch into possibility, a shared readiness to step forward together into a world that had always seemed just beyond reach.

"Then we'll go," she said softly. "Together."

Jisoo reached for her hand again, this time holding it longer, his thumb brushing against her knuckles. Across the table, Micah was already imagining the cameras, the lights, the thrill of stepping into something that had once seemed impossibly far away.

The next morning broke clear and bright, the city humming awake as they piled into the car. Jisoo slid behind the wheel, his usual calm anchored in something steadier, more deliberate. Celeste sat beside him, her hands folded in her lap, while Micah leaned forward from the back seat, practically vibrating with questions.

"Will there be cameras on when we get there?" he asked.

"I will have to shoot a couple of scenes," Jisoo said, glancing at him in the rearview mirror with a reassuring smile. "But the main reason is for you to meet the staff."

Micah nodded, though his eyes still danced with curiosity. "Do they really build whole houses inside the studio? Like, entire rooms that look real but aren't?"

Jisoo chuckled. "Yes. You'll see walls that don't connect, windows that look out on painted skies, and doors that lead nowhere. That's the magic of it."

Celeste turned her head, watching Jisoo as he spoke, her own nerves quieting in the rhythm of his voice. "And the staff? They'll know who we are?"

"They already do," Jisoo said softly. "I told them you're important to me. They'll treat you with respect."

For a moment, the only sound was the steady hum of the car and the muffled city beyond the windows. Micah leaned back in his seat, eyes wide as if trying to picture it all. Celeste let out a slow breath, her hand brushing against Jisoo's on the console between them.

"It feels strange," she admitted. "Crossing into your world like this."

Jisoo tightened his fingers around hers. "It's not just my world anymore. It's ours. I want you both to feel that—before anyone else sees you, before the fans, before the cameras. This is where we begin."

Micah grinned from the back seat. "Then let's go see how a movie gets made."

Jisoo's laugh, low and genuine, filled the car as they turned onto the wide boulevard leading toward the studio gates.

Celeste continued to watch Jisoo, her fingers curled around the edges of her jacket as a crisp breeze swept through the set. Never in her wildest dreams did she ever expect to be in Korea with the love of her life, standing in the shadow of cameras and stage lights, watching him slip into a world that had once seemed untouchable.

She had memorized his face through letters, late-night calls, and fleeting visits across oceans. But here, under the sharp gaze of the director, surrounded by crew members bustling with quiet efficiency, he seemed different. Every movement was deliberate, every word measured. It was a version of him she had never known, and yet, he was still hers.

A cue was called, and the scene reset. Jisoo's eyes lifted for just a moment, scanning the set—until they found her. The softest flicker of recognition crossed his face, just enough to make her breath hitch. In that moment, Solmere and the quiet life they had built there felt impossibly distant. Here, in the heart of his world, she wondered if she truly belonged, or whether she was a mere visitor in his dream, waiting to wake.

The invitation only event was held in a private hall in Seoul, tightly secured and for Jisoo's most devoted fans. Rows of chairs filled with excited faces, phones already out, cameras raised. The stage was lit softly, the anticipation thick in the air.

Jisoo stepped out to a wave of cheers and flashing lights. He looked every inch the movie star calm, composed, charismatic in his sleek dark suit.

"Hello," he greeted with a warm smile. "Thank you all for coming."

His fans leaned in, hanging onto his every word.

"I know there's been a lot of curiosity. I want to say first—I'm grateful for your support. It means more to me than I can ever express. I've been working on a new film, which I hope you'll all love. It's a story about love, courage, and belonging… something that's been very personal for me lately."

He signed a few autographs, exchanged some quick pleasantries, and then paused as the crowd quieted.

"There's something more I want to share," he said. "Two people who have become everything to me."

The side curtain parted.

Jisoo stepped forward and walked to greet them, extending a hand as Celeste and Micah entered the stage.

Gasps echoed across the room.

Celeste was stunning. Dressed impeccably in an elegant yet understated ensemble, her long jet-black hair flowing over her shoulders, her regal posture matched by her serene confidence. Her caramel brown skin glowed under the stage lights, and her features were graceful, striking—radiating strength, warmth, and poise.

Beside her, Micah stood tall and athletic, his youthful frame a clear product of his training as a track and swim star. His thick, jet-black curls framed a face with sharp features, intense eyes, and a disarmingly beautiful smile.

Jisoo led them to the center of the stage, his hand resting on Celeste's lower back with quiet pride.

"This is my wife, Celeste Monroe. And this," he said, looking fondly at Micah, "is our son, Micah."

Celeste stepped forward with a gentle bow. Speaking perfect Korean, she said "Hello. Thank you so much."

Micah followed suit, bowing respectfully. Speaking perfect Korean, he said, "Hello. Thank You."

And just like that, they stepped back, offering warm smiles before exiting the stage, leaving behind a stunned and silent crowd.

The moment settled over them like a revelation. There was no speech needed. No defense. Just truth. Beauty. Dignity. Family.

Jisoo remained a moment longer. "Thank you," he said. "For seeing us."

Then he too left the stage, hand in hand with his wife, and their son steps behind.

The applause didn't erupt until after they were gone, but when it did, it was thunderous. Not everyone would be swayed. But for many, seeing was believing.

And what they saw… was love.

Backstage, the quiet after the storm was filled with unspoken tension and the distant hum of applause still echoing from the hall.

Celeste exhaled slowly as the curtain closed behind them. Jisoo immediately reached for her hand and squeezed it gently.

"You were incredible," he whispered.

Celeste gave a faint smile, still processing. "I felt like I couldn't breathe walking out there… but then I looked at you, and I knew I could."

Micah leaned against the wall, one hand still in his pocket, the other running through his curls. "They stared like we were aliens at first."

Jisoo chuckled softly. "Well, they've never seen perfection in motion."

Micah groaned. "Appa…"

"You were perfect," Celeste said, pulling Micah into a quick side hug. "You made us proud."

One of Jisoo's managers stepped in with wide eyes and a tight smile. "That was... a moment," she said. "I've never seen a crowd so still before an ovation."

Another manager added, "We're already getting responses online. Mixed, of course, but there's a definite shift. They saw what they weren't expecting: dignity, grace, and real love. That's hard to argue with."

Jisoo nodded, wiping a hand across his brow. "Let's get home. This day's done its work."

Chapter 38

Micah Celebrates

As their car pulled away from the venue, Celeste watched the city blur past the window, Seoul glowing under the late evening lights.

Jisoo looked at her. "You okay?"

She turned toward him. "Yes… I think so. I've never felt so exposed, but also… seen."

Micah chimed in from the back seat, earbuds out for once. "They were staring. Like they were trying to figure out what kind of woman you'd have to be to end up with someone like Jisoo."

"And what did they see?" Jisoo asked, glancing at him in the rearview mirror.

Micah smirked. "A boss."

Celeste laughed softly. "Well, good."

At a cozy café in Little Hanseong, Mrs. Moon and Hana sat at a corner table, phones in hand.

Mrs. Moon adjusted her glasses and watched the replay of the event on her screen. "She's a queen," she said.

"She looked like a first lady," Hana whispered. "And Jisoo—he never looked surer about anything in his life."

Back at the Park family restaurant, Mr. Park watched the video with arms crossed, nodding slowly. "They'll still whisper," he said. "But they won't be able to unsee what they saw today."

Jiyeon held the remote, tears in her eyes as the final bow replayed again on their living room screen. Si-woo sat beside her, silent, unmoving.

"She was beautiful," Jiyeon said softly. "And Micah… such presence." Si-woo finally spoke. "Our son looked like a man. A man with a family. And no regrets."

Jiyeon leaned against him. "I'm proud of them."

He nodded. "So am I."

The house was quiet. Micah had long since gone to bed, exhausted from the emotional weight of the day.

Celeste stood in the kitchen, sipping tea. Jisoo walked in, still in his event suit, tie undone, shirt sleeves rolled back. He came up behind her and wrapped his arms around her waist.

"You really are my leading lady," he murmured into her shoulder.

She leaned into him, warm and safe. "And you're the star who finally stopped hiding."

They stood like that in silence for a long time, knowing tomorrow the world might spin again with gossip and speculation.

But tonight… the stage belonged to them.

Lying in bed, Jisoo tells Celeste I have an idea for Micah's perfect PSAT score. I want to take him to a K-pop concert, just the two of us, if you don't mind. Jisoo, I think that would be a fantastic idea.

The energy outside the arena was electric. Fans were buzzing with anticipation, lightsticks glowing in every imaginable color, and music thumping faintly through the stadium walls. Micah stepped out of the car, wide-eyed at the sight.

"Whoa," he whispered, taking in the sheer number of people and the chaotic excitement.

Jisoo grinned beside him. "You ready for this?"

"I didn't think you'd be the one bringing me to a K-pop concert," Micah said, laughing. "I thought you were more jazz and ballads."

"I contain multitudes," Jisoo said with a wink, then leaned closer. "Besides, you've been working hard. Thought you deserved a night out."

They were ushered in through a private entrance—no lines, no chaos, just smooth access all the way to a VIP box overlooking the stage. The lights dimmed, and the crowd roared to life as the headlining idol group burst onto the stage, the performance a dazzling spectacle of synchronized dance, flawless vocals, and fireworks.

Micah watched in awe, mouthing the lyrics and bouncing slightly in his seat. Jisoo glanced over, satisfied to see the boy so completely in his element.

After the final encore, a staff member led them through a series of corridors to a private backstage lounge. The members of the idol group, fresh from the stage and still buzzing with adrenaline, greeted them warmly.

One of the performers recognized Jisoo and bowed deeply in respect. "Jisoo-ssi, it's an honor," he said with a smile.

Jisoo waved it off with casual humility. "This guy," he said, gesturing to Micah, "is the real VIP tonight."

Micah gave a respectful bow. "Thank you for letting me meet you."

"Thank you for coming," one of the group's vocalists replied as he handed Micah two shirts—both autographed. "One for you, and one for your friend Kai, right?"

Micah's eyes widened. "You remembered? That's awesome. He's gonna flip!"

Photos were taken, polite conversation shared, and then it was time to go. As they left the venue, Jisoo clapped a hand on Micah's shoulder.

"Hungry?"

"Starving," Micah grinned. "That concert burned calories I didn't know I had."

Jisoo leaned forward to the driver. "Can we stop at that spot you like near the bridge? The one with the dumplings and jjajangmyeon."

The driver nodded, already turning toward the late-night takeout stand.

Twenty minutes later, Jisoo and Micah sat in the backseat with steaming containers in their laps, chopsticks in hand, slurping noodles and trading stories.

Micah looked out the window at the city lights. "Thanks, Appa," he said quietly. "This was one of the coolest nights of my life."

Jisoo smiled, wiping a bit of sauce from his lip. "You've earned it. And hey—remind me to get that Kai shirt into your bag before you forget."

Micah nodded, already texting Kai a full recap.

Chapter 39

Busan Sunrises

By late Friday afternoon, the Seoul sky had turned soft and gray, the city bathed in a gentle drizzle as Celeste zipped the last suitcase shut. Jisoo had arranged for a discreet driver—one the management company trusted to pick them up early Saturday morning for the drive to Busan. No public train, no airport frenzy. Just a quiet, comfortable ride down the coast.

"Micah, double-check your bag," Celeste called out from the hallway. "Toothbrush? Chargers? Swimsuit?"

Micah appeared in his doorway, holding his duffel bag like a trophy. "Triple checked. I'm good, Mom."

Jisoo came out of the bedroom, his phone tucked between his ear and shoulder, as he confirmed details with the driver. "Yes, 7 a.m. pick-up. Back entrance of the building. Thank you. See you then."

He hung up and turned to them. "Okay. Bags packed, snacks ready, playlist curatcd. We're good to go."

That night, they shared a quiet dinner in the apartment—bibimbap from Jiyeon's favorite local spot, fresh-cut fruit, and herbal tea. Afterwards, Jisoo and Celeste curled up in bed, the windows open to the soft nighttime air.

"Busan," Celeste murmured. "It feels like we've been moving nonstop since we got here."

"I know," Jisoo said, brushing her hair back gently. "This trip, it'll be good. For all of us."

Before leaving, Celeste took a moment to glance around the apartment, letting the familiar warmth of home sink in. The quiet hum of the city outside, the faint scent of leftover tea and bibimbap, even the soft creak of the floorboards—they all felt like anchors. "We'll be back soon," she said softly, more to herself than anyone else, as Jisoo slipped an arm around her shoulder. "Together," he added, and she nodded, comforted by the steadiness in his voice.

The next morning, they met the driver just before dawn. He greeted them with a low bow and helped load their luggage quickly, glancing around for potential onlookers—no fans in sight—just the still city and the soft promise of a quieter day.

Micah fell asleep within minutes of settling into the back seat, headphones in, hoodie up. Celeste leaned into Jisoo's side, lulled by the motion of the car and the low hum of the road beneath them.

The sun began to rise as the city gave way to the countryside. Rolling hills dotted with greenhouses and coastal towns replaced skyscrapers and neon lights. Celeste stirred, glancing out the window at the shifting landscape.

"Is this still Korea?" she teased softly.

Jisoo smiled. "Wait until we get to the beach. You'll see the real magic of Busan."

They arrived at the Min family's seaside home by midday. The traditional hanok-inspired house stood proud against the coastline, its curved tiled roof and wooden latticework glowing warmly in the light. The sound of waves crashing against the rocks greeted them before anyone else did.

Jisoo's mother stepped onto the stone path just as they exited the car, apron tied at her waist, her face glowing with anticipation.

"You made it safely," she said, pulling Celeste into a hug before reaching for Micah.

Jisoo's father appeared behind her, nodding at the driver as he carried in the bags. "Welcome back," he said to his son.

"It's good to be home," Jisoo replied.

Micah's eyes widened as he took in the house. "This is where you grew up?"

"Some of my best years," Jisoo said with a grin. "We spent our summers down the hill, at the water."

Celeste stood at the edge of the stone porch, breathing in the salty air. "It's beautiful, Jisoo."

"I thought you'd like it."

After a warm lunch of grilled fish, seaweed soup, and side dishes lovingly prepared by Jiyeon, the house slowly settled into the soft quiet of a coastal afternoon. The windows were open to the sound of gulls and crashing waves, the scent of salt air mixing with the last traces of sesame oil and garlic.

Jisoo changed into a loose linen shirt and shorts, barefoot as he walked out to the wooden deck at the back of the house. Celeste followed, her sundress catching the breeze, a soft scarf wrapped around her shoulders. She carried two cups of barley tea.

The morning air was crisp, carrying the faint saltiness of the sea and the soft hum of distant waves against the rocks. Jisoo took a slow sip of his tea, letting the warmth spread through his chest, while Celeste's fingers found his instinctively. For a moment, neither spoke, content to let the rhythm of the water and the whisper of the wind fill the space between them—a quiet pause that felt as essential as the sun rising over the horizon.

They sat side by side on the low wooden bench, facing the sea, the horizon stretched wide before them like the edge of a dream.

"Your parents' home… it feels sacred," Celeste said quietly.

Jisoo nodded, his gaze far out. "It always does. There's something about this place that strips everything down to the truth."

Behind them, the sliding doors opened and closed with a soft thud—Micah stepping outside with a towel slung over his shoulder and a ball in hand. Si-woo followed, pointing toward the hill that led to a small, secluded cove.

"I told him we could toss the ball around for a bit," Si-woo said, his tone light but firm. "If you don't mind."

"Not at all," Celeste said with a smile. "He could use the fresh air."

As the two walked down toward the shore, Jisoo leaned closer to Celeste. "This is good for them," he said. "My father is connecting with Micah. It means something."

Celeste rested her head on his shoulder. "It means everything."

Later that afternoon, Jiyeon invited Celeste to walk with her down to the beach path. The two women strolled slowly, Jiyeon carrying a small woven basket of tangerines from the tree behind the house. Celeste bent down to admire the wildflowers along the trail, her sandals brushing over smooth stones and driftwood.

"I've never had a daughter," Jiyeon said softly as they walked. "I didn't know what to expect when Jisoo told us he was serious about you. But now… I see why he chose you."

Celeste glanced at her, touched by her words, and a little caught off guard. "Thank you. I know we come from different worlds, but I love him. I love him with everything I am."

Jiyeon stopped, holding out a perfectly ripened tangerine. "Then that is enough."

They sat on a low rock near the shore, peeling the fruit and watching the tide roll in. The waves sang a lullaby neither needed to interpret.

As the sun lowered, casting orange and pink streaks across the water, the family gathered under the paper lanterns on the porch for dinner. Grilled vegetables, cold noodles, fresh pickles, and fruit filled the table. Micah was relaxed, chatting easily with Jiyeon about Korean idioms he'd picked up. Celeste laughed when she misunderstood one and accidentally said someone "had an egg in their nose."

Celeste reached across the table, lightly touching Jisoo's hand. "It feels… peaceful here. Like no one is expecting anything from us but to just be." Jisoo turned to her, a small smile tugging at his lips. "Exactly. No cameras, no fans, no scripts. Just us. And somehow, it makes everything else seem less important." Micah laughed, nudging his chopsticks against a bowl. "I vote we stay here forever. Honestly, Appa, this is way cooler than any concert or movie set."

Jisoo smiled as he watched them, quietly thinking. This is the life I never knew I needed. My wife, my son, and my parents are all under one roof, in harmony.

Near the end of the meal, Jisoo leaned forward. "I'll call my management team tomorrow. See if we can get a driver and extra security to take us back to Seoul. With everything online, we should avoid attention."

Jiyeon nodded. "That's wise. But for tonight, we rest. We're together. That is what matters."

The early light poured gently through the woven blinds of the coastal hanok home. Waves lapped softly against the shore in the distance, and the air smelled of pine and sea. It was a peaceful morning except inside the guest room, where Celeste stirred, frowning slightly.

She sat up slowly, pressing a hand to her stomach.

Jisoo rolled over, blinking awake. "Honey… are you okay?"

Celeste gave a soft groan. "I don't know. My stomach's upset. It started in the middle of the night, but I thought it would pass."

Jisoo sat up immediately, his eyes filled with concern. "Something you ate?"

"Maybe. Or just the travel, all the new food, stress... who knows," she said, managing a small smile. "Don't worry. It's not terrible. Just uncomfortable."

"I'll make you some porridge," Jisoo said, already getting up. "Stay in bed. I've got you."

In the kitchen, Jiyeon was already bustling around, the kettle whistling and a fresh batch of kimchi pancakes sizzling in the pan.

Jisoo entered, hair tousled, still in sleepwear. "Mother, Celeste has an upset stomach. I'm going to make her some rice porridge."

Jiyeon turned, immediately concerned. "Poor thing. Let me help. I have fresh ginger, which is good for nausea."

Together, they worked quietly while Min Si-woo entered from the backyard with a small box of herbs he'd been growing.

Celeste rested in bed, sipping warm water with lemon. Micah peeked in.

"You okay, Mom?"

She nodded, touched by the concern in his voice. "Just a little off today. Thanks for checking on me, baby."

Micah lingered for a moment. "I was gonna walk down to the shore with Grandpa again. Want me to stay?"

"No," she said softly. "Go on and enjoy it. I'll be okay. I've got Jisoo watching over me like a hawk."

Micah grinned and left the room, his footsteps light.

Later, after Celeste had finished her porridge and fallen back asleep, Jisoo stepped out onto the back deck with his phone. The sun was warm against his skin, the sea breeze cool.

He called his management office in Seoul.

"Yes, I'd like to arrange for a driver to meet us discreetly near the ferry terminal when we return. I want the safest, least public route back to the apartment. The fans are already talking. I don't want them disrupting our trip or overwhelming my family."

He listened, nodded, then confirmed details. "We'll be back in the city by Tuesday. Please make sure the apartment is ready—and tell security to be on alert."

He ended the call, exhaled slowly, and looked out at the water. Just then, Jiyeon came out with a fresh cup of tea.

"How is she?" she asked gently.

"Sleeping," Jisoo said. "She said it's not bad. Just… off."

Jiyeon nodded. "It happens. We'll take care of her."

Jisoo smiled, grateful. "Thank you, Mother."

The family gathered around the low wooden table in the airy dining room, sunlight filtering through the latticed windows. Jiyeon had prepared a light, comforting spread: steamed vegetables, grilled fish, a small bowl of kimchi, and Jisoo's homemade porridge for Celeste.

Celeste, dressed in soft cotton and moving slowly, managed a few spoonfuls of the porridge with a faint smile.

"This is perfect," she said softly, reaching for Jisoo's hand. "Thank you."

"You sure you're feeling up to eating?" Jiyeon asked gently, concern still etched in her eyes.

Celeste nodded, though her stomach hadn't quite settled. "I think I'll be okay. I just wanted to sit with everyone."

Micah glanced at her from across the table. "You don't have to eat much, Mom. Just chill."

Jisoo gave her an encouraging look. "We're just happy you're here. No pressure."

Celeste nodded again and slowly finished half the small bowl of porridge. But as she leaned back with a soft sigh, her expression changed—her face paled, and her eyes widened.

"Oh no—" she whispered, then shot up from the table.

Everyone froze for a moment before they heard her footsteps running down the hallway toward the guest bathroom. A second later, the sound of the bathroom door slamming shut and the unmistakable retching behind it filled the silence.

Jisoo stood immediately, his heart pounding. Jiyeon reached for a towel and a cool compress without hesitation. Micah looked worried, unsure whether to follow or stay seated.

Si-woo rose calmly. "Let them take care of her," he said gently to Micah. "She'll be all right."

Jisoo knelt beside the bathroom door, listening with a worried frown.

"Honey? Can I come in?"

A weak voice came back. "Y-yeah."

He opened the door gently. Celeste was sitting on the cool tile floor, her back against the wall, flushed and shaky. Her hair was pinned up loosely. "I'm so sorry," she murmured, wiping her mouth with a tissue. "It just… came on all of a sudden."

Jisoo knelt beside her, pressing the cool towel to her neck. "No apologies. We'll take care of you, okay? Just breathe."

Jiyeon appeared a moment later with water and a change of clothes. She gave her daughter-in-law a soft smile. "Let's get you cleaned up and back in bed."

Celeste nodded, embarrassed but grateful.

Jisoo helped Celeste settle into bed with a cool compress on her forehead and a fan running gently in the corner of the room. Jiyeon brought a thermos of barley tea and whispered a few comforting words before leaving them alone.

"Do you think it's just a bug?" Celeste asked quietly, eyes half-lidded from exhaustion.

"Could be travel stress… or something you ate. Maybe just your body saying it needs rest," Jisoo said, brushing her curls from her forehead. "But if it doesn't pass by morning, we're going to the clinic. Deal?"

Celeste nodded, closing her eyes. "Deal."

Jisoo leaned down and kissed her temple. "Sleep, my leading lady. I've got you."

Soft morning light crept through the hanok's paper-covered windows, casting delicate shadows across the floor. The house was quiet, save for the distant sound of waves breaking along the shore and the soft clinking of teacups from the kitchen.

Celeste stirred in bed; her head nestled into Jisoo's shoulder. She blinked slowly, her body aching but her mind clearer than the night before. She lay still for a moment, listening to the rhythm of Jisoo's breathing—deep and even—and the peaceful hum of the world outside.

Still it felt like morning sickness.

Then came the twist. Change can feel a faint flutter. Not gas. Not nerves.

It was something else. Low in her belly, something she hadn't felt in years. Something impossible… but unmistakable.

She sat up slowly, a hand moving instinctively to her abdomen. Jisoo stirred beside her.

"Honey?" he mumbled, voice thick with sleep. "Are you okay?"

She turned to him, eyes wide and blinking rapidly.

"Jisoo… I need you to wake up."

He sat up, immediately alert. "What is it? Is it your stomach? Do we need to go to the clinic?"

"No, no, just… I need you to listen." She looked down at her hand, resting gently over the flutter. "I felt something. I don't know how else to describe it."

Jisoo blinked, trying to process. "Something… like what?"

She hesitated, the words catching in her throat. "Like… movement. Inside me."

There was a long silence. Then Jisoo whispered, "Like… a baby?"

Celeste exhaled shakily. "I don't want to jump to anything. I thought I couldn't have more children, Jisoo. That's what they told me after Micah…"

Jisoo stared at her, his expression a mixture of wonder, disbelief, and cautious hope. "Do you want to go to the clinic? We could find out. Today."

She nodded, overwhelmed. "Yes. Please. I just… I need to know."

Jisoo reached for her hand, squeezing it tightly. "No matter what it is—we face it together."

Later that morning at the clinic in Busan

The waiting room was quiet, its clean, minimalist interior calming yet clinical. Jiyeon and Si-woo sat with Micah outside, giving Jisoo and Celeste space and privacy inside the small exam room.

Celeste lay on the examination table, Jisoo holding her hand, eyes fixed on the monitor as the doctor moved the ultrasound wand over her lower abdomen.

The screen flickered.

A heartbeat. Small. Steady. Real.

The room fell still.

Jisoo's breath caught. Celeste's eyes filled with tears.

The doctor smiled softly. "You're pregnant, Ms. Monroe. About 12 weeks along."

Celeste let out a breathless laugh, her hand flying to her mouth.

Jisoo turned to her, his eyes shimmering. "Celeste… we're having a baby."

"I didn't think I could…" she whispered, overwhelmed.

He leaned in and kissed her forehead. "And yet, here you are. Stronger than every impossibility."

They held each other, stunned, joyful, breathless, already changed by the tiny life growing quietly between them.

The soft hush of evening had settled over the coastal hanok, the sky outside painted in strokes of lavender and rose gold. The sea air drifted through the open windows, carrying with it the scent of salt and pine. Inside, the lamps cast a warm amber glow across the house's wooden beams, and the world felt, for a rare and fleeting moment, perfectly still.

Celeste sat curled up on the low couch in their guest room, wrapped in a soft blanket, a cup of warm barley tea cradled in her hands. Her gaze was far away—distant, reflective—as she tried to take it all in.

Jisoo entered quietly, freshly showered, his hair damp and tousled, his expression thoughtful. He carried a small tray with a few pear slices and a folded note tucked beneath. Setting it down, he knelt beside her.

"You okay?" he asked gently.

She looked at him, her eyes still wide with wonder. "I don't even know what I'm feeling, Jisoo. I didn't think this was possible. I'd accepted it… that Micah would be my only one. That part of my life was closed."

Jisoo nodded slowly. "And yet, somehow… life opened it again."

She smiled softly, a little shakily. "It feels like a miracle. But also… terrifying. I'm older now. My body's different. What if"

Jisoo took her tea from her hands and set it aside. He pulled her into his arms, holding her close.

"We don't have to figure everything out tonight," he whispered into her hair. "All we have to do is breathe. Just… be here. Together."

She let out a shaky breath, the tension in her shoulders slowly unwinding. "I'm glad we found out here. In this place. It feels right."

Jisoo smiled and reached over to the tray, pulling out the small, folded note. "I wrote this in the clinic parking lot while you were speaking with the nurse."

She took it carefully, unfolded it. Inside was a single line written in his elegant script.

Her throat tightened, and she pressed the note to her chest.

"Jisoo," she whispered, "you are going to be the most beautiful father… all over again."

"And you," he said, brushing her cheek with the back of his fingers, "will be the heart of this family. Always."

They sat like that in silence, the waves murmuring in the distance, the gentle creak of wood and wind around them like the breath of the house itself.

They weren't ready to tell the world just yet.

But in this quiet moment, it didn't matter.

Their world had already changed.

Morning broke gently over the hanok, the golden sunlight spilling through the paper-paneled windows. The sea was calm, its rhythmic waves a soft lullaby that gave the house a sense of peace—of something sacred beginning.

Celeste sat at the kitchen table in one of Jisoo's oversized sweaters, her hands wrapped around a warm mug of ginger tea. Her appetite had barely returned, but her mind was already racing. She'd been up since dawn, lying in bed with Jisoo's arm draped protectively across her waist, wondering how and when they should say the words out loud: We're expecting.

Jisoo appeared a few minutes later, barefoot, hair slightly wild, stretching his arms above his head as he yawned. "Smells like ginger. You're feeling a little better?"

"Yeah," she said softly, watching him pour his coffee. "Still queasy. But better."

He leaned down to kiss the top of her head. "One day at a time."

They sat together for a few quiet minutes, the only sound the soft clinking of their mugs and the breeze rustling the trees outside. Then Celeste broke the silence.

"So… when do we tell people?"

Jisoo looked thoughtful. "We don't have to rush. But we should probably talk to Micah first. Before anyone else."

She nodded slowly. "He deserves to hear it from us. I just… I want to make sure he knows this doesn't change anything. He'll always be—"

"Our first," Jisoo finished gently. "The one who taught us how to be parents. He knows. But we'll tell him together."

Celeste smiled at that. "And after Micah?"

Jisoo took a sip of his coffee, considering. "My parents, definitely. Maybe we can do it when we get back to Seoul. They'll be thrilled. Well, after the initial shock."

Celeste chuckled. "Your mother might cry."

"She will," Jisoo agreed. "And father will get quiet and serious and then tell me to build a nursery with reinforced windows."

They both laughed at the image.

"And your family?" he asked gently.

Celeste leaned back in her chair. "My parents will be overjoyed. Diane's probably going to start knitting the moment we tell her. Elijah and Nadia might faint. But they'll come around."

Jisoo reached across the table and took her hand. "So, we take it slow. First Micah. Then the parents. Then everyone else."

"And the press?"

He exhaled. "Let's not worry about that yet. Sang-ho still hasn't run the follow-up piece. We can control the narrative when we're ready."

Celeste nodded, the plan grounding her. "Okay. Then… after Busan?"

"After Busan," he confirmed. "We start this new chapter one heartbeat at a time."

They stayed like that for a while—hands entwined, coffee cooling, morning light warming their skin—holding space for what was to come. The beginning of a new story, waiting to be written.

The morning air in Busan was crisp, with a soft breeze drifting through the open kitchen windows. Jiyeon had already set the table with a light breakfast: rice porridge with chestnuts, grilled mackerel, seasoned spinach, and a small plate of pickled radish. The house smelled like warmth and care.

Celeste shuffled in wearing soft house slippers and a pale blue wrap dress, her skin still a bit pale but her eyes bright with something more than just morning calm. Jisoo followed a step behind, freshly showered, hair slightly damp, his expression unreadable but peaceful.

Micah looked up from his seat, spoon halfway to his mouth. "Hey, Mom. You okay now?"

Celeste smiled as she took the seat beside him. "Much better, sweetheart. Thanks for asking."

Jiyeon and Min Si-woo joined them, both dressed neatly but comfortably, their curiosity simmering just below the surface.

Everyone began eating, but the questions hung in the air like steam from the porridge. Jiyeon finally broke the silence, her voice gentle.

"Celeste, Jisoo… Did the doctor say what was wrong?"

Jisoo and Celeste exchanged a quick glance. He nodded slightly.

Celeste set down her spoon and turned to her son. "Micah, can you look at me for a second?"

Micah looked up, chewing slowly. "What's going on?"

Jisoo reached for Celeste's hand under the table. "The doctor said she's okay… but there's a reason she hasn't been feeling well."

Micah's brow furrowed. "Okay…"

Celeste inhaled deeply. "I'm pregnant."

Micah blinked. "Wait… what?"

Jisoo leaned in. "You're going to be a big brother."

The table went still. Jiyeon gasped softly, one hand covering her mouth. Si-woo's brows lifted in surprise, but a smile was already forming.

Micah stared, mouth slightly open. "Seriously?"

Celeste nodded, her voice soft but steady. "Seriously."

Micah sat back in his chair, silent for a long beat. Then—

"Whoa," he said, eyes wide. "I mean… whoa."

Everyone chuckled, and Jiyeon finally reached across the table to touch Celeste's hand, her eyes glistening. "Congratulations, my dear. What a blessing."

Si-woo gave Jisoo a proud, quiet nod. "That is good news, son."

Micah scratched his head. "I mean, I didn't see that coming. But… cool.

Micah gave them a slight, crooked grin. "So… when's the baby due?"

"Probably early spring," Celeste said.

Jiyeon stood up and started bustling around the kitchen, already muttering about making seaweed soup and starting a prenatal care schedule.

Si-woo reached for his teacup with a small chuckle. "Well… this breakfast just got a lot more interesting."

Micah looked down at his bowl, then up at Celeste again. "I'm happy for you, Mom. For you both."

Celeste reached for his hand, squeezing it. "Thanks, baby."

As they continued eating, the table filled with excited chatter, questions, and planning. A new chapter had quietly begun—at the breakfast table, with family, love, and the promise of new life.